The Emotional Life of Populism

The Emotional Life of Populism

How Fear, Disgust, Resentment, and Love Undermine Democracy

EVA ILLOUZ

with Avital Sicron

polity

Copyright © Eva Illouz 2023

Copyright © Suhrkamp Verlag AG Berlin 2023

All rights reserved by and controlled through Suhrkamp Verlag Berlin.

The right of Eva Illouz to be identified as Author of this Work has been asserted in accordance with the UK Copyright, Designs and Patents Act 1988.

First published in English in 2023 by Polity Press

First published in German in 2023 by Suhrkamp Verlag AG as *Undemokratische Emotionen. Das Beispiel Israel*

Polity Press
65 Bridge Street
Cambridge CB2 1UR, UK

Polity Press
111 River Street
Hoboken, NJ 07030, USA

All rights reserved. Except for the quotation of short passages for the purpose of criticism and review, no part of this publication may be reproduced, stored in a retrieval system or transmitted, in any form or by any means, electronic, mechanical, photocopying, recording or otherwise, without the prior permission of the publisher.

ISBN-13: 978-1-5095-5818-6
ISBN-13: 978-1-5095-5819-3(pb)

A catalogue record for this book is available from the British Library.

Library of Congress Control Number: 2022948539

Typeset in 11 on 14pt Warnock Pro
by Cheshire Typesetting Ltd, Cuddington, Cheshire
Printed and bound in Great Britain by CPI Group (UK) Ltd, Croydon

The publisher has used its best endeavours to ensure that the URLs for external websites referred to in this book are correct and active at the time of going to press. However, the publisher has no responsibility for the websites and can make no guarantee that a site will remain live or that the content is or will remain appropriate.

Every effort has been made to trace all copyright holders, but if any have been overlooked the publisher will be pleased to include any necessary credits in any subsequent reprint or edition.

For further information on Polity, visit our website:
politybooks.com

Contents

Acknowledgements	vii
Introduction: The Worm Inside the Apple	1
1 Securitist Democracy and Fear	21
2 Disgust and Identity	58
3 Resentment, or The Hidden Eros of Nationalist Populism	92
4 National Pride as Loyalty	125
Conclusion: The Emotions of a Decent Society	162
Notes	178
Index	222

To the memory of my father Haim Illouz,
who loved Israel so much.

Acknowledgements

This book was researched and written long before the profound political and constitutional crisis faced by Israel as of March 2023. Tragically, its analysis has turned out to be more than amply confirmed by current events: what we can only call a new form of Jewish fascism is in power, threatening to turn Israel into a full-blown religious dictatorship. By the time this book is published, it is possible that civil society will have won and that Israel will have returned to the *status quo ante*. Or not. But whatever the outcome of the crisis pitting a fascist government against hundreds of thousands of protesters, two key points of this book remain valid: populism is the antechamber of radical and authoritarian political regimes. And some emotions come to saturate the political arena so that they obfuscate facts, evidence and self-interest. Despite overwhelming evidence that Israel will see its economy and security seriously jeopardized if the government stays on course, this path is the one preferred by a large proportion of the population.

The study of populism has, reluctantly, made me return to a notion I have rejected for most of my sociological career – that of ideology. Cognitive psychology has accumulated considerable evidence that our thinking is full of flaws and biases. Sociology cannot ignore these powerful findings, however different cognitive psychology may be from our discipline. These biases and errors in thinking are effects of the inherent limitations of our attention and reasoning, but they are also systematically shaped by the set of ideas spread through various organizations funded by conservative and libertarian billionaires who aim to undermine and destroy democracy. Jeff Yass and Arthur Dantchick – two Jewish billionaires who have financed the highly conservative think tank Forum Kohelet which masterminded the regime change in Israel – provide examples of the ways in which money distorts and undermines democratic processes. Ideas become ideology when they serve so crudely a small group at the expense of the majority.

This book would not have seen the light of day without generous funds from the Van Leer Institute, which helped support Avital Sikron, a PhD candidate at Hebrew University and a crucial researcher for this book. It was also supported by the Institute for Israeli Thought and by its generous fellowship.

Shai Lavi was a privileged interlocutor early in the project, long before it turned into actual text on a page: he encouraged and supported it when it was only an idea; he deconstructed and reconstructed the argument numerous times. My gratitude goes to him. Avner Ben-Zaken and Mordechai Cohen have also played an important role in probing my thinking on the faults and flaws of identity politics and on the ways in which real victims go astray with the politics of victimhood. Tamar Brandes has been an ongoing source of inspiration, as a colleague and as a friend. Her thinking about the nature of constitutional culture has profoundly enriched me. Finally, Boaz Amitai – who has enabled me to probe questions about the decent society – is an inspiration for us all and a model of what a decent citizen is.

Introduction:
The Worm Inside the Apple

In a lecture he gave in Vienna in 1967, Adorno offered his audience remarks strikingly relevant to our times,[1] and this despite the vast differences which separate us from his period. Although fascism had officially collapsed, the conditions for fascist movements, he averred, were still active in society. The main culprit for this was the still prevailing tendency towards concentration of capital, a tendency which "still creates the possibility of constantly downgrading strata of society that were clearly bourgeois in terms of their subjective class consciousness, and want to cling to, and possibly reinforce, their privileges and social status." It is the same groups of bourgeois moving down who "develop a hatred of socialism, or what they call socialism; that is, they lay the blame for their own potential downgrading not on the apparatus that causes it, but on those who were critical towards the system in which they once had a status, at least in a traditional sense."

In these short lines, Adorno packed some of the key insights of critical theory. Fascism, for him, is not an accident of history. Nor is it an aberration. Rather, it works inside democracy and is contiguous with it. It is, to use a worn-out metaphor, a worm lodged inside the apple, rotting the fruit from within, invisible to the naked eye. As an anthology on the Frankfurt School put it: "It was a major theme of the early Frankfurt School that no sharp line could be drawn between the extremity of political fascism and the more everyday social pathologies of bourgeois capitalism in the West."[2] This also means that fascism need not be a full-blown regime. It could in fact be a tendency, a cluster of pragmatic orientations and ideas which work from within the framework of democracies. Contained in Adorno's remarks is also the claim that capitalism deploys tendencies towards a concentration of capital and power (a rather unsurprising idea for a Marxist which even non-Marxists would have a hard time disputing). Adorno had not yet witnessed the spectacular way in which democratic electoral processes would be hijacked by concentrated capital. He was thus referring to the class dynamics which the concentration of capital created inside liberal societies. Such dynamics threatened to constantly downgrade the very same bourgeois classes who had previously contributed to and benefited from the capitalist system. Note that Adorno focuses on the bourgeois (a mixture of segments of the upper and middle classes) and not on the proletariat as the agent for this new fascism. Echoing a tradition in sociology that viewed fascism as the expression of fear of downward mobility,[3] Adorno suggests that the same class which had, and continues to have, privileges is the same one which, when it sees these privileges threatened, will support it. Loss of privilege thus seems to be a key motivation for endorsing anti-democratic leaders. (In the 2016 election, support for Trump tended to be higher among groups with high and middle incomes. People with very low salaries were more likely to side with Clinton.)[4] Desire to maintain privilege or the fear of losing privilege is, as Adorno suggests, a driving force of politics in general and of fascist politics in particular. The third and perhaps (at least for this book) most significant move contained in Adorno's succinct remarks suggests that identification with fascism finds its roots in a certain way of thinking about causes (how we think about why things are the way they are) and a certain way of assigning blame and responsibility. The downgraded bourgeois class will not blame the very capitalist system of economic concentration which undermines its loss of status and privilege. Instead, it will transpose blame onto those who criticize that same system. Adorno is laconic, but we are left to understand that they will grasp their social world as if in a camera obscura, an inverted image of the outside world. Continuing the Marxist tradition of *Ideologiekritik*, Adorno identifies here a very important cognitive process at work in proto fascism: the lack of capacity to understand the chain of causes which explain one's social situation. Perception of the social world, Adorno suggests, can be fundamentally distorted. The bourgeois (and probably other classes) cannot properly identify the causes of their losses and thus cannot rally behind those who, without exactly defending their interests, at the very least question the system responsible for their downgrading.

In these short lines, Adorno thus makes a claim about the persistence of fascist tendencies in our societies, due both to economic processes of accumulation and concentration of capital and to certain distorted or incomplete forms of thinking, to be found particularly in the ways in which we build causality, make events intelligible, and attribute blame, pointing to what in another context Jason Stanley has called a flawed ideology.[5] A flawed ideology – as Stanley defines it in *How Propaganda Works* – robs "groups of knowledge of their own mental states by systematically concealing their interests from them."[6] What the *real* interests of a class or group of people are, of course, is not self-evident. Any judgment about this is based on certain presuppositions on the part of the researcher who makes distinctions between real and false interests, thus claiming a certain epistemic authority for herself. When trying to understand the social world, adopting such a position of epistemic authority seems inevitable. As a citizen, I do not believe the theories advanced by QAnon and other conspiracy groups. Pretending their view of the world is the same as that of a piece of investigative journalism would amount to bad faith. Thinking, all thinking, contains erasures, displacements, errors, and denials. Recovering these denials and erasures remains the vocation of critical social analysis.

The idea of *Idiologiekritik* has been abundantly criticized, yet recent political developments suggest it is not one we can easily give up. Some have argued that *Idiologiekritik* is usually conducted in bad faith (criticizing others but not oneself),[7] or that it bestows too much authority on the researcher, or that, whatever choice people make, it is always a rational one because their thinking reflects their preferences. Indeed, sociological analysis should respect the reasons citizens have for holding their opinions and choices: it should not mock or dismiss an opinion, but, in an era where outlandish conspiracy theories flourish and obstruct democratic processes of opinion-making, we can no longer afford the luxury of assuming that all points of view are equal or equally knowledgeable; nor can we afford to ignore the manipulations of opinion that are engineered by an increasingly sophisticated political class, extraordinarily well versed in the various arts of the manipulation of opinion and rumor. The power of these arts of manipulation have become decoupled by the rapid transmission of information through social media.[8] Thus, against our will, we must return to the idea of *Idiologiekritik* because, when accounting for reality, not all ideas are equal.

An ideology will be flawed if it meets the following conditions: it contradicts the basic tenets of democracy while citizens actually want political institutions to represent them; its concrete policies (for example, claiming to represent the simple people and yet privileging policies which make home ownership very difficult) conflict with its avowed ideological principles or aims; it displaces and distorts the causes of a social group's discontent; and it is oblivious or blind to the flaws of the leader (for example, self-serving corruption or his indifference to the welfare of the nation). It should be clear, however, that it is not only the supporters of populist proto-fascists who fall into this cognitive trap and blind spot. There are many illustrations of such cases. Jerome McGann has argued, for example, that romantic poetry denied the material conditions in which it was produced through evasions or erasures.[9] The French communists who believed in the Soviet communist regime during the 1950s, when Stalin's murderousness could have been known, are no less a cogent example of a flawed ideology.[10]

To pursue Adorno's thought, fascism continues to work from within the heart of democratic societies because those who are hurt by the logic of economic concentration cannot connect the dots of its causal chain and may actually oppose those who work to expose it, curiously creating antagonism between those who work to denounce injustice and inequality and those who suffer from them. This antagonism has become a key feature of many democracies around the world. The question of flawed ideology is particularly relevant to the present time because everywhere around the world, and especially in Israel, democracy is under the assault of what Francis Fukuyama calls "nationalist populism," a political form that undermines the institutions of democracy from within and which thus lets the most powerful actors in society – corporations and lobbies – use the state to meet their own interests to the detriment of the demos, which curiously feels alienated from the institutions that have historically guaranteed its sovereignty. As political scientists Steven Levitsky and Daniel Ziblatt claim, democracies do not die only through military coups or other such dramatic events. They also die slowly.[11] Populism is one political form taken by this slow death.

Populism is not fascism per se but, rather, a fascist tendency, a line of force which puts pressure on the political field, pushing it towards towards regressive tendencies and anti-democratic predispositions. An enormous amount of research has tried to explain the emergence of such fascist tendencies.[12]

Some explain it by the globalization of the workforce, which has left the working class in a precarious condition, others by a shift in cultural values to which populism is a reaction. False consciousness or flawed ideologies are also explained by the transformation of mediascapes, which in many countries have been consolidated and purchased with the explicit intent of changing the "liberal agenda" of the mainstream press. For instance, in France, the billionaire businessman Vincent Bolloré owns several French television stations, including Cnews, a 24-hour news channel that promotes a decisively right-wing agenda. Bolloré has been named as the funder of the campaign of the far-right French populist Éric Zemmour.[13] Another example is the Australian-born American billionaire Rupert Murdoch, who owns hundreds of media outlets worldwide – among them the propaganda machine Fox News in the United States – and has been accused of using these to support his political allies.[14] In Israel, in turn, the free newspaper *Israel Hayom*, financed by a now deceased casino mogul, wields enormous political influence. So the concentration of capital throughout the world has had the effect of forging formidable weapons to distort consciousness.

Along with this increasing control of information, the globalization of the economy has left the working classes in a precarious condition.[15] Bill Clinton's globalist policies, such as signing the North American Free Trade Agreement (NAFTA), angered many working-class voters, with the president of the electrical workers' union quoted as saying "Clinton screwed us and we won't forget it."[16] The working classes no longer feel represented by the left and contest its very capacity to articulate their interests, a fact which reflects the implosion of social-democratic ideology throughout the world, and perhaps signaling the very exhaustion of liberalism.[17] The combination of these factors explains why, in many countries around the democratic world, we are witnessing the rise of fascist tendencies – not quite fascism yet, but a mindset that certainly predisposes one to it.

This book focuses on one aspect of this complex tapestry: the perception of the social world through flawed social causal frameworks – that is, false explanations of social and economic processes. "Flawed" may seem uncomfortably close to the word "false" and may appear to bring us back to the epistemological and moral pitfalls of *Ideologiekritik*. And yet, "flawed" should be differentiated from "false" because it does not dismiss and negate the thinking and feeling of citizens. It contains the possibility that, while not perfect, thinking is not false but simply flawed. It is not false in the sense that it contains the trace of a real social experience which must be recovered by the analyst. These traces produce reasons which must be both understood and reckoned with. I am attentive to these reasons, as made clear in interviews I conducted with people who subscribe to right-wing, populist, ultra-nationalist worldviews and tried to understand the inner coherence of their views in order to ask just where and how thoughts about our social environment become distorted. This book focuses on causal frames (how we explain our social world) and the ways in which they profoundly affect political cognition and behavior.

If we want to understand why some frameworks can come to distort our perception of the social world, why we are unable to correctly name a real malaise, we must push Adorno's thought to new realms and grasp more firmly than he did the intertwining of social thought with emotions. Only emotions have the multifold power to deny empirical evidence, to shape motivation, to overwhelm self-interest, and to be responsive to concrete social situations. Thus, this book follows the suggestion of the Swedish sociologist Helena Flam to look into the influence of emotions on macro-politics and "map out emotions which uphold social structures and relations of domination."[18] Politics is charged with affective structures without which we would not be able to understand how flawed ideologies slip through the social experiences of actors and shape their meaning. This is the broad theme of this book. It takes Israel as its main case study with the hope that its findings can either be generalized or at least compared to those in other countries.

Structures of Feeling

Raymond Williams, the great British literary theorist, coined the expression "structures of feeling" to designate the forms of thinking that were vying to emerge between the hegemony of institutions, the popular responses to official regulations and literary texts accounting for these responses. A structure of feeling[19] points to experience that is inchoate, what we may today call an affect, something that is beneath coherent meaning. It is a shared way of thinking and feeling that influences and is influenced by the culture and way of life of a particular group.[20] And the notion of structure also suggests that this level of experience has an underlying pattern, which means it is systematic. These structures may play an important role in shaping individual and group identities.[21] Politics shapes and is shaped by such structures of feelings,[22] whether they come in the form of fear, resentment, disgust or national pride, as studied in this book. Political actors are particularly powerful in shaping narratives which bestow emotional meanings on social experiences.[23] They address voters directly with narratives they forge with the help of consultants, experts, and advertisers. These narratives, shaped by political and media elites, may resonate with emotional habitus formed during one's socialization (for example, indignation at perceived injustice or disdain for 'lower' social groups are typically formed through family),[24] or they may give meaning to social experiences in process (such as downward mobility). Sometimes emotions sustain material socio-economic interests, and sometimes the latter can be overwhelmed by emotions[25] and can even contradict them, as when working-class people vote for leaders who lower taxes for the rich, weaken trade unions, deregulate labor laws, and lower social benefits. Emotions play a crucial role in shaping and influencing voting patterns and other political choices of citizens.[26]

Emotions can turn into affects or less conscious modes of feeling. Such affects are not only based in one's social position or social experiences. They also pervade spaces, images, stories that circulate in the social bond, creating public atmospheres to which we respond beneath and beyond our self-awareness.[27] We respond to them by absorbing the key emotional associations which words, events, stories, or symbols create. Affect is a non-cognitive or pre-cognitive level of experience. It is "deposited" so to speak in public and collective objects or events, such as public speeches, national holidays, military marches, symbols, and policies of the state.[28] It can also be actively engineered by political marketers and the clients they serve. This symbolic and emotional material is both the effect of conscious manipulations by powerful political actors and a kind of raw energy circulating in civil society through social media, interpersonal interactions, and non-state organizations.[29] Such emotions have a particular stickiness when they come attached to stories which orient us in social space and shape our social identity and our understanding of the world. In this perspective, then, emotions are sometimes implicit in orienting one's sense of the issues that matter or explicit when they are manipulated by actors in the political field. They are neither fully rational (since they often disregard self-interest and ignore the real causes of events) nor irrational (since they express one's position in the social world).[30] Because emotions are eudaimonic – they express one's perception of one's well-being in a given situation – they do not fit neatly into the rational–irrational divide. In the analysis to follow, then, emotions are understood as responses to social conditions, responses that take the form of collective narratives that deliberately connect causes and effects in a specific way, assign blame, and offer solutions to predicaments. Emotions, as Arlie Hochschild argued in her remarkable study of Louisiana Trump voters, are embedded in deep stories which need neither be true nor rely on any fact, only *feel* true.[31] That emotions guide our political orientations is true for the entire political spectrum, but some leaders, some ideologies, and some historical circumstances make this fact even more cogent, as is the case with contemporary populism. The predominance of emotional orientations may be the reason why, for example, Trump's popularity has changed very little throughout the years, no matter which new scandal he was involved in.[32]

Structures of feelings can be said to have a dual property: they can point to a social experience shared by members of a social group, accumulated through time, which may or may not be explicitly named and which may or may not become a part of the political discourse.[33] For example, at the turn of the twentieth century, Austrians envied the Jews who were disproportionately present in professions as medicine, law, and journalism.[34] That envy probably constituted an important element of the virulent ideological antisemitism which gave rise to Nazism, yet that affective experience, while grounded in the vertiginous social mobility of Jews, did not bear an explicit name – social envy. It took the circuitous route of a demonization of the Jews in pamphlets, newspaper articles, caricatures, rumors, and pseudo-scientific theories. It constituted a climate of opinion and a public atmosphere.

The other dimension of structure of feeling pertains to the public character of politics and policies and to their capacity to shape the affect of their recipients. It refers to the capacity of leaders, public media and government policies, official political actors, and heads of parties to shape emotions or affective atmospheres more or less consciously and more or less manipulatively by labeling events (past, present, or future) and by bestowing on them public interpretative frames. Political leaders often invoke their own sentiments in order to induce those of their constituents as well as their identification. As Walter Lippman put it in *The Phantom Public* in 1927:

> Since the general opinions of large numbers of persons are almost certain to be a vague and confusing medley, action cannot be taken until these opinions have been factored down, canalized, compressed and made uniform. The making of one general will out of the multitude of general wishes is not a Hegelian mystery, as so many social philosophers have imagined, but an art well known to leaders, politicians and steering committees. It consists essentially in the use of symbols which assemble emotions after they have been detached from their ideas.[35]

These two types of frame – deriving from social experience and consciously crafted – sometimes become intricately intertwined and reflect the cognitive and affective meanings with which citizens and constituents interpret their social world. This process of assembling symbols and extracting from them, so to speak, their affective meaning is key to understanding how emotions and affects, once transformed in public speech and images, connect to flawed ideologies. A structure of feeling has thus a double property: it is a social experience shared by people who may have a common economic, cultural, and social experience; and it can also designate the ways in which this experience is named and framed by various groups that control the public arena, these groups being media, political actors, lobbyists, influencers, and politicians. Political structures of feeling consist of the successful encounter between the two. To be sure, a social experience can be one of general and vague malaise. To become politically relevant and operational it needs to be incorporated into a frame of meaning which recodes the malaise into a specific set of ideas and emotions.

Populism is one such (often successful) way of recoding social malaise. This book argues that, in the Israeli context, populist politics recoded three powerful social experiences: one is to be found in the various collective traumas lived by the Jews throughout their history, including the birth of the state of Israel, which entailed a war against the British colonial powers and surrounding Arab countries. These traumas have been translated into a generalized fear of the enemy. The second powerful social experience is the conquest of land, which, since 1967, has increasingly become the object of intense ideological struggles over the nature of Israeli nationalism, while the land has become an economic resource.[36] The Occupation generates emotional practices of separation and even disgust between various groups in Israeli society. The third social experience on which runs the powerful emotion of resentment is the long-lasting discrimination and exclusion of Mizrahim, Jews who were born in Arab countries or whose parents or grandparents were born in Arab countries. This resentment in turn operated a radical transformation of the political map, tipping it to the extreme right. These three so-called negative emotions (fear, disgust, and resentment) are all transcended into the love of the nation and/or the Jewish people. These emotions are generated by narrative frames which are anchored in concrete social experiences. In other words, social experiences become translated into emotions and motivations, creating narratives which become operative in the political sphere. These narratives are invoked by political actors and are mobilized by them in their struggles to claim power and authority. Once these emotions are mobilized in the public sphere, they become imbued with what I would call surplus imaginary affects: emotions feed on social experiences as much as on the invocation of imagined narrative scripts – for example, of the enemy or of the true and authentic people – which in turn generate strong affective orientations. The deployment of emotions in the public sphere thus invites the analysis of the ways in which concrete social experiences are framed and recoded in public narratives which yield surplus imaginary affects. Emotions are as much a response to reality as they are to imagined objects.

Emotions, Character and Politics

This book aims to characterize Israeli populist politics by viewing it as a politics which blends four specific emotions – fear, disgust, resentment, and love – and makes these emotions dominant vectors of the political process. Despite its very unique problems and geography, Israel can be seen as paradigmatic of the nationalist and populist political style that has unfolded throughout the world. No doubt it is, in many ways, an outlier because it is a Jewish state tucked within a predominantly Arab area, with a significant Palestinian minority, thus creating a breeding ground for military conflict, which is absent or played in a minor key in many countries in which populism has become a dominant voice. Yet, this makes it also a prime case for the development of populist movements because, as the Israeli political scientist Dani Filc suggests, populism is a "political project supported by some common ideological premises that appear in societies where conflicts around the inclusion or exclusion of subordinate groups prevail."[37] To be sure, this book does not claim Israel is worse than other democracies in its turn to populism. In fact, the opposite is true. Given the considerable number of external conflicts and inner tensions this young democracy has faced, its institutions have been remarkably resilient for an astonishingly long time. (They are now threatened with collapse under the assault of the populist and messianic right.). Especially when compared to such countries as Poland, Hungary, the United States or Brazil, which have no enemies at their borders (the first two are even relatively homogeneous), we can only be impressed by the fact that Israel did not yet resort to a more muscular military democracy. And yet, Benjamin Netanyahu was among the first leaders to adopt a populist style of governance. Choosing Israel is all the more justified in that Netanyahu forged bonds of diplomatic, political, and personal friendship with many anti-democratic leaders of the world, such as Duterte, Bolsonaro, Trump, Putin, Modi, and Orban.[38] These leaders share in common a distinctive political style and common interests:[39] they are hyper-masculinist (Netanyahu never had any known or visible feminist agenda in an era where all social democratic leaders are committed to this issue); they attack the rule of law and established democratic institutions; they foment conspiracy theories about a deep state (the very same state they are supposed to represent); they identify enemies threatening the borders or integrity of the majority group; they play social groups against each other; and, finally and most importantly, they claim to represent the people against the elites, a point which has often been made in the increasingly large literature on populism. Even though these leaders often control and overwhelm the party they claim to represent, their ideological platform is carried through a party apparatus. All of them distrust international law and organizations, many of them loathe the EU, and they all would like a freer hand to rule their country without a strong parliament or judicial system.

It is often said that the current Likud is an extreme version of its predecessor, the Herut party that was led by Menachem Begin. Yet, we forget that Herut had been viewed, at least initially, as a terror organization, outside the Zionist consensus. On December 4, 1948, a group of American intellectuals published a damning evaluation of the party of Menachem Begin (upon his visit in the USA). Their letter read as follows:

> Among the most disturbing political phenomena of our times is the emergence in the newly created state of Israel of the "Freedom Party" (Tnuat Haherut), a political party closely akin in its organization, methods, political philosophy and social appeal to the Nazi and Fascist parties. It was formed out of the

membership and following of the former Irgun Zvai Leumi, a terrorist, right-wing, chauvinist organization in Palestine. . . . The Deir Yassin incident exemplifies the character and actions of the Freedom Party.

Within the Jewish community they have preached an admixture of ultra-nationalism, religious mysticism, and racial superiority. Like other Fascist parties they have been used to break strikes, and have themselves pressed for the destruction of free trade unions. In their stead they have proposed corporate unions on the Italian Fascist model.

During the last years of sporadic anti-British violence, the IZL and Stern groups inaugurated a reign of terror in the Palestine Jewish community. Teachers were beaten up for speaking against them, adults were shot for not letting their children join them. By gangster methods, beatings, window-smashing, and widespread robberies, the terrorists intimidated the population and exacted a heavy tribute.

The people of the Freedom Party have had no part in the constructive achievements in Palestine. They have reclaimed no land, built no settlements, and only detracted from the Jewish defense activity.[40]

This letter was signed by such luminaries as Albert Einstein, Hannah Arendt, and Sidney Hook. In the view of these liberal Jews, the Herut party was a dangerous radical right-wing party. It wanted to annex more land, refused to recognize Jordan's sovereignty, and did not want peace with Arabs. Begin was even likened by Ben-Gurion (to the latter's discredit) to Hitler, and it was the fact that he joined the unity government in the wake of the Six Day War that started the process of legitimation of the right, which morphed into a moderate version of itself. Netanyahu inherited an ambiguous heritage when he became the head of the Likud party, which was founded in 1973 and which was then in many respects a moderate one, resembling the moderate right of its European or North American equivalents. In the 1990s that party had achieved the capacity to rally the middle classes and be the party of liberals (defending free markets as well as the rule of law and human rights). Netanyahu forever changed that party into a populist one and in many ways took it back to the radical ideology of its predecessor, albeit through a different route.

Israel is a very good case study to understand populist politics for a few other reasons. As Yonatan Levi and Shai Agmon explain: first, "because of the longevity of its populist regime ... Israel has been ruled by populist governments for at least ten years ... It is, therefore, an instructive example of what a full decade of uninterrupted populist rule looks like."[41] In fact, according to the authors, the key attributes of populism – from the delegitimization of the press and the legal establishment to the politicization of state bureaucracy – have been present in Israeli politics for at least a decade.[42] Additionally, "Israel plays a central role in the emerging populist axis on the international stage – as evidenced by its tightening relationship with Brazil and India and the invitation it received to join the Visegrád Group, an alliance of Central European countries led by right-wing populists."[43] I would add another important reason: Netanyahu implemented neo-liberal policies yet has steadily enjoyed the support of a variety of downtrodden social groups[44] and, to this extent, is exemplary of the same conundrum which characterizes populist politics at large: it is a politics which has no compunction in lowering taxes for the rich, reducing the public sector, and increasing inequalities – and yet it enjoys the support of those most hurt by these policies. For example, house prices in Israel rose by a whopping 345.7 percent between 2011 and 2021, the highest increase in the world. During this period, Israeli wages increased by only 17.5 percent.[45] Clearly, this type of change would benefit only the very top echelons of society and hurts people of lower socio-economic status, as it makes it virtually impossible for them to find affordable housing. Despite this, Likud recruits its followers mostly from the less wealthy sectors of society. This fact clearly indicates that, as has often been noticed by a wide variety of commentators and scholars, populism is able to be immensely attractive despite the ways in which it hurts the economic interests of its supporters.[46] It also suggests that populism is mostly a politics of identity: it aims to strengthen the identity of the majority group, to repair symbolic injuries (real or imagined), and to play various identities against one another.

Dani Filc has described what he dubs Netanyahu's post-populism, a politics built around three dimensions: a material one in the form of economic neo-liberalism, a political one in the form of authoritarianism, and a symbolic one in the form of conservative nationalism.[47] The three dimensions of Netanyahu's (post-)populism cohere and coalesce seamlessly around a core emotional style that glues citizens to beliefs and stories that become particularly "sticky," viewed as persuasive by a wide variety of people because they resonate with real social conditions and with powerful symbols and meanings at work in culture. The argument of this book uses Filc's triptych as its departure point; it does not aim to explain populism as much as to describe it through the prism of emotions. It argues that authoritarianism and conservative nationalism rest on four emotions: authoritarianism is legitimized through fear, and conservative nationalism (a view of the nation based on tradition and rejection of the stranger) rests on disgust, resentment, and a carefully cultivated love for one's country. This book studies these four key emotions, the intertwining of which is crucial to understand the shift to a populist politics. Privileging such emotions does not exclude the relevance of other emotions, as they are indeed contiguous with others (anger, for example, is closely intertwined with resentment, disgust with hatred). Yet, at least in the Israeli case, they seem to capture most concisely the affective structure of populism, which, despite being versatile, has a common ideological core – one that is differently inflected in varied political cultures.

This book offers a grid of analysis which can and should be modulated in other countries. To be sure, these same emotions may also be present in left-wing populism (with different contents), but I focus on right-wing populism because it is this version which has come to dominate Israeli politics and which is far more widespread in the world. It is the *combination* of these four emotions and their relentless presence in the political arena that might be a characteristic of populist politics. This is in line with findings such as those of Salmela and Von Scheve, who attribute the rise of right-wing populism to a combination of several emotions working together (in their case, this includes resentment, fear, shame, and anger).[48] Therefore, despite dedicating a different chapter to each emotion, fear, disgust, resentment, and love of one's nation should be viewed as forming a compact cluster. In real social life, they come enmeshed with each other and may in fact form a single narrative made of multiple narrative threads.

*

In his *Politics*, Aristotle famously asked "whether the virtue of the good man and the excellent citizen is to be regarded as the same or as not the same."[49] In asking whether the virtues of the citizen and the virtues of a human being are the same, he invited us to question whether it is the same virtues that make particular people and citizens commendable. Inasmuch as virtue presupposes certain emotional dispositions (for example, we cannot imagine envy as a character trait of a virtuous person), Aristotle's is an invitation to think about the set of emotions which should or should not be cultivated in a good society. More specifically, he invites us to ask how, beyond the simple invocation of emotions in the rhetoric of certain leaders, some emotions come to redefine the horizon of thinking of a citizenry. Although Aristotle was not an unqualified supporter of democracy (he preferred a mixed form of government with democratic and oligarchic elements), we may follow his example and view the worm inside democracy as promoted by a specific set of emotional dispositions cultivated by populist leaders. Martha Nussbaum started such an analysis in her magnum opus *Political Emotions*, asking which emotions should be privileged or discouraged in liberal democracies (she cites disgust as an example of the former and love and compassion as examples of the latter).[50] This book pursues her analysis by viewing emotions as part and parcel of what Pierre Bourdieu called the habitus, the set of dispositions which structure a matrix of thinking and acting.[51] But where Bourdieu was interested in the ways in which habitus reflected and reproduced social inequalities, this book explores the formation of specific emotional habitus or dispositions in the political sphere. This in turn invites the question: Which criteria should we follow to define an emotion as a populist one – that is, how should we differentiate between the emotions which are routinely exercised in many political regimes and those that are particularly at work in populist regimes? Surely democratic public life is routinely rife with emotions (indignation, compassion, hope are the most obvious examples), yet *some* emotions may and do take a democratic public sphere away from its vocation.

Jan-Werner Müller, one of the most prominent world specialists on populism, has suggested that populism is "a permanent shadowy effect of representative democracy,"[52] a diagnostic astonishingly congruent with that of Adorno. His striking formulation suggests precisely one of the key findings of this book: how difficult it is to extricate populist claims from democratic ones. This task is made all the more complicated when we deal with emotions. With a group of Israeli MA students – professional lawyers with law degrees – we drew up the following criteria to try and differentiate between populist and ordinary emotions at work in democracies: populist emotions divide the people and pitch groups against groups; they are geared to divide the citizens of the same country; they tend to be animated by the perception of stark distinctions between groups; they engender or call for direct or indirect forms of violence, ostracism, censorship, or direct physical harm; they cancel the very legitimacy of positions different from their own; they are quick to perceive political rivals as traitors; they appeal to an imaginary core of greatness and authenticity of the nation which people are summoned to revere and love unconditionally; and they are often fed by narratives of victimhood and impending danger. Finally, these emotions, while aimed at inflaming the imagination of a people, often are used in an opportunistic way by the leader to promote or maintain his power. Indeed a key characteristic of such emotions is that they derive from the mistrust in institutions of the state and thus create a deep sense of alienation from the same institutions that are tasked with protecting democracy, while creating strong identification with and even love of a leader. This book does not claim it has exhausted the range of possibilities to understand the Israeli public sphere. It only offers an interpretative grid which may perhaps be applied to other countries, modulated and modified accordingly. The four emotions selected for this study constitute a matrix to explain how the political process becomes marred by anti-democratic populist impulses, what we may call fascist tendencies. How such emotions come to structure the field of vision of social actors in Israel is the theme of this book.

1
Securitist Democracy and Fear

"Oderint dum metuant"
Caligula

In a famous work addressed to Lorenzo de' Medici, Niccolò Machiavelli recommended that the prince should learn how to elicit love and fear in his subjects. Being loved and feared was the best way to exercise power, but, if you have to choose, Machiavelli admonished, better to be feared, for fear of the prince will at least maintain social order (on condition that the prince is not cruel).[1] Fear (instilled in others) is undoubtedly the emotion most relished by tyrants.

Fear was also central to the thought of another thinker, Thomas Hobbes – the seventeenth-century English philosopher – who claimed that two key passions guided people's political desires: the fear of death and the desire for comfort.[2] This is why people would abandon their natural freedom and let a strong state govern their lives, as long as it guaranteed security. In this view, fear would be progressively eliminated if the state were the only entity allowed both to monopolize the instruments of fear and to assuage it by guaranteeing the security of all. The Harvard political philosopher Judith Shklar went as far as defining liberalism as the political regime which abhors fear.[3] Freedom, for her, could be properly exercised only if the liberal state created the conditions of the removal of fear from citizens' everyday lives. The rule of law, democratically shared power, and constitutionally guaranteed human rights were supposed to make fear obsolete.

Yet, even democratically elected leaders sometimes find it difficult to give up on the Machiavellian insight regarding the usefulness and expediency of fear. Many populist leaders such as Netanyahu owe their long and deep grip on power to something Renaissance princes and tyrants could only envy: the capacity to *be loved through the fear* they sow.

Israel and Security

Thomas Hobbes claimed that, when he was born, his mother gave birth to twins, himself and fear.[4] The same can be said of Israel. When it was born, fear was born as its twin.

The Shoah forever changed Jewish consciousness. The pan-European massacre of the Jews made antisemitism take on quasi-metaphysical significance, making the hatred of Jews eternal, inescapable, and total, inscribed in the order of the world itself. Enemies formed a continuous and unending chain of evil: Amalek, the personification of the quasi-theological principle intent on destroying the Jews, Haman, who plotted to destroy the Jews in the Babylonian Empire; the Romans who wanted to dominate the Jews; the Christians and the Inquisition who tortured, killed, or expelled the Jews; the Polish peasants who executed pogroms; their lords who gave the quiet signals to do so – all of these came to look as elements of the same historical chain leading to and culminating in Hitler. The radicality of the Shoah made it very difficult if not impossible not to view the world through its intent and determination to annihilate the Jews.

It is with no small historical irony that the early Zionists chose as a land for their national project a small territory tucked in a large area dominated by Arabs and Muslims, none of whom had any particular reason to welcome a handful of people from Eastern Europe initially backed by a foreign colonial power. Muslims had been far less privy to the vicious antisemitism of Christian countries (or of secular movements such as Nazism), but the Arabs opposed the Zionist enterprise, as most people would, because the Jews made national claims on their land. In reference to the Arab opposition to the Jews in Palestine, Zeev Jabotinsky, the founder and leader of the right-wing Revisionist movement, lucidly wrote in 1923 that "The native populations, civilized or uncivilized, have always stubbornly resisted the colonists, irrespective of whether they were civilized or savage."[5]

But instead of viewing their opposition to Zionism as Jabotinsky did – that is, as the predictable opposition to dispossession and colonization – in the nascent Zionist consciousness the Arabs' rejection of Zionism slowly melded with ancestral antisemitism. The shift happened gradually, perhaps in 1929 (with the Hebron massacre which left almost seventy Jews dead), or after 1936, in the wake of the Arab revolts in Palestine, and certainly once the scope and magnitude of the European massacre of the Jews became clear. While in the 1920s Jabotinsky had been able to view the Arabs' opposition to the Jews as a predictable and understandable political reaction to colonialism, in the nascent Israeli consciousness, Arabs' opposition to the Zionist project started filling the place left vacant by Amalek, the demonic figure of Jewish history – "They want to drive us into the sea" – combined all in one the reality of Arab anti-colonial hostility with the plots and characters of Jewish unconscious, forever traumatized by an unredeemable history.

In its short history, which is just about the average life expectancy of a human being, Israel has been involved in at least twelve military conflicts or wars and at least fifty or more operations of various scales, such as shelling, bombing, strikes from the air, and incursions into territory. This is without even mentioning the state of low-key war with the Palestinians of the Occupied Territories since 1967. While Israel is not the only country to be engaged in protracted hostilities (Armenia, Afghanistan, and South Sudan are examples of countries involved in long-term conflict), it is the only nation to have been the object of direct attacks by at least seven countries in a span of seventy years, to be engaged in an ongoing low-intensity military conflict with a population intertwined with its own, and to identify 20 percent of its citizens as aligned with (potential or actual) enemies. Israel is thus entirely unique in that it is defined by its enemies outside its borders, by enemies close to its nonborders, and by the presence (real and imagined) of similar enemies inside its borders. In that sense, Israel displays what Carl Schmitt defined as the essence of "the political" – that is, the distinction between friend and enemy.[6] When groups face each other as enemies, it means there is the potentiality of war and killing between them, and this, for Schmitt, is the essence of the political. (This is the reason why Schmitt held liberalism in contempt, precisely for its inability to understand the constitutive role of enmity in politics.) This distinction – between friend and foe – is at the heart of the self-understanding of the Israeli polity. This is why we may say that Israel is not a democracy like others. Because of its geography and inner vulnerability, it was compelled to become a securitist democracy, perhaps with no equivalent in the world. This means that the state and the citizens are not only concerned with but constantly and actively mobilized to defend Israel. *Survival* is the key modus operandi of the country. Institutionally, this means that its army, police, and secret services play a key role in the daily conduct of the state and that "security" has become a key mental feature of citizens. Political life, morality, and culture are a matrix of habits of thinking and acting which, in Israel, can be called securitism.

*

The key category that came to prevail in the Zionist leadership was that of "survival." This key motif already appeared on the night of 14–15 May 1948, when the Arab states attacked the country immediately after it declared independence. Other important stages were attacks by Egyptian-trained *fedayeen* on civilians in Israeli territory in the 1950s. During the month of April 1956, Egyptian soldiers killed three Israelis. Israel responded by shelling Gaza and killed sixty-two people, among them civilians. At the end of April, Arabs ambushed the 21-year-old security officer of Kibbutz Nahal Oz, Roi Rotberg. He was killed, his eyes were gouged from their sockets, and his mutilated body was handed to UN observers. Moshe Dayan, the legendary one-eyed Israeli general, gave a eulogy considered to be one of the most influential speeches of Israeli history:

> Let us not today cast blame on the murderers. Who are we to argue against their potent hatred for us? . . . We are the generation of settlement, and without steel helmets and the maw of the canon we will not be able to plant a tree or build a home. Our children will not live if we do not dig shelters, and without barbed wire fences and machine guns we will not be able to pave roads and drill for water. Millions of Jews, annihilated because they had no country, gaze at us from the dust of Jewish history and command us to settle and raise up a land for our people. . . . We must not flinch from seeing the hatred that accompanies and fills the lives of hundreds of thousands of Arabs who live around us and await the moment when they are strong enough to get our blood. We will not avert our gaze lest our hands grow weak. This is our generation's destiny.[7]

Dayan's speech is exemplary of what would become the essential blueprint of the Israeli psyche. Dayan puts here annihilated Jews throughout history and throughout the world at the center of Israeli consciousness. It is to them the nation now addresses itself and it is this group the nation represents. Arabs become an undifferentiated mass, full of hatred, mirroring the ancestral threat of annihilation. A small group of *fedayeen* became a vast threatening entity. There is no doubt this speech was still in the minds of many when Israel invaded Egypt six months later, upon the Suez Canal crisis, provoking an international diplomatic predicament but asserting its military might. Barbed wire fences and machine guns became unavoidable and necessary in what emerged as a survivalist conception of the body politic clarifying the meaning of a securitist democracy: protecting oneself from the enemy and killing the enemy became two key imperatives to survive. A securitist democracy orients its mental, moral, political, and economic resources towards "survival" which overrides other considerations; it divides the world into friends and enemies, and defeating the enemy looms large in its decisions. Because of the permanent perception of threat, the law is regularly tramped over for the sake of survival. This was to become the fundamental political blueprint of Israel's politics as well as of its legal system.[8]

A decade after Dayan's speech and three weeks after the Six Day War, a war in which Israel had been the first to strike (in reaction to Nasser's closing of the Straits of Tiran) and after it had seized a considerable amount of territory, the words of Yitzhak Rabin (who was then chief of staff) resonated with those of Dayan a decade earlier:

> Our airmen, who struck the enemies' planes so accurately that no one in the world understands how it was done and people seek technological explanations or secret weapons; our armored troops who beat the enemy even when their equipment

was inferior to his; our soldiers in all other branches ... who overcame our enemies everywhere, despite the latter's superior numbers and fortifications – all these revealed not only coolness and courage in the battle but ... an understanding that only their personal stand against the greatest dangers would achieve victory for their country and for their families, and *that if victory was not theirs the alternative was annihilation*.[9]

Rabin drew here the contours of the alternatives as they came to be increasingly perceived by Israelis: either beat the enemy or be obliterated. In the same breath that Rabin boasted of Israeli military prowess, precision, courage, and force, he invoked annihilation. "Either force or annihilation" became the basic political and moral blueprint of the Israeli psyche.

In an official document, Israeli security doctrine of many decades was aptly summarized: "The assumptions underlying the traditional national security doctrine were that the state faced an existential threat; there was clear asymmetry in favor of the Arab states (with respect to area, population, economic base, political and military backing, and the ability to decisively resolve the conflict); and that Israel had no allies upon which it could depend."[10]

After the Eichmann trial in 1961 and the Six Day War, Israel became militarily and territorially stronger, yet the fear of annihilation took on larger, quasi-mythical proportions, because the Shoah emerged in international consciousness as a radical evil[11] and started occupying a central role in the Israeli collective psyche. In Idith Zertal's words, the enemy (Arabs) was Nazified,[12] even though this enemy had actually had very little to do with the pan-European massacre of the Jews. In 1982, explaining why he was waging the Lebanon War, Menachem Begin declared: "The alternative is Treblinka, and we have decided that there will not be another Treblinka."[13] Lebanon was a military target which replayed the monstrous history of European Jews.

Zionism started as a set of militias fighting on three fronts: all of them (Lehi, Etzel, Hagana) fought against the Arab natives and the British authorities, and, in addition, they fought each other. These three simultaneous fronts made military combat into a key component of the nascent Zionist identity. Most national struggles end once the nation is created; soldiers become pacified and surrender their arms to the state, which goes on to the task of building a civil society. But this was not the case of Israel, as military forces and secret services went on to become the spine of the state apparatus, shaping public policy as well as the ordinary language and outlook of citizens, instilling what Baruch Kimmerling called cognitive militarism.[14] Cognitive militarism is a state of mind in which civil society adopts, wholesale, the way of thinking of the military – civilians are military in waiting, civil institutions are constantly preparing for the possibility of war, war is the horizon of thinking and planning, problems are conceived as a power struggle, and victory is always the aim.

Two examples will suffice to illustrate how "security" shaped the Israeli style of governance and Israeli culture in a deep and long-lasting way: as Ronen Bergman shows in his remarkable book *Rise and Kill First*, targeted assassinations were embedded in the state apparatus of Israel from the beginning.[15] According to him, through Mossad, Israel has assassinated more people than the secret service of any other Western country since World War II. British officials, German scientists (who were ex-Nazis working with Egyptians to develop missiles), the PLO, Hamas, Hezbollah, and Iranian nuclear scientists have been regularly and almost routinely assassinated by Israel in order to prevent them from developing weapons or undertaking terror attacks against the country. It became taken for granted that Israel could and should ensure its security extra-territorially by executing murders outside the legal system (I do not think one can say with certainty whether there was or was not an alternative way to ensure its security;

for myself, I cannot say). The second example is demography, which in most countries in the world is viewed as an economic matter, but in Israel it became a security matter. To be sure, immigration is no less cast in Europe as a threat to one's values and identity. In Israel, however, such a threat is viewed in more literal terms, as entailing the annihilation of the Jewish people as such. "Demographic threat" became an ordinary expression, easily understood by everyone: Jewish babies needed to supersede non-Jewish babies (a view uncomfortably reminiscent of the view held today by white supremacists, the only group for whom demography is also a security threat – with the difference, however, that Jews are a tiny fraction of humanity and include several different so-called races). Securitism is also the source of the 2003 Citizenship Law which prevented Palestinians marrying Israelis from acquiring Israeli nationality (as is the case in most countries where marriage grants the possibility of citizenship). As Samara Asmir has claimed, in Israel, the term "security" has become a metaphorical "black hole" that can eclipse many issues related to the relationships between Israelis and Palestinians. In addition to the birth rates of Palestinians and Arab Israelis, Arab land ownership is described by some Jewish Israelis as a security issue. Given that international legal standards acknowledge that civil rights may be suspended in order to act against a breach of security, framing an issue in terms of a security threat allows the state to act in an illiberal manner towards those who are so identified. This is the situation created for Palestinian citizens of Israel – mechanisms that act in the name of security dictate and manage many areas of their lives. Asmir further claims that Arab Israelis are seen as an inherent threat to Israeli security, and therefore in many cases their rights are institutionally and legally denied.[16]

To be sure, many countries have reacted to terror attacks by reinforcing surveillance and security and suspending civil liberties. The response of the United States to the attacks on 9/11, which included expanding police surveillance of civilians and limiting certain civil privacy protections,[17] is just one example of this. However, Israel's case is slightly different because it does not distinguish between states of quiet and states of threat. Rather, its entire existence is viewed as marred by a continuous, unending existential threat, a state defined by Uriel Abulof as "deep securitization": "Deep securitization is defined and identified through its distinct scale and scope: threats are explicitly framed as probable and protracted, endangering the very existence of the nation/state and that discourse is incessantly and widely employed by the society."[18]

One of the most interesting features of a state and a culture which make security into its default option is that it makes fear into an invisible and intrinsic part of national consciousness. Imagine while I am walking in the street in a nonchalant way, thinking about my dinner, I see two guards heavily armed with rifles patrolling the street. This will change the course of my thinking and feeling: I will be made aware of the possible terror threats I had not thought about a moment ago when I was thinking about my vegetables. The rifles will simultaneously make me worried about a threat that had not been on my mind and reassure me that the threat will be offset. A military state works in the same way: its constant display of force and power, military emergencies, weapons, military language, celebration of victory, and memorialization of military victims produces a permanent awareness of the enemy and fear of the same enemy at the same time that it deploys the means to ensure security. Fear of the enemy becomes embedded in the entire state apparatus and in civil society; military power appears as necessary and the only antidote. Once fear is at the center of the collective psyche, it becomes virtually impossible to oppose it, because fear is a primary emotion concerned with survival. Thinking becomes an automatic "us vs. them" or "there will never be peace" or "you can never trust an Arab." The world is either for us or against us; problems are dealt with in terms of victory or defeat. Israel is one of the countries with the highest defense spending in relation to GDP (behind countries such as Eritrea and some Gulf states).[19] It has the most advanced industries of surveillance, security, and cyber security in the world (along with that of the United States), some of which specialize in helping both rogue states and wealthy individuals evade the law and commit various crimes (see the various scandals around security and spying companies Black Cube and NSO, which spy on behalf of rogue states and rich individuals).[20] With the exception of China, Israel's population is probably the most surveilled in the world (tapping a phone requires two signatures and no judge to approve)[21] and perhaps on the cusp of being *the most* surveilled in the world (there are plans to install cameras for face recognition throughout the country).[22] Security, military combat, and fear form a single matrix at the heart of Israeli politics and the nation's psyche.

Security is not only a vast array of weapons, technologies, and techniques of combat. It is first and foremost an idea, a concept, and a way to orient ourselves in the world. Concepts that are constantly present in consciousness and actions create "pathways" of thinking, feeling, and acting. "Security" divides the world between foes and friends: enemies and fear of the enemy become an entrenched part of consciousness. Ilana Hammerman, a left-wing activist and writer, describes what it feels like to grow up with such consciousness in which fear occupies a center place.

> The shooting and explosions and later the bombardments we heard from the lower city instilled in me a huge fear of the Arabs. I just wanted them to leave and to have quiet.
> This fear stayed with me for many years. During the 1956 war, I fled in terror from our apartment balcony on the top floor, because I saw a face in a red kaffiyeh looking back at me from the roof. I can still remember it. Maybe it was just an Arab

worker fixing the elevator motor, or maybe it was the face from my nightmares that suddenly appeared to me. At any rate, as a child and a teen, in the mixed city where I was born, I never met an Arab in regular social circumstances, not as a classmate or in the youth movement. In middle school, when it was time for me to choose a second language to study, I chose French and not Arabic. Our "French" group stood out in the schoolyard and taunted the smaller group that chose Arabic. Most of them probably went on to serve in intelligence.[23]

Hammerman describes here the subjective consciousness of those Israelis who lived in the incipient nation in the shadow of real enemies; such enemies become so present in consciousness that they are also sometimes imagined. Such fear connects the individual to the collective; one fears for the collective all the more because only the collective protects the individual. In her description of the child who was scared, the enemy is a specter, real and unreal, and fear ends up confusing real enemies and innocent strangers. Fear ascribes the enemy to a given essence and congeals him in that essence; it makes him both incomprehensible and evil, evil because incomprehensible.

This is also the basic mode of thinking instilled in soldiers, especially those that serve closer to the Palestinians.

Nadav Weiman is the vice-president and head of the pedagogical department of the NGO "Shovrim Shtika," or Breaking the Silence. This NGO encourages former Israeli soldiers to speak out about human rights infringements that they may have seen during their service and provides various public platforms for these stories to be heard. He has been a member of the organization since 2012. In the army he served in a Nahal elite unit as a member of a sniper team from 2005 to 2008. He joined the organization after he realized what the Israeli army was doing. I interviewed him through Zoom during the Covid pandemic.

Eva: From what you remember, as a soldier, what perception did you have of Palestinians?

NW: We did not call them Palestinians, but Arabs. Arabs are an entity, not individuals or people with desires. They are an entity, and this entity is the enemy and you should be afraid of all of them. You really are scared. We are constantly told that the Palestinians are terrorists, that they teach their children to murder. I was in high school during the Second Intifada. I am from Tel Aviv: buses were exploding around us, my brother's friends were killed in the army. So, when I joined, my friends and I thought they [the Palestinians] were all terrorists until proven otherwise. Even a pregnant woman who walks by you may be hiding something in her stomach; even a child on the way to school, his bag might have explosives.

Eva: Where do you learn to see it this way? Where does it come from? Did you arrive at the military with this concept? Or did you acquire it while training in the military?

NW: I came with it to the army. I was raised in Ramat Aviv gimel, the north area of Tel Aviv [an affluent and secular neighborhood], but I didn't speak to Palestinians. I had friends from sea scouts in Jaffa, and I didn't realize they were Palestinians. So, for me, Palestinians were something far away, a kind of enemy that is beyond the mountains of darkness. During the Second Intifada, it was our greatest fear – encountering a terror attack or something. In this respect they [the Palestinians] are evil and they are our enemies. Then in the army they teach you from morning to evening. There are "enemy consciousness" lessons that teach you who your enemy is. You learn about the different Palestinian organizations and all their branches, and which types of weapons they have. And every week you learn about problems in other operations, where soldiers were wounded or killed. The perspective on this is always what the soldiers are doing right or wrong in their jobs, not what you feel – that's how you are taught. You go on the job, you go back; before you even take off your face paint you make black coffee, sit down to drink the coffee, and every person says what he did well and what he did not do well. For instance, when we entered the room together we went shoulder to shoulder too much . . . You're not referring to the fact that you drag a kid who is peeing his pants out of bed in the middle of the night and how you feel about it. The whole discourse is a machoistic military discourse – whether or not we succeeded as soldiers. The goal is to protect the state of Israel, the mission is to seize terrorists in the Jenin area, the task of the team is to get on the roof and cover the other team. My mission as their observation officer was to find the targets, to measure the distance with the laser, to count "three, two, one, fire." So from defending the state of Israel to Nadav sitting on the roof of a Palestinian family home and directing a sniper.

So who taught me? On the one hand, reality taught me, and the fear within which I grew up and the very militaristic family from which I came, and on the other hand in the army they taught me that there is no such thing as an innocent or a guilty Palestinian – there is a Palestinian who is involved or uninvolved. When we came to arrest Palestinians we called them terrorists, and we never said the Palestinian's name – we called him Johnny. It's a sort of . . . [generic] name that keeps it distant. It sounds like I'm catching someone in the Wild West. We would say "The Johnny is in our custody. With the Johnny on the way to the car." So the language keeps you away from it and reality brings you into all the hate and anger about the Palestinians who just want to kill us. The moment comes when you finish your military training . . . You are on the top of the world . . . Then you reach the Occupied Territories, you suddenly leave the base. You . . . are a soldier with weapons, and suddenly all the Palestinians you see are all looking at you with a look of fear and hatred. They are terribly scared of me because I am a soldier, and in one second the situation can flare up and I will do what I want – violence or arrests or I don't know what – but they also hate me because I'm an occupying soldier. It took me a few weeks to figure it out, but all of a sudden you feel that everyone is looking at you with those looks and you are scared of everyone and you hate everyone back. So it's not just what we're taught or the military language, it's also the reality itself. No matter how much I tried to be a good soldier, or the moral soldier, the moral occupier, the reality itself was stronger than anything else. Even if I stroked every Palestinian we met with a silk glove, everyone would still look at me with hatred. Even if I would seat him nicely on the chair or tie him up not too tightly, I would still be an occupying soldier. I came from a Mapainik, Labor Party household, I support the two-state solution, but still the Palestinians are trying to murder us. And I felt that I was doing everything I could, but everyone hates me, everyone fears me. This means they're my enemy, period.

Nadav Weiman recounts in somewhat striking terms how fear pervades the entire military service of young soldiers (this is a tangible fear with a real object, since soldiers can be, and frequently are, targeted or killed). Fear is also what enabled him to develop the disposition to kill an enemy. Without his own fear, it would be much more difficult to execute his role as a soldier, to subscribe wholeheartedly to the vast security apparatus deployed by Israel. Fear helps burn into one's consciousness that Palestinians are the enemy, thus enabling their dehumanization. Fear then sits squarely at the center of the Israeli psyche for many reasons: it is anchored in the traumatic history of the Jews; it is an expression of the embattled geography of Israel; and it is routinized by a security doctrine which has viewed existential threat as permanently looming over the country.

Netanyahu intuitively understood that the core of the Israeli soul was fear and perfected the formula that was invented by his Labor predecessors (Arabs = Shoah). He used this understanding relentlessly, manipulatively, not for the collective interest (as Ben-Gurion, arguably, did) but for his own electoral interests. Few democratically elected heads of legitimate democracies have used fear as blatantly as Netanyahu. However, in comparison to regimes that are rated as less democratic than Israel, a similar case comes to mind: in the Philippines,[24] former President Duterte enacted what some scholars call "penal populism" by enhancing and utilizing fear of crime and drugs in the country.[25] While Duterte did not seek a second term in office, for Netanyahu, the fear he has known to instill may explain the fact he has been the longest serving prime minister in Israeli history. Peter Beinart summarizes this very aptly: "For Benjamin Netanyahu, Israel always faces the same enemy. Call it Amalek, call it Haman, call it Nazi Germany – it seeks the same thing: the destruction of the Jewish people."[26] Netanyahu intermingled more cynically than any other Israeli politician the biblical and theological characters of Jewish history with the geopolitical entanglements of Israel.

In his 2000 book *A Durable Peace*, Netanyahu wrote that the idea that the Palestinians are a separate people who deserve the right of self-determination is borrowed directly from the Nazis.[27] In 2002, he urged the United States to invade Iraq because "we now know that had democracies taken preemptive action to bring down Hitler in the 1930s, the worst horrors in history could have been avoided."[28] In 2006, he said: "It's 1938 and Iran is Germany."[29] In 2010, he vowed that "we won't forget to be prepared for the new Amalek [the eternal figure intent on destroying the Jews], who is making an appearance on the stage of history and once again threatening to destroy the Jews."[30]

Much earlier, in 1994, Netanyahu cast Rabin as a traitor and shrouded the Oslo Accords in a climate of fear.[31] He demonized

Iran by combining it with the mouth-shutting analogy of the Holocaust.[32] He made up the historical lie that the Palestinian Mufti was the first to think of the Nazi final solution.[33] At the Munich security conference in 2018, Netanyahu spoke about the Holocaust,[34] and at the Yad Vashem conference that same year he talked about security,[35] blending perfectly security and the Shoah. So it was in his 2015 speech to the American Congress. Netanyahu started by comparing Iran's regime to Haman, Amalek's genocidal heir from the Book of Esther, and ended by comparing it to Nazi Germany. "The days when the Jewish people remained passive in the face of genocidal enemies," he declared, "those days are over."[36] In an analysis comparing the current Serbian leader Aleksandar Vučić and Netanyahu, Dahlia Scheindlin argues that

> Both men insisted to the world that their countries' aggression was justified because their people were the victims. Vucic [in his then role as Serbian minister of information] argued that military force was necessary to defend against the Kosovo Liberation Army, which Serbia viewed as a terrorist organization. Netanyahu staked his career on Israel's war of survival against terrorism. Both criticized the Western press for maligning their countries and denounced news organizations for falling for propaganda.[37]

Both leaders promoted a distinctly illiberal style of democracy, precisely because they are able to project the victimhood of their country and generate an attendant sense of fear.

Once he cast political and diplomatic issues as threats of annihilation, Netanyahu obliterated discussions on strategy. Instead, he created two camps: one that would defend the survival of the state, another that would threaten it. This is how emotions work: they address their object in an immediate way and push aside calculation. Fear enabled Netanyahu to cast Arab members of the Knesset (MK) and human rights

NGOs as dangerous, and he did what fascist leaders routinely do: draw a straight line between external enemy and internal rival. He brought fear inside the borders of Israel and cast the left parties and their Arab partners as an enemy, equivalent to other enemies.

During the 2015 elections, in an attempt to encourage as many Likud voters as possible to go out and vote, Netanyahu addressed them by using the stern military language used during wars:

> The Arab voters are going in droves to vote. The leftist organizations are driving them there in buses . . . We now have "Tzav 8" (an emergency call to reserve forces in times of war). We only have you. Go out and vote. Take your friends, your family, vote Mahal [Likud], we'll close the gap between us and the Avoda party. With your help and with God's help, we'll establish a national government that will keep Israel safe.[38]

In this short but striking speech, Netanyahu's strategy became crystal clear: the leftist parties and Arabs were equivalent; both are enemies of the state and should be a source of fear. The political struggle is framed in the language that is most familiar to Israelis – a military one. Fear of and hatred for Arabs are indistinguishable from the fear of and hatred for the left. Netanyahu is as comfortable invoking Iran's nuclear power as he is in instilling fear of his political opponents (who are presumably about to destroy the Jewish people). The cynicism of this strategy sometimes takes on almost comical features, for example when the Likud party accuses Isaac Herzog, a veteran Zionist leader of the moderate left, of discrediting Netanyahu and endangering the country's security by giving a critical speech at the Munich Security Conference, possibly betting that the historical associations associated with the venue alone would bring this appearance close to treason.[39]

Accusing political rivals of threatening the security of the country has been a consistent strategy of Netanyahu and the main political content of the Israeli right.[40] Perhaps because it can no longer justify its opposition to the peace process on rational grounds, the right has increasingly resorted to fear, justifying its opposition by casting the other side as dangerous, wicked, and criminal.

In an article published in *Haaretz* on October 6, 1993, Doron Rosenblum illustrated this logic: he quotes Uzi Landau, a Likud MK:

> If Rabin's policies toward Syria are followed, one morning they [Israeli Jews] will awaken to see columns of Syrian tanks descending from the Golan Heights like herds of sheep ... The settlements of the Galilee will then be attacked by firepower stronger than that used in [the war of] 1973 ... Since the idea of extermination of Israelis remains a topic in the Syrian consciousness ... any [Israeli] withdrawal from the Golan Heights will only precipitate the moment that the Syrian knife will approach the throat of every inhabitant of the Galilee ... Syrian policies are fixed by a genetic code not subject to rapid changes.[41]

MK Benny Begin, Menachem Begin's son and, before his resignation, himself an important figure of the right-wing Likud, was also quoted in this 1993 article and went even further. The imagined Syrian invasion, he claimed, had the same aim as "the Pogromists of Kishinev," and this aim was "to cut Jewish throats." Alongside the image of past pogroms, Begin made sure to include, as a courtesy, the image of an impending apocalypse by adding that nuclear scientists would help in the Syrian venture.[42] Eternal hatred of Jews, pogroms, and nuclear warfare intertwine here smoothly and cannot fail to provoke an affect of fear. It should be stressed that antisemitism is indeed the oldest hatred known to our civilization. And while early Zionism aimed to find a solution to it by ending the state of subservience of the Jews, it never intended to place it at the center of Israel's political bond and psyche.

Fear, both imagined and real, is a potent political tool. It trumps and overrides all emotions and considerations. It bulldozes the entire political arena and justifies the suspension of basic rights and liberties. It is the commander in chief of all emotions. Therefore, whoever credibly commands fear is able to command the political arena. In drawing a straight line between external and internal enemies, Netanyahu bullied the entire electoral process.

Even when he started his campaign against Netanyahu, Benny Gantz had already been bullied. In 2019, Gantz was not only a contender for the post of Israeli prime minister, he also more loftily aspired to replace Netanyahu on *moral grounds*. To establish his status, he made a series of videos called "Only the Strong Survive." In one video, Gantz took credit for having commanded the operations which killed 1,364 Hamas terrorists in the 2014 Gaza war.[43] That this man was supposed to be the man who would replace Bibi on moral grounds only shows the extent to which the pairing fear–security has *de facto* pulverized norms of public morality.

We may thus say this: through a combination of historical memory, the reality of Arab hostility (along with the fear-inducing rhetoric of some Muslim and Arab leaders),[44] the persistence of antisemitism in many parts of the world, the prevalence of the memory of the Shoah, and the manipulations created by Netanyahu, fear has come to occupy the central place in the Israeli psyche. This fear makes it virtually impossible to think in terms other than security, enmity, force, power, survival, crushing the enemy. Such an agenda renders plausible the delegitimation of the liberal left and is undoubtedly responsible for the fact that the left is now only a tiny and marginal fraction in Israeli politics. This is evinced by the Israeli chapter of Amnesty International. Moran Avital and Yariv Mohar, two activists who work at the Israeli branch of the international organization, confirm this. In an official report of Amnesty International, *The Initiative for National Security and Human Rights* (yet to be published), they state that, on the basis of research as well as conversations with government officials and ordinary people, they have found that the idea of human rights is often viewed in Israel as suspicious because antithetical to "security." Because security trumps all other values, government officials and ordinary citizens are willing to weaken human rights.

Similar processes may be happening elsewhere in the world as well, albeit less markedly. In France, fear of immigration has been tied to the dwindling support of the public for left-wing parties.[45] During the 2014 European Parliament elections in the UK, the right-wing populist UK Independence Party arranged its platform around the issue of fear of immigration and gained huge electoral support in regions previously identified with the Labour Party.[46] In many ways, the fear of immigration in Europe and the USA bears an increasing resemblance to the politics of fear in Israel: it identifies immigrants and refugees as enemies threatening the nation at its borders and, as the theory of "great replacement" (the fear that the minority will replace the majority) suggests, it also makes demography a key political issue.[47]

*

In relentlessly invoking the annihilation of Israel, fear feeds on and mixes facts and fiction. Populist fear creates affective imaginary surpluses that are difficult to prove or disprove and take hold of the political psyche.

This fear differs from the fear felt by ordinary citizens living in dangerous parts of Israel. To better understand what we may call "real fear," provoked by real bombardments and concrete threats to one's life, quite different from the fictitious one invoked in political speeches to achieve political aims, in January of 2020 I traveled with Avital Sicron (a graduate student in sociology at the Hebrew University, who assisted in conducting this research) to a kibbutz in the northwestern part of the Negev, in Otef Aza, in the very same region where Roi Rotberg was killed almost seventy years ago. I interviewed three women from the kibbutz, Shelly, Rouhama, and Efrat, who have all been living there for all their adult lives. They arrived in the region forty-five years ago, in 1975, with Hashomer Hatsair, a socialist Zionist group. Their intent was to settle the land and create a Jewish presence in the remote corners of Israel. In Shelly's spacious and clean kitchen, we had a long conversation around a cup of hot tea, and I tried to understand what it feels like to live with a constant fear.

> *Eva*: Has your general feeling about life and living here changed in this time?
> *Rouhama*: I can say that I used to hitchhike all the time, and we weren't scared at all. Arabs would drive on this road too, and we never felt fear. I think that one of the reasons why I chose to live here was the distance and the quiet. It was quiet. Now it isn't. I think it happened gradually. Gaza used to be open; we went to visit there, around 1976. Then settlements started popping up there, and the Arabs weren't permitted to keep using our roads. It was gradual, not sudden. I think that, when the Gaza settlements were evacuated, that's when the shooting started.
> *Efrat*: It started small. Today it's big. Small means that it wasn't really scary yet. We didn't have alarm systems; it wasn't announced on TV. It wasn't organized yet; we weren't shielded yet [the buildings of the kibbutz did not include shelters]. The army told us to stand in the corridor [when there was shooting]. Today it seems crazy, standing in the corridor, but we thought it was fine. It was the army saying. . . . We were very naïve, thinking that we would stand in

the corridor and it would be alright. I realized the danger when a kid was killed in Nahal Oz, when he was in his house, which was shielded. That's the first time I realized that people actually die from this. It's dangerous. This was about five years ago. . . . when it started my daughter was a teenager, and she used to call me, and I told her to stand in the hallway. It became part of our regular routine. Then they started to shield the buildings. They added a shelter room to every house. Even before that, they covered all the children's buildings, the kindergartens, in cement. And every time there was an event [bombing], we were supposed to bring the kids there.

Rouhama: At this time our houses weren't shielded yet.

Shelly: People used to sleep in the kindergartens.

Efrat: Yes, it was like we went back to communal sleeping. Parents and children used to go sleep there, or in the shelters during the wars. And I know people that used to go sleep there with their families even when there were small events.

Shelly: Or they would just leave.

Efrat: At first, I barely felt it. We would just move on after every event. And then a good friend from a kibbutz nearby was killed. On the same day that they said that the war was over [operation "Protective Edge"], a missile hit the kibbutz and killed Zevik and Shachar. Zevik's wife works here at the kindergartens. That was scary. . . . We used to run between buildings, from my house to hers, because the "in-between" spaces, that's the scariest part. . . .

Eva: Could you expand on the point of continuing with the normal routine? . . .

Shelly: When it's quiet, I'm in denial. I don't think about it. But once something happens, even something small, like a few alarms ["Tzeva Adom"], maybe not even here, it just paralyzes me. I don't leave the house; I sit near my shelter [mamad, a secure room built of heavy concrete]. I plan my bathroom breaks and my shower in advance. It paralyzes me. But when it's quiet it's like . . .

Efrat: We transferred our bedroom to our shelter.

Shelly: Me too.

Efrat: That's the safest option.

Shelly: I know when this . . . when it started. I went for a walk with a friend, in the field, and we had to lie on the ground. A missile passed above us, we saw it and we couldn't do anything. There was an alarm and we were in the field. So, when the situation is like that, I don't go for walks in the field. If I want to see my grandkids, who live just nearby, they come and pick me up in the car, because I feel safer with someone else. . . .

Eva: So, what have you stopped doing?

Efrat: I don't leave the kibbutz when I go on walks. Because I'm afraid to be in the field when it happens. So, I walk in the yard, along the fence. And even then, after an event, it takes me about a week to go back to taking walks. It's scary. My daughter was on a walk [during a bombing]. I'll never forget it. She called me, terrified, they were shooting, she was in the middle, and there's nothing you can do, you're completely helpless. . . . A few times missiles went just over our heads. You hear this whistle. I can't describe it. It's like a physical pain. It's before the alarm. It feels like you're having a heart attack. And then you hear BOOM. I close my eyes and just wait for it to fall, so we know where it fell. Once, it fell really close to my house, near the petting zoo, it's really close. And there was silence for a few moments. You're afraid to move because you don't know what you'll find when you open the door.

Fear, real fear, grips the body of these women and has transformed the ordinary decisions of their lives and what they do in their own houses. Habits inside the home, the distribution of bedrooms, windows, daily walks, family gatherings, driving, even standing inside one's home, all of these bear the mark of fear because one's life can suddenly stop, at any moment. This fear is importantly different from the one that is activated by the threat of a new holocaust. Responding to the possibility of another holocaust mobilizes history and imagined objects. A fear that responds to imagined threats cannot find ways to modulate its responses to the world. We may perhaps suggest that imagined fears become closer to anxiety, as defined by Freud. For him, fear has an object while anxiety lacks an object; the first is transient while the second is long-lasting.[48] Fear may help us survive by a fight or flight reaction, while anxiety is more likely to paralyze the body or the mind and to be diffuse in one's daily life. We may also add that the latter feeds on imagination whose grip is probably more powerful than that of reality, since it does not really respond to the world. It can persist even when objective conditions change.

*

Ami Ayalon was a model soldier. Many times decorated for courage, he was major general and served as commander of the Israeli Navy from 1992 through 1995. Following Yitzhak Rabin's assassination in 1995, Ayalon became head of the Shabak (Israel's internal security service) and made a few incursions into the realm of politics on a slate we could qualify as center-left. I interviewed him in the headquarters of Akim, an association that aims to assist people with intellectual disabilities, of which he was the chairman at the time.

> For Israelis, the past events (exile of Babylon, exile from Spain, the pogroms, the Holocaust) are embedded in the present. It's the only state in the world where its citizens aren't certain of its survival in the near future (forty years ahead). The concept of existential threat is a daily reality for many Israelis. It's part of the DNA that shapes the perception of security. One of the key concepts of this perception is the assumption that, when an

> existential threat presents itself, we will have to deal with it on our own; no one will come to our aid.
>
> ... The state of Israel is the most protected in the world, from any threat of missiles, rockets, airplanes, terror – our borders are closed. There is no other state so protected on quantifiable parameters when you measure the amount and the quality of the army and its systems in relation to the quantifiable threats that we face. But Israeli citizens feel less secure than in most countries, maybe even less than any other people. This gap between defense [the quantifiable aspect of security] and security [an existential feeling of security] is the basis for our behavior, that shapes the Israeli perception of security.

Fear, Ayalon says, is key to the Israeli collective psyche at the same time that Israel has the strongest security system in the world. This means that Israelis' fear bears no relation to the actual defense system they have. He goes further.

> In a reality of fear, citizens will always prefer security over [human and civil] rights, especially if it's not the rights of the majority, but of the "others." They are perceived as a threat. Courts have used this policy in wars that have a definite end, understanding that rights can be "put aside" for security, but the war on terror doesn't have a definite end. So, every time, we take a little bit more of their rights. ... A rational leader should have said that a scared society collapses upon itself, so he will do anything to create security, but the leaders need to be re-elected. So, in a time of fear, we don't elect a leader who gives us a better education system, better health, or culture, we vote for leaders who are better at killing our enemies, who are better at "pushing the red button."

Ami Ayalon exposes very lucidly the tension between a political culture of rights and securitism. "Ilan" is a senior member of the Israeli Shabak who preferred to remain anonymous and with whom I spoke separately. Ami Ayalon's opinion unknowingly resonated with him:

> *Ilan*: I don't think there is another country in the world where exercising these powers [of the Shabak] is so easy. For example, getting a warrant to tap someone's communications is radically easier in Israel than in other Western countries. Here you only need two signatures: the head of the Shabak and the prime minister. Few prime ministers have really deliberated before giving these signatures. This doesn't exist in the rest of the world, where a judge always has to sign.
> *Eva*: Do you think this undermines a culture of human rights?
> *Ilan*: Potentially, yes. This power exists and the question is how we use it. But, in principle, the powers that are in the hands of the head of Shabak are unmatched in the democratic world. And every day that passes, and technology increases, those powers grow.

Ilan goes on about the ways in which the organization of the Shabak penetrates all areas of social and political life.

> *Ilan*: An organization like the Shabak is built for big outbursts, like the Intifada. What do all these people do when there is no outbreak? So, I think sometimes there is a tendency to invent problems, if only to justify this system. Because the Shabak doesn't have a reserve force, so a very heavy system has to be held in order to respond to large events, but between such events there isn't necessarily a job for everyone. So, organizationally, you need to find ways to justify this system, so it's always necessary to create an opponent that justifies it. So, for example, there is the question of how much Shabak should oversee minorities in Israel. As a democratic state, overly extreme surveillance is bad because it creates a negative social impact [between the lines, we understand that the impact is chronic suspicion]. Ami

[Ayalon] was the first to understand this and ask how much coverage is needed. It is very difficult for an organization to analyze this for itself, because it needs external observation. How can an organization say, okay I have too much? You have to decide to take a little risk and reduce sources as much as possible, but the Shabak is measured by the ability to enforce security, so it basically has no interest in taking that risk.

Eva: Do you think there is an unjustified use of security while discussing legal issues like these? What would you do as a legislator? Do you think there is security fundamentalism in Israel? . . .

Ilan: This thinking gives excess weight to all security considerations. For example, when the government dealt with infiltrators from Sinai or the unification of Palestinian families, there was tremendous pressure for the Shabak to provide a security justification, even though the problems are not inherently related to security. The reason for this is that security issues are a winning argument. This pressure, that I experienced personally, to provide a justification based on security . . .

Even within issues of security there are things that are being misused. For example, the evacuation of Amona [a West Bank settlement]. This is a security issue. A court ruled that they must evacuate. They contacted the head of the service and asked for his professional opinion that clearing Amona is problematic for security, that it can cause bloodshed and the like. Which is ridiculous because this can always be true. Does anyone imagine not complying with a court order because someone wouldn't like it? But on this issue, they asked for our opinion, and the court didn't accept it. A smart head of Shabak should be wary of these things. In the first six months after the appointment of a Shabak head, such a situation is likely. There's a danger that the Shabak head will try to please the political echelon.

Ilan, who plays an important role in the Shabak, offers a striking view: the security agency is an organization which can artificially inflate its role. There is a clear trajectory, he says, which consists in using and mobilizing the Shabak and the idea of security to justify crass political, partisan decisions, such as the refusal to evacuate illegal settlements. Shabak bestows an aura of legitimacy to policies that infringe human rights and international law by making them into security issues, showing how security becomes an empty category, a fiction to implement controversial policies. Ilan suggests clearly the ways in which an institution such as the secret service agency translates and converts political issues into security matters.

The Effects of Fear on the Political Body

Corey Robin distinguishes between the fear that is mobilized to create unity among the people (as in a state of war, for example) and fear that works on the divisions and inequalities of the society in which it is deployed.[49] In the Israeli context, Netanyahu has mixed these two types of fear while privileging the latter over the former, as he has relentlessly promoted fear of Arabs and left-wing people. Because the left is almost defined by its trust in moral progress and in the capacity of institutions to foster cooperation, fear has been the privileged emotion of the right. More exactly, research has shown that fear tends to make people move rightward on the political spectrum[50] in the sense of taking precautionary measures to undermine a threat. Fear is the ally of the right because it enables people to live in what Carl Schmitt called states of exception, or the ability of the state to transcend and ignore the rule of law in the name of the state, the nation, and their security.[51] In other words, fear enables cost-free social control and cost-free bypassing of laws by the state. A little-known fact about Israel is that it has been in a state of emergency since its inception. The official website of the Israeli Knesset stipulates:

> Despite the fact that the circumstances which prevailed during the first years of the State of Israel's existence have changed, a national state of emergency has existed since the country's inception in 1948. It has been regularly extended by the Knesset and the Government due to the fact that over the years the Knesset has enacted many laws which include directives that are conditioned by the existence of a state of emergency. The cancellation of the state of emergency will lead to the annulment of these directives.[52]

This includes laws and directives that are geared towards security (such as a law that enables placing individuals in administrative detention without charge or court order), as well as laws concerning economic affairs (such as the authority of the state to supervise and regulate the sale and manufacture of certain products).[53]

This permanent state of exception authorizes forms of action which bypass the law, which in turn generate specific habits and styles of thought, namely, responding immediately to threats rather than devising long-term policies. As Ilan emphasized, Israel knows very well how to think about responding to threats but does not know how to think about consequences. In addition, fear enables rule through chaos and makes chaos and disorder into a mode of governance. The greater the chaos in a country (because public services are neglected, because social groups are increasingly set against each other, because some groups are made so alien that they can be easily cast as enemies) the more acutely felt is the need for a strong leader who will alleviate the fear and the anxiety generated by disorder. Third, as the remarkable testimony of Nadav Weiman suggests, fear makes the enemy into an incomprehensible entity, an animal hidden in the dark, invisible and dangerous, someone we can neither see, nor grasp, nor understand. When one fears an entity perceived to be emotionless, it is much easier to kill, torture, harass, arrest, or terrorize them, since they are emptied of any content other than the fear they elicit in me. Fourth: fear always privileges the right-wing side of politics, since the right is always the one which prefers security and order over almost any other issue and sometimes does not hesitate to suspend human rights and civil liberties in order to defend security.[54] As the US terrorism expert Brian Jenkins writes, "Democracy does not preclude voluntary submission to despotism. A frightened populace demands protection."[55] The constant threats in Israel have meant that the army has always been deeply involved in Israeli society. What is new over the last three decades is that, thanks to the hi-tech industry, security has become a multi-billion dollar industry, in which the private sector, the military, and the state converge smoothly. In fact, similar trends are apparent worldwide: the size of the global security services market has grown from $78 billion in 2011 to $132 billion in 2020. North America is responsible for a considerable part of this growth, with its market increasing during that period from $18 billion to $32 billion. Another leading force in this shift is Asia, where the numbers increased from $15 billion to $37 billion.[56] These security services are private companies, but in many cases they take on duties that have formerly been provided by the state, thus melding together the economic logic of the capitalist market with the enactment of state-sanctioned violence.

This represents a dramatic departure from the civic culture of democratic societies. As Rosa Brooks, a professor of law, former analyst at the Pentagon and senior advisor to Obama, suggests in an illuminating analysis,[57] human societies throughout history draw clear separations between war and peace and between warriors and civilians, and that this is all the more true in a democratic society. In so-called primitive societies, men are turned into warriors through the use of war paint and initiation rituals, and when they return they must also undergo reintegration rituals. The reason why this is the case is that what is permissible in wartime becomes morally and legally unacceptable in peacetime. Killing others in peacetime is a crime, but in wartime, as Brooks puts it, it might get one a medal.[58] But when fear justifies the pervasive presence of military action and thinking, it has a potent effect on political culture: it blunts and blurs the distinction between the civilian and the military modes of thinking, acting, and feeling.

Indeed, the most significant effect of fear is not to understand that the enemy is also a scared human being living in our midst. Living in a state of fear blocks the understanding that *the very same people who live in fear* create conditions of fear for others through a tremendous security apparatus.

*

Since 2006, Israel has fired thousands and thousands of rockets into Gaza, killing and maiming thousands. In 2006, *The Guardian* in the UK reported that Gazans who had been killed or wounded had suffered previously unseen injuries:[59] internal organs were severely burned and damaged, resulting in amputations or death. Bodies were severely fragmented, melted, and disfigured. It was rumored that a new experimental weapon, a Dense Inert Metal Explosive (DIME), was used. (Israel has declined to comment regarding the use of the bomb, which has presumably been designed to limit the radius of the attack and its collateral damage).[60] Since then, many operations, attacks, missiles, and counter-missiles have been launched on both sides. According to the organization B'Tselem, since 2006 5,713 Palestinians have been killed by Israeli security forces in Gaza[61] and 106 Israelis have been killed by Palestinian forces (this includes civilians and security forces).[62] If we count the numbers of the wounded and the traumatized, then the effects of this continuous low-density war are far wider and reach the tens of thousands. It is safe to argue that, in Gaza, almost no one has been able to escape constant fear of hunger, deprivation, terror, maiming, or death.

Gaza has practically no economy; there are regular severe medical crises with no supplies of medicine and hardly functioning hospitals; little food; no work. The lives of ordinary Gazans have been destroyed to the core, but the conditions in which they live are hardly perceptible to the minds of Israelis. And they are not the only ones who live in misery and fear, albeit of a much lesser kind. Much closer are Arabs living in East Jerusalem. Nisreen Alyan is a lawyer working at the legal clinic at Hebrew University. She represents Arabs living in East Jerusalem:

> An ordinary Arab lives with the constant threat of incarceration, of stop and frisk [an indiscriminate policing measure used on a large scale by the New York Police Department under Mayor Michael Bloomberg], the fear that you will "fall" on someone while walking down the street who will take you to prison. Also, when you live in East Jerusalem, you need to prove that your main residence is in East Jerusalem, otherwise you are thrown out of your home. Imagine ever fearing to lose your home. You are in constant fear of being in the wrong place.

East Jerusalem residents lack two basic human rights which most people around the world take for granted: the right of citizenship and the right to be at home in their home (they can vote in municipal elections but not in national ones). They are stateless people and therefore utterly without any protection and defense. In this state of political dispossession, they run the risk of losing their homes, the very source of most people's identity.

A 2010 survey showed that, among Israeli Jews, 54 percent are worried that they or their relatives could be attacked by

Arabs during their everyday routines, while 43 percent are not worried. Among Palestinians, 75 percent are worried that they could be attacked, or their property confiscated or their house bulldozed, by Israeli forces, while 25 percent are not worried.[63] The overwhelming majority of Palestinians live with the constant fear of being dispossessed of their right to make it back home or to walk freely in the streets.

Fear has a key political property: in fear, the other is perceived as wanting to annihilate us, and so it is therefore easily "otherized" – that is, viewed both as far from our group and as threatening our group. It derives from enmity but also further deepens that enmity. Moreover, fear is ceaselessly manipulated by leaders to divide and sow divisions, to seize more power, and to justify authoritarian rule and supremacy. This truth is relevant on all sides of the Palestinian–Israeli conflict. The report by Amnesty International, mentioned above, goes even further and highlights a deep paradox at the heart of securitism: once human rights take the back seat because they are perceived as inimical to security, this state of affairs tends to make Israel *less* rather than more secure because the erosion of human rights tends to pitch groups against each other and to actually promote violence. Ironically, securitist political cultures may end up being far less secure, thus further justifying the fear on which they are built.

Conclusion

Some people manage to go beyond their own fear, beyond the automatic mechanisms of thinking and feeling that fear produces. Curiously, when fear derives from a real object, it seems that people are better able to cope with it than when that fear rests on an imaginary narrative. The three women mentioned earlier – Efrat, Shelly and Rouhama – who live very close to the Gazan border, offer a striking example of the ways in which fear from a real object can be modulated in a rational point of view.

> *Eva*: Has your attitude towards the Arabs changed over the years? Both as individuals and as a community?
> *Efrat*: I've become more pro-Arab.
> *Rouhama*: I still think we have to talk to them. People don't agree with me, but I still think that saving the place that I live in can happen only if we talk with them.
> *Efrat*: I'm not ashamed to say this to my family. At work as well. My place of work is considered leftist. If things continue in the way they have been, they'll close it eventually. Everything we told you about here, the shielding and the money, they [the Palestinians] don't have any of it. No shielding, no community, no medical help, nothing.
> *Rouhama*: Why wouldn't they be mad?
> *Shelly*: They have nothing left to lose.
> *Efrat*: I think they're extraordinarily creative. Today a bunch of balloons attached to a soccer ball was sent over [from Gaza]. The first thing I said to my grandkids was "Look, you can't touch this." We had a balloon with explosives fall in the playground here; luckily the children weren't there. That's the kind of thing that makes me anxious, since the grandkids were born.
> *Rouhama*: When they started with the balloons, I asked myself how it hadn't happened sooner. Because they have nothing to lose. It's so creative, using a balloon, so simple, you can find it anywhere. And where do you shoot at when this balloon lands here?
> *Eva*: Is it hard not being on "your own" side? To identify more with the other side, sometimes?
> *Efrat*: Not for me.
> *Rouhama*: Me neither.
> *Shelly*: It's difficult because I find myself not being able to talk about it in certain forums, because I can tell it's no use.

Rouhama: I don't argue.
Shelly: Yes, me too. Because I see that the other side isn't even listening. In our community it's better, but when I'm at work it's like that.
Eva: Who are these people that you don't want to talk to?
Shelly: People who repeat what they heard on TV, that the other side is always to blame. I can't talk to them.
Rouhama: They treat us as if we're stupid.
Efrat: Sometimes I hear people saying "We need to hit them hard" . . . I don't even respond anymore. Who is even left over there to hit?
Eva: So, you all learned to keep quiet.
Rouhama: Yes. I don't argue.

These women undoubtedly do not represent the majority in Israel. But they represent an alternative response to fear: they refuse to yield to its yoke because they understand that, of all collective emotions, fear might be the worst, as it makes it difficult to distinguish between real and imagined dangers; it willingly makes us give up our freedom under the banner of security; it stifles complex thinking, since it divides the world into friends and enemies; it replaces moral thinking and deliberation with survivalism and transforms self-defense into a reflex reaction which pervades the body politic. Finally, fear fuels hatred in helping justify it. Citizens need to be extraordinarily mature to distinguish between the fear that rides on collective and imagined scenarios of catastrophe and fear that reacts to actual dangers, however intertwined the two may sometimes be; they need to be mature to see through the bluff of manipulators and distinguish between real threats and invented ones. Citizens such as Israelis who live in the shadow of historic and ongoing trauma and are mentally and emotionally trained to live in fear, often for good reasons, cannot, perhaps, have the maturity of citizenries who can balance democratic freedoms with their security. They will be tempted to yield to the surplus of imagined threats entailed by permanent fear. In *The Origins of Totalitarianism*, Hannah Arendt analyzes in striking words the nature of such ways to enlist citizenry:

> The effectiveness of this kind of [fascist] propaganda demonstrates one of the chief characteristics of modern masses. They do not believe in anything visible, in the reality of their own experiences; they do not trust their eyes and ears but only their imaginations, which may be caught by anything that is at once universal and consistent in itself. What convinces masses are not facts, and not even invented facts, but only the consistency of the system of which they are presumably part. Repetition . . . is only important because it convinces them of consistency in time.[64]

The Israeli public sphere, as the meeting place for a sovereign people, could and should have been a site to heal from the collective traumas inflicted on the Jewish people. Instead, these traumas have been drilled into their consciousness, partly because they seemed to resonate with a hostile geography, making it virtually impossible to establish the complex differences between the past destructions of the Jews and the geopolitical and diplomatic challenges involved in the protracted conflict with Palestinians. Scared citizens rely on and "trust their imagination" too heavily indeed.

2
Disgust and Identity

> Every kingdom divided against itself is brought to desolation; and every city or house divided against itself shall not stand.
> Matthew 12:25

Hitler likened Jews to "a maggot inside a rotting body."[1] The metaphors he used were far from fortuitous. A maggot is the larva of a fly. It is small, viscous, slimy, and invasive. Slime is a soft, wet substance, typically disgusting to touch. Rotting bodies are horrible to look at and emit a distinct stench difficult to bear. What Hitler managed to do in this double image of the maggot and the rotting body is to mobilize three senses (touch, smell, and sight) to create maximum repulsion and disgust. It is probably the same impulse which, at an anti-lockdown rally in the USA during the Covid crisis in 2020, made someone bear the sign of a rat standing on its back legs with a star of David, provided with the stereotypical head of a Jewish man with a long pointed nose, rubbing his hands together and the caption "The Real Plague."[2] The combined association of rats and plagues evokes repulsion. If fear is the privileged emotion of tyrants, disgust is the privileged emotion of racists.

As an emotion, disgust is characterized in particular by the fact that the sight of disgusting things, such as waste, feces or decay, is accompanied by immediate physiological reactions and urges one to move away from an object or remove it from the field of sensory perception. For evolutionary psychologists, this reflex reaction helped us to adaptively avoid the danger of bacteria, germs, viruses, or diseases.[3] Disgust is thus at the borderline between nature and culture: it is not only a reflex-like reaction to biologically dangerous substances, but it is also, as Hitler's quote illustrates, an emotion which can be bestowed on persons and groups of people through speech.

As a way to illustrate his research, the psychologist Paul Rozin offers the following example:

> A man sniffing decay odors from two opaque vials. The man (who likes cheese) is told that one vial contains feces, the other cheese. Unknown to him, however, the same decay odor emanates from both (the real odors are in fact confusable). The man is then asked to sniff a vial and try to distinguish between the two substances. If he thinks it is cheese, he likes the smell. If told the odor is in fact from feces, though, he suddenly finds it repellent and unpleasant. It is the subject's conception of the object, rather than the sensory properties of the object, that primarily determines the hedonic value. Although certain strong negative tastes (e.g., bitter tastes) may not be reversible by manipulation of the object source or context, we suspect that any positive taste can be reversed by contextual or object information.[4]

One word was enough to cast a sensory experience either as pleasant or as disgusting, suggesting that disgust is, as Hitler well understood, a matter of the words, images, and metaphors we associate with specific objects.

Disgust as Fear of Mixing

The British anthropologist Mary Douglas made a stunning suggestion: all cultural systems make some kind of separation between things defined as dirty (pork in Judaism and Islam, for example) and things defined as clean.[5] Dirt, Douglas claimed, is not only and not primarily real dirt; it is first and foremost symbolic, and it is defined by the fact that it deviates from an established symbolic order. If someone places shoes on a table, this is considered a violation of the order with which we normally draw a line between cleanliness and dirt, even if the shoes are freshly polished and there is no food on the table at all. Uncleanliness is fundamentally about disturbing a pre-established symbolic order. As Douglas observed, religions revolve not only around a sense of the sacred and the profane but also around providing such a symbolic order which makes certain things dirty and impure and designate others as pure.[6] These ideas are apparent in many religions, but, because the focus of this book is Israel, we will concentrate on the importance of the separation between the pure and the impure in Judaism. In Jewish law, impurity has to do with the spilling of certain bodily fluids out of the body. A woman menstruating is deemed "unclean" (*niddah*), as a result of which her husband may not touch her. A man who has a nocturnal emission is also deemed impure. Both the menstruating woman and the man with the nocturnal emission are rendered clean again by immersion in a ritual bath, a *mikve*. These instances of pollution make sense to the believer in reference to the whole cultural system and laws pertaining to the purity of the family (*teharat hamishpaha*). Similarly, only the general dietary laws (*kashrout*) make comprehensible why the flesh of a cow is allowed for consumption while camel meat, seafood or pork are polluted. Faithful Jews disdain these foods not only because they are forbidden but also because they have internalized these prohibitions to such an extent that they feel revulsion towards them anyway. So profound is this type of social learning and conditioning that non-religious Jews who grew up in religious homes often continue to find pork or seafood repulsive.

The emotion of disgust is comprehensible only in the context of a cultural system which defines where the boundary exists between purity and pollution. Disgust chiefly concerns the body, what we can touch and what we cannot touch, what we can ingest and what we can't, and which substances defile our body and which don't. Disgust is key to many religions because the categorization of substances is crucial to their symbolic structure.[7] It also has a social function, namely to enforce social hierarchies embedded in the distinction between pure and impure entities.[8] Disgust expresses separation in order to maintain symbolic order: it is the emotion which abhors mixing.

Disgust has another key attribute: it spreads quickly to other objects, thus generating chains of contamination.[9] You are happily eating your spinach and you suddenly see rotting mold in a small corner of the plate. Even if the rest of the plate looks fine, that small corner will most likely compromise the whole plate. You will throw away not only the piece with mold but everything on your plate, and not only what is on your plate but probably the whole pot. For hours or even days after, you will refrain from eating spinach, because you now associate it with the image of rotting mold. Disgust of a small specific object may thus widen through a psychological mechanism of contamination. In the same way, if feces or corpses are disgusting, anyone touching them becomes, by contamination, also disgusting. The best example of the law of contamination is found again in Judaism: a menstruating woman renders her bed, her chair, her drinking glass impure because her impurity contaminates the objects she touches. Her husband (or any man in fact) is forbidden to touch her bed, chair, and drinking glass. Wine that has been touched by a non-Jew or by a Jew who violates Shabbat follows the same logic and becomes automatically non-kosher,[10] as if the impurity of a person (the non-Jew or Shabbat-violating Jew) was transferable from person to object – that is, as if it was contaminating. Disgust and revulsion are thus triggered by a central (possibly symbolic) object (menstrual blood, pork, rot, mold). The emotion is then transmitted chain-like to other objects or people, even if they are far away from the epicenter.

We may thus state that religions are not only about the worship of deities or founders of beliefs but also about enforcing categories of purity and impurity. These categories may seem purely theological at first glance, but in reality they also have very important social functions, as they produce and enforce an unbridgeable distance between social groups.

In India, the entire caste system is based on hierarchies of purity and impurity, with the Dalits (or Untouchables) at the lowest scale of the hierarchy of purity. As the *Encyclopedia of the Developing World* put it, the Dalits worked with leather, human waste, dead animals, or cremation grounds.[11] The same encyclopedia states that "A theory of purity (the Brahmins, the priestly caste) and pollution (the Untouchables), the top and bottom of a graded hierarchy, was the religious justification for denying water and temple rights, a place in the village itself, and even literacy until the modern period."[12] In the example of the Dalits, hierarchies of purity and impurity create and overlap social hierarchies: the people who clean the feces of others or touch dead skin are impure, and become untouchable, and *thus* are *legitimately* at the bottom of the social ladder. In fact disgust relieves society of the need to present elaborate explanations as to why social groups are unequal and separate. It compels the disgusted subject to move away, beyond words or arguments, and thereby enforces domination in a way that seems both natural and irresistible.

By doing things defined as impure or defiling, a person situates herself as inferior to the pure group, which is thereby defined as socially superior: The Jewish class of priests

– *cohanim* – are forbidden to touch a corpse or even be near it, precisely in order to retain their purity status. Jewish religion contains a whole social system based on purity. For example, priests rank higher than Levites, who rank higher than Israelites, who rank higher than converts, who are themselves higher than non-Jews. The inner logic of this hierarchy is one of family purity which combines with proximity to the temple and priestly caste. It is not only people but also forms of uncleanliness that have an inner hierarchy: the impurity of a corpse is greater than that of a leper, which is greater than of a menstruating woman, which is itself greater than that of a man who has spilled his semen.

The system of social differentiation is also a system of gender differentiation. If a menstruating woman cannot be touched, this in turn enforces and reinforces a radical difference between men and women and a hierarchy between them (unlike women, men are not per se biologically impure; only certain acts may make them so). The law of *niddah* is obviously written from the standpoint of men (as men probably found menstrual blood disgusting, and possibly still do so today) and reflects the masculine point of view in deciding what is impure.

Disgust thus shapes social hierarchies and makes them look natural. It is also a powerful ingredient in maintaining such hierarchies. This is why marriage was closely safeguarded. It aimed at reproducing the purity of family lines (marrying a *bnei Israel* – born Jew – is superior to marrying a convert, which is better than marrying a freed slave). The marriage of the *cohanim* (priests) was the most closed. They cannot marry a divorced woman (presumably because this has compromised the blood line) and must marry within the caste. Thus the dichotomy of pure and impure has a powerful social role: social identity becomes grounded in the capacity to remain separate and to know how to enforce boundaries. This strategy, it should be noticed, has been critical in maintaining the

Jewish people throughout history despite the endless attempts at forcible conversions.

Disgust and the Logic of Racism

As a social emotion, disgust is the emotion which expresses fear of closeness, proximity and mixing; it is an emotion which characterizes quite well, for example, the racist, as shown by this testimony posted on Reddit by someone living in France.[13]

> I recently moved into a neighborhood where there are a lot of blacks, and everything they do disgusts me. I don't want to be a racist, I don't want to be xenophobic, but yesterday I found myself crossing the street as soon as a black person walked up from the other side, and I can only conclude that I am.
> Some of the things that go trough my mind (and apply to 95% of the blacks I've encountered; it's not just *some* of them):
>
> - they smell SO bad! I feel like, if you take public transportation, you should at least make sure that your body odour isn't that pungent that it can be noticed by people sitting next to you (with reasonable distance; it *is* public transport so you're close to each other but it's not like sitting on each others lap)
> - They talk SO loud! Even in the library, of all places. They talk and laugh extremely loud constantly as if they were the only people on the planet. I'm not sure if this is a lack of education or a cultural difference.
> - another thing showing lack of education: they NEVER get up in the bus/tram/train when an old person enters
> - They don't lift their feet when they walk. I can hear them coming from miles away
> - I can't help but think all the african third world countries are, despite all the help, still third world because of their "lazy culture". You can't attribute their poverty to the bad climate

because there are a lot of countries with even worse climates and they *did* manage to develop
- deseases like HIV and ebola spread so fast in africa because of african people's lack of hygiene.

As with Hitler's quote above about the Jews, black people elicit disgust, and this disgust is amply evoked in this testimony: smell, touch, hearing, and sight are all elicited to make black people sensorially repulsive, thus eliciting the fear of proximity and contamination. Disgust mobilizes the senses precisely because it is a physiological reaction that guarantees distance from an object. Moreover, these disgusting properties are converted into moral evaluations (they are lazy, uneducated, do not get up on the bus for others) and illustrate a property of racism, namely its ability to convert physiological, visual, olfactory, and auditory reactions to a specific group into moral statements which make disgust both sensorial and moral (laziness being a manifestation of moral degeneracy).

Disgust Entrepreneurs and Fear of Contamination

In the last two decades, Israel has seen the burgeoning of new normative entrepreneurs, whose vocation has been to affirm and encourage values of Jewish and religious supremacy antithetical to liberal values. Liberal morality is universalist, views all human beings as equal, aims to foster fair relationships between the majority and minorities, and believes in separation of religion and the state. The new moral entrepreneurs have decided to change the content of the public sphere by promoting new forms of disgust of specific social groups. They are "disgust entrepreneurs": politicians and new NGOs have as their function to create, engineer, and reinforce disgust from some groups to others. They represent the point of view of various religious and religious-nationalist factions. Judaism defines holiness itself as the act of separating and making distinctions (conceptual and practical) between cleanliness and uncleanliness. The ultra-orthodox have a strong sense of cleanliness and uncleanliness (visible, for example, in the intensive use of *mikve*, the stringency with which they observe laws of menstrual impurity, the laws of semen spill, and the laws pertaining to kosher food).

In contemporary democratic societies, such distinctions between pure and impure are legitimate as long as they are a part of a private religious belief. But one of the key changes in Israeli politics has been the introduction of issues of cleanliness and pollution into the public political sphere. If one had to pick the defining moment during which disgust started playing a role in Israeli public life, the creation of the right-wing party Kach would be a good candidate. Kach was a religious radical right-wing party founded in 1971 by an American Jew, Rabbi Meir Kahane. For over a decade after its foundation, Kach did not receive enough votes to make it into the Knesset. But in 1984 the party won its first seat. Kahane made numerous legislative proposals whose content was to revoke the Israeli citizenship of non-Jews, to outlaw Jewish–Gentile marriages, and to ban sexual relations between the two groups. Kahane's party shifted the focus from land to people: the issue was no longer to make territorial compromises but, rather, to erect laws that would *de facto* prevent Arabs from entering, let alone assimilating to Israeli society. For example, Kahane proposed a law "to prevent assimilation between Jews and non-Jews and for the preservation of the sanctity of the People of Israel," the purpose of which was to separate completely Jews and non-Jews in the public space, in conformity with the logic of contamination and purity.[14] Kahane's legislative proposals, as he claimed, were based on the *Mishnei Torah*, Maimonides' magnum opus.[15] Yet, it is no less likely that his ideas were shaped by the formal racism which was in vigor in the United States until the civil rights movement. Kahane was born in

Brooklyn in 1932 and lived in America until 1971. He was as much an American as he was an observant Jew. He could not have been a stranger to the deep segregation in the USA of black people, justified by white supremacist ideology which was embedded in so many American institutions (let us not forget that the Nazis found the American "one drop rule," which defined as black any person with any black ancestry whatsoever, too stringent for them, and instead limited their definition of Jews to anyone with one Jewish grandparent).[16] Kahane's ideology was thus characterized by his wish to bring Jewish laws of purity to the public sphere and a deeply racialized view of ethnic and racial supremacy that was entrenched in the USA until long after the desegregation in the 1960s (Kahane decided to emigrate to Israel in 1971, soon after the civil rights movement).

Kahane's party Kach was outlawed in 1988 but was defunct only in name. In fact, it started a small ideological revolution, as its ideas were resuscitated through various and vibrant small political parties and organizations. For instance, the name of the Lehava organization, founded in 2009, is an acronym for the Prevention of Assimilation in the Holy Land. It opposes marriages between Jewish and non-Jewish people, especially with Muslims. Its mission is to help extricate Jewish women from such "harmful" relationships,[17] when most of these women never sought their help. Another example is Im Tirzu, founded in 2006, which defines its activities as promoting Zionism in Israel.[18] This involves innocuous activities such as giving small gifts to IDF soldiers, but it also includes far less innocuous activities, such as harassing scholars and those who identify with the left, dubbing them "anti-Zionist," traitors, and dangerous people. Despite being a secular movement with strong affinities to McCarthysm (for example, drawing up blacklists of left-wing scholars), Im Tirzu, like the religious Lehava, frequently casts groups or their individual members as morally repulsive – that is, disgusting. It is animated by the same impulse to expel from public institutions any contaminating ideas or people. Otzma Yehudit (Jewish Strength), HaIchud HaLeumi – Tkuma (The National Front – Resurrection), HaBayit HaYehudi (the Jewish Home), Eretz Israel Shelanu (Our Land of Israel) – all of these parties, despite some slight differences in emphasis in rhetoric and orientation, point to the ideological liveliness of the ideas that were harbored by Kahane and subsequently outlawed. These ideas have gradually migrated to the center of society and to that extent have become mainstream, a process that found its ultimate confirmation in the elections of 2022, when the "Religious Zionism" list, a union of parties from the extreme right, Noam (anti-LGBT), Otzma Yehudit, led by the Kahanist Itamar Ben-Gvir, and HaIchud HaLeumi – Tkuma, headed by Bezalel Smotrich (a religious settler with ideas close to Kahane's about the sanctity of the land and the people), received 10.84 percent of the vote, earning fourteen seats in the Knesset.[19] All three factions represent portions of the religious public and all are orthodox and draw their first inspiration from religious texts; they are also ultra-nationalists and believe in the sanctity of the land of Israel; for them, Palestinians have no rights to the land in which they have lived, and in general these factions do not seem bothered by the violation of international law or the absence of human rights. They view all of the contested territory as belonging rightfully and morally to the Jews, thereby justifying expropriation, expulsion, and domination of the Arabs. Mostly, they are all committed to a definition of the Jewish people based in Jewish Law (Halacha) and care a great deal about preserving the ethnic purity of the Jewish people. It is because they aim to preserve the purity of the people and the sanctity of land that they attack those who threaten such purity. These parties have become a very active sector of Israeli society, and since December 2022 they have been part of Netanyahu's right-wing government. Even before that, they influenced discourse and politics in many indirect ways

– through money, through pressure groups, and by spreading new norms of speech.

In fact, what many have called the radicalization of the Likud in the first decade of the 2000s was mostly characterized by the fact that it conveyed new political messaging based on disgust. For instance, in 2004, twenty-two members of the Likud voted in favor of a law that would allow towns and villages to be legally defined as serving only certain ethnic or national groups (i.e., allowing the legal category of a "purely Jewish" town). The law was proposed by a member of the National Front party and supported by several other religious parties, but it was rejected in the Knesset by a narrow margin (thirty-eight in support, forty opposed).[20] In cases such as this, the Likud's ideological platform was deeply reshaped by religious messages which insist on a radical, abyssal separation between Jews and non-Jews, religious and secular people, pure and impure modes of life.

This bears certain similarities to white evangelical Christians in the United States, of whom 34 percent say that there should not be separation between church and state (as compared to 19 percent in the general US population),[21] thereby supporting the use of religious principles in political decision-making. One of the most obvious examples of this is the decades-long campaign by white evangelicals against abortion. This includes, among other things, featuring the faces of doctors who provide abortions in "wanted"-style posters,[22] a disgust-eliciting tactic that extreme-right organizations in Israel have also frequently utilized (albeit for ethnic and nationalist purposes).

Consistent with other far-right movements in the world (Victor Orbán's Fidesz party in Hungary; American white supremacists such as the American Front and the American Freedom Party (formerly the American Third Position Party); the Serbian Radical Party; Narendra Modi's BJP; Giorgia Meloni's "Brothers of Italy"), the Israeli extreme right also defends the purity of the Jewish people, an idea and ideal which is both political and religious (it has a solid basis in Jewish law). Consider the Lehava organization: it has hardly any ideological equivalent in most countries, where miscegenation, interfaith marriage, and interracial relationships are protected by the law and are not on the agenda of any legitimate political party in the Western world. One would have to look at the Ku Klux Klan of the 1920s to find similar ideological platforms explicitly forbidding and fighting inter-ethnic, interracial, and interfaith marriages and sexual relations. However, we may see a more recent resemblance to this in Modi's India, where, since 2020, several districts have passed laws making interfaith marriage more difficult by forbidding newlyweds to convert to their spouse's religion.[23]

An organization such as Lehava pushes forward on the political scene an item which is not (yet) on the official agenda of a political party but which in fact corresponds to the worldview and values of many religious parties currently in power in Israel (and other parts of the world). For example, Bezalel Smotrich, the leader of the Religious Zionism list, the union of religious right-wing parties mentioned above, and since December 2022 Israeli minister of finance, declared that his wife, after giving birth to a child, should not have to share a room with an Arab woman.[24]

Not only does Lehava actively oppose interfaith marriages, but it has even encouraged Israelis to report to the organization the names of Jews who rent their apartments to Arabs,[25] so that they can be "named and shamed" publicly. It has also campaigned against Jews and Arabs mixing on beaches,[26] another illustration of the fear of mixing that is at the core of this politics. All these injunctions and prohibitions follow the logic of disgust and contamination: the presence of non-Jews in the body collective endangers the purity of the people as a whole. In short, Lehava defends the principle that pure and impure categories (Jews vs. non-Jews) should not be mixed. Organizations such as Lehava take their direct inspiration from many strands of Orthodox Judaism that conceive of the

Jewish people as an entity whose purity can be threatened (by intermarriage for example) and which actively works at maintaining such purity by insulating Jews from non-Jews.

In the Israeli context, this symbolic structure grounded in religion resonates with the social and geographical structure of the Occupation, which is not only a military fact; it also involves an active and constant separation between Jewish settlers and Arabs, and this despite their existence being tightly intertwined. Jews living in settlements often reside in gated communities, have a separate school system, and do not interact with Arabs as friends, co-workers or sexual partners. An elaborate system of roads and checkpoints attempt to create maximum separation between two populations who could easily live in close symbiosis. It is the army which has the role of ensuring the separation of the two groups.

Ultra-orthodox Jews apply the laws of purity and impurity only to their own closed communities. But extreme-right national-religious people (many of whom are settlers) are different: they are far more missionary in their attempts to divide adjacent communities by spreading a forceful sense of separation (of which one might say that it is the result of fabricated disgust) throughout society. Religion and the army are two powerful institutional systems enforcing strict separation. In fact, the main difference between ultra-orthodox and extreme-right religious-nationalists is that the latter actively try to engineer disgust in the public sphere towards various groups through their rabbis. The groups supposed to elicit disgust are secular people, left-wing people, reform Jews, feminists, homosexuals, and of course, first and foremost, Arabs. These ideas are conveyed by some members of the settlers' elites, many of whom are rabbis who teach the students at pre-military schools[27] or rabbis in the military.[28] Such rabbis represent the perfect conjunction and convergence of the religious ethos and the military's active involvement in the physical separation between the two groups.

The Yeshiva Bnei David in the settlement of Eli (viewed by the international community as illegal) is a pre-military academy which prepares religious students for the army. It has several rabbis who exert a deep influence on an increasing number of army officers and politicians. According to Yair Nehorai, a lawyer who has monitored the speeches of highly influential rabbis who operate behind the scenes of political parties and ideological platforms, these rabbis constitute a possible future direction of Israel. This is worth examining further.

Rabbi Eli Sadan, head of the religious pre-military school at Yeshiva Eli, the recipient of the 2016 prestigious Israel prize, and a very influential figure of messianic Judaism, refers to reform Jews and secular people in metaphors that clarify their dangerous and contaminating nature. "It [reform Judaism] is a snake venom, and many of those who carry it do not understand at all what venom they carry. In the shallowness of their education and knowledge, they carry this venom in them, because it seems to them the nicest and the best and all is well . . ."[29]

Rabbi Kashtiel, in the same Yeshiva Eli, compares secular literature to a pile of garbage. One can appreciate the choice of metaphors whose sole aim is indeed to elicit disgust:

> If a person has some garbage, it's not a reason for the whole environment to suffer . . . just because you have some garbage in the house, you have to go out and put up stalls, lots and lots of stalls and lots and lots of tables, with lots of piles of rubbish. And ask for more money for it. I sell garbage, who wants to buy it? But if the subject of literature is not [religious] redemption, or at least there is no atmosphere of redemption in the background, then what is the point of it? They just present the impurity that is in a person as it is, and this is . . . Every person has all kinds of passions and urges, and they put them on the table, and everyone has to buy this huge mixture of urges and

pay for it . . . It's good that we buy garbage from time to time, so we can distinguish between a good cucumber and a cucumber that is garbage, so we can put up a stand near the grocery store with rotten cucumbers, and buy there . . . and it's good to have such neat shelves at home, with lots of rotten cucumbers, so we know better to distinguish [between them]. How can one live when everything is full of this stench?[30]

Another rabbi, known for his pronouncements against gay people and for being the spiritual force behind the Noam party, uses a similar imagery to elicit disgust.[31] Says Rabbi Thau:

There is no denying that until today this virus [Covid-19] was known to harm animals but did not attack humans. *Gemara* [Talmud] tells us: . . . There is no beast that controls man, unless man seems to be as a beast . . . the postmodern culture with the iPhones flooded with abomination films, with the perverted organizations that make man all over the world resemble a beast. Is polyamory not an act of beasts?

But the most striking speech is undoubtedly this one, given by Rabbi Kashtiel to his students, which views Arabs as genetically and inherently inferior and suggests that the aim of the Occupation is in fact to elevate them – that is, to take them out of their terrible lowly situation.[32] The Occupation and the domination of Arabs become part and parcel of the civilizing mission of Israel.

Yes, we are racists, for sure. Yes, there are races in the world and there are genetic traits of peoples, and that requires us (the Jewish people) to think about how to help them. The fact that there is someone who is less than you – this is not a reason to mock or to destroy him, but to help him. True, there are differences between races, and this is exactly the reason to reach out and help. As we know, there are genetic defects, let's say, within society; unfortunately, a child is born with a defect. Is this a reason to mock him? No, it's a reason to help him . . . I see that I reach much more impressive achievements than him. In the fields of morality, mentality, personality, I reach much higher achievements – so it is my duty to help him, not to leave him that way, poor and miserable, but to reach out to him, tell him, "come." Come be my slave, be a partner in my success. . . . If the Occupation means humiliating you, mocking you, destroying you – then it's bad. But if the Occupation means, "I'm successful, come on," I call on you to be a partner in my success, why are you alone, why are you separated from me, I want to conquer you, to attach you – then you are a partner in great success. You should be my slave. Now, you live a miserable life. Come be my slave, see what a life you will live, what a spiritual and moral level [you will achieve] . . . There is a genetic defect here, objectively, what can you do? . . . The Bible is full of things like this, and traditional rabbinical wisdom [Chazal] is full of it . . . It is not a reason to celebrate, it is not a reason to be arrogant, it is a reason to help. It is better to state things clearly and say, "It's true, there is a genetic problem here and we need to help them," than to say, "No, no, there are no genetic problems here," and in the end you do not help them . . . There are such peoples around us with genetic problems . . . Ask a simple Arab, I asked a simple Arab, where do you want to be, under the Palestinian Authority or under the State of Israel? The answer is unequivocal. Everyone will tell you the same unequivocal answer that they want to be under occupation . . . Why? Because they have a genetic problem, they do not know how to run a country, they do not know how to do anything, just see what they look like . . . they do not know how to run anything. Savage. . . . Let them [the Arabs] manage things for one moment – everything falls apart. Immediately. They do not know. So they have a genetic problem. Let's help them. The simple Arab, working every day, what's the question? Which employer does he prefer, ask him? A Jewish employer or an

Arab employer? There is no question at all. They know it, so let's say things clearly and say, "Come be our slaves"... Instead of making excuses, it's better to say true and correct things and not to be condescending.

This last quote is particularly interesting, since it presents Arabs' inferiority not only as genetic and natural but also as the opportunity to feel and display Jews' greater morality in helping the inferior species. While these rabbis are all of Ashkenazi origin, the Sephardic Rabbi Ovadia Yosef – the spiritual leader of the Mizrahi Shas party – has nothing to envy where his Ashkenazi counterparts are concerned. Regarding a conflict that he recalled between Muslims and Jews in Baghdad (a specific date was not cited in his speech, but it should be noted that the general conflict ended in Jews being persecuted and fleeing their country), Yosef had even less compassion for the "inferior" species: "[the Arabs] got up the next day, did some demonstrations. This is the power of these wicked Arab people. They must not be pitied, they should be blasted with missiles, destroyed, they are cursed and wicked."[33] (It must be said, however, that Shas, the ultra-orthodox party representing Mizrahim (non-Ashkenazi Jews), was often more tolerant and mindful of Israeli Arabs than many other Israeli parties).[34]

Venom, garbage, abomination, stench, beasts, snakes, animals, murderers, spoiled minds, wickedness, all form the matrix designating Arabs and secular Jews as representing pollution which can, in turn, only invoke disgust. Arabs and secularity form the impure core which will contaminate other groups: left-wing people, homosexuals (homosexuality in Hebrew is *to'eva*, a word meaning something disgusting) and feminist women. People who meet, touch, like, love members of these groups or read their books will be contaminated by the vermin. These views are extreme, no doubt, and are articulated by specific rabbinical figures: their ferocity is not shared by a majority of the Jewish Israeli population. Yet, such views have the power to shift the norms of discourse, and they find an echo in the key secular institution of Israel, the army, most conspicuously deployed in the territories to enforce separation between Jews and Arabs (an echo is not a sound but the reflection of a sound wave).

Nadav Weiman, encountered in the previous chapter (the vice-president of the NGO Breaking the Silence), did his army service in an elite sniper unit and came out convinced that the Occupation was both inhuman and inefficient. Our interview started by evoking the ways in which disgust and contempt towards Arabs is structurally embedded in the military service.

> *Eva*: You talked about sewage. Is there a perception that Arabs are dirty?
> *NW*: Yeah, sure. By the way, when you see armed men you call them "dirty" on the radio phone. That's literally the official word. "Identifying two 'dirties' four hundred meters."
> *Eva*: What does the dirt manifest as?
> *NW*: In a few things. First of all, because the infrastructure in the West Bank and the Gaza Strip is terrible, there are many houses with sewage pits, so there is a bad smell. And there is no drainage and the infrastructure of houses and things like that are not good. So there really is a smell of sewage, and garbage, and stuff like that. It's also the physical dirt in the street, the smell. But also a man who burns garbage, who are you? Don't you realize you are hurting the Earth? Don't you realize that there is a waste-disposal site for these things? We didn't realize there was no such thing. Also physically. A lot of Palestinians that you come across work in manual labor, they are farmers, they work within Israel. They are not dressed like I'm used to on a regular street in Tel Aviv. Although my first response when I drove in Nablus was, "Wow, it really looks like Allenby Street in Tel Aviv." A lot of times you see barefoot kids hanging out; they are a little

dirty. And even when you stop and arrest someone, many times what happens is that you throw him on the floor of the jeep or the armored vehicle, or place him at the entrance to the base, and then they get covered in dirt.... you call it to "hand back" [*lehizdakot*, the word soldiers use to describe returning military equipment]. When you "hand back" the Palestinian and bring him to the military police, then they physically wash him with a hose, apart from the medical examination they do. All of this together gives you a perception that they are just dirty. In a lot of Palestinian houses you enter and there is no toilet, there is a hole in the floor like in India. I remember in training they explained to us that the Palestinians do not have toilet paper and they wipe their ass with their hands and wash with water.

Eva: Who explained?

NW: One of the commanders in the training.

Eva: Is that something that had any basis?

NW: I don't think so. I never got to have a conversation with a Palestinian [about this subject], even today after all the years I spent in the field.

Eva: It's very interesting that it's a story that goes around.

NW: Because we were a sniper team, we used a lot of night vision and thermal gear, so there are always the stories of snipers or IDF observers who at night see a Palestinian having sex with a sheep or goat. They say there's a video of it. I've never seen such a video.

As Nadav Weiman suggests, soldiers have a pre-established image of the Palestinians they are supposed to control, monitor, beat, incarcerate, and even kill. That image mixes key emotions of fear and contempt, which in turn generate disgust. We may thus say that the continuous domination over a population that is poor and lacking in basic sanitary conditions generates a disgust that becomes integrated in an ideology that justifies continuous violence in turn based on disgust.

These views are not limited to rabbis and soldiers. In the 2016 documentary film *The Settlers*, by the Israeli director Shimon Dotan, one of the interviewees who lives in Esh Kodesh, a settlement in Shilo valley, which was established in 2001 and today houses around 350 people, declares: "The people of Israel have a role to play: to conquer the land. To bequeath it. To expel the Gentiles who live in it ... I do not see a place for Arabs in our country."[35] Asked if he does not mind being called a racist, he answered:

> I am a racist. I say every morning in prayer Blessed are you G–d that I was not made a gentile. I'm a racist. I will give a ride to a Jew and I will not give a ride to an Arab because I am a racist. And I will also only employ Jews and not Arabs because I am a racist. Nor will I give charity to an Arab woman who asks for money because I am a racist. She should go to their organizations, go to Hamas, maybe there they will give her a few shekels.[36]

It is difficult to evaluate how representative such claims are of the entire population of settlers. There is no doubt that many settlers do not harbor racist attitudes. There is also no doubt that, in the background of a protracted conflict over land, such racism is mixed with territorial enmity and a military conflict (as was certainly the case between France and Germany at the end of the nineteenth century). Yet it is safe to suggest, minimally, that such language is not unusual or terribly shocking to many Jewish residents of the West Bank. Disgust and fear of the enemy are here so tightly intertwined that they become virtually indistinguishable, the latter legitimizing the former. An eighteen-year-old woman to whom I spoke was born in a settlement, is religious, self-declaredly on the right, and a strong believer in the idea of "Greater Israel" (*Eretz Israel Hashlema*), the belief that the state of Israel should encompass any lands that were part of biblical Israel, including the areas controlled by the Palestinian authorities. At the same time, she participates in a discussion group made up of Palestinians and Jews. When I interviewed her, she reported that one of her biggest surprises in attending the group was to discover that one of the Palestinian boys "read books and painted" during his leisure time. Before that, she had viewed Arabs as frightening and primitive and could not associate them with reading and painting, thus suggesting that, as the legal scholar William Ian Miller argues, disgust is subtly intertwined with contempt.[37] Another surprising form of moral disgust takes a circuitous form but is commonly heard. A rabbi from the West Bank living in Shilo declared (all) Arabs inferior because they have neither democracy nor do they recognize the rights of homosexuals and women. This is an interesting form of disgust, because democracy in many respects is not upheld by many members of ultra-orthodox communities. Orthodox Judaism does not recognize the notion of human rights in general and the rights of women and homosexuals in particular. It therefore points to a kind of appropriation of the language of rights by groups who actually do not fully believe in them to justify an "enlightened" disgust. Disgust is another key social emotion because it creates an impermeable barrier between social groups through the pure/impure divide, with deep political implications.

In what way is disgust connected to populism in Israel? In addition to the NGOs and the settlement rabbis mentioned above, the Likud's closest ally, the Shas party, has played a key role in the spread and legitimation of disgust, as it has controlled the Ministry of the Interior for twenty-four years in the nine government coalitions with the Likud. In Netanyahu's sixth government, which has been in office since December 2022, Shas has once again taken over the Ministry of the Interior. In this office, the party was and is responsible for regulating the relationship between Jews and non-Jews in Israel.

Shas is usually classified as an ultra-orthodox party and initially seemed to be removed from the left/right divide. It has in fact morphed into an extreme right-wing party, in the worst tradition of European xenophobic parties. Two examples will suffice to make this point.

In the campaign for the 2013 elections, a promotional video by Shas presented a young couple getting married. Moments before the ceremony, the woman (Marina, who is very pale and blonde, and obviously from the former USSR) gets a certificate of conversion to Judaism (*Giur*) by fax, after having dialed *Giur, using the fax given to her by Yisrael Beiteinu, a secular Russian-Israeli party. For Israelis, the implication is clear: she is not a proper Jew according to the strict law of orthodoxy, and Yisrael Beiteinu, the secular (right-wing) party, aids in that process of dilution of the Jewish people.[38] This video unabashedly puts forward what has been an electoral slogan of Shas and other extreme right-wing parties, namely the danger of "mixed" marriages.

Due to the same fear of mixing, Eli Yishai, one of the leaders of the ultra-orthodox Shas and minister of the interior from 2009 to 2013, was famously opposed to accepting asylum seekers from Africa, claiming that all asylum seekers are criminals and that they should be put in jail or in a closed facility and given money to leave Israel.[39] The demonization of immigrants and asylum seekers is one of the most prominent tropes of the populist extreme right in many countries: while declaring his presidential bid in 2015, Donald Trump accused Mexico of sending drugs, criminals, and rapists to the United States;[40] in the Netherlands, Geert Wilders, the leader of the far-right Party for Freedom, called Moroccan migrants "scum";[41] in the UK, the former leader of the UK Independence party (UKIP), Nigel Farage, described refugees arriving in Britain as an "invasion."[42]

According to the political scientist Anna Bagaini, Shas can be considered a populist party on account of three features of populism that it exhibits: "appeal to people who perceive themselves as marginalized, strong anti-élite rhetoric and xenophobic attitudes."[43] For instance, the party gained political traction in the 1999 electoral campaign by making "strong attacks against the institutions and the judiciary... in the attempt to support the party's leader Aryeh Deri who was facing conviction for bribery and fraud."[44] The party has also expressed xenophobic attitudes against Israeli Arabs, immigrants from the former Soviet Union and foreign workers.[45] Thus Shas is as much an ultra-orthodox party as a member of the family of extreme right-wing parties precisely because the emotion of disgust is present.

We may wonder if this does not rely on another binary distinction. As Jason Stanley has argued, the division between cities (as places of corruption) and the countryside (as still holding on to the right moral values) has been a key axis of fascist ideologies.[46] People living in small towns, in the countryside, on the periphery, on the frontier, are viewed as representing the true and pure values of the nation and "the people," while people from the cities represent cosmopolitan, pluralistic, and secular values which endanger the integrity of the nation as a whole.[47] Tel-Aviv is perceived by religious and national-religious movements as a place of decadence because it symbolizes the cosmopolitan values they revile. An example of this was the right-wing condemnation of the gesture by Mayor Ron Huldai to light up Tel Aviv City Hall in the colors of the Lebanese flag to mark the devastating explosion in Beirut Harbor.[48] Disgust reached as far as simple humanitarian gestures of solidarity.

This form of disgust emerges from the tangled and complex relationship which populism entertains with religion. Inasmuch as populism fosters a binary distinction between "us" and "them," it is bound to find an echo within religions that are based on a strong distinction between the faithful and the infidels. It is particularly likely to be true in the case of Judaism, which draws an almost unbridgeable distinction between Jews and non-Jews (such distinction, it must be added, explains the remarkable survival of Jews despite the forcible attempts to destroy or assimilate them). In populism, the Austrian theologian Wolfgang Palaver writes, "an imagined homogeneous people distinguishes itself from all foreign others, often also claiming its own superiority. Frequently, religion plays a role in this self-understanding of people who feel threatened by religious or cultural others."[49] Populist movements and religion entertain more than an affinity with each other: in India, France, Italy, the United States, and of course Israel, religious people seem to vote in significant numbers for xenophobic policies where religion comes to play a key part in identity and reinforces the boundaries between one's group and another.[50]

*

Nadav Weiman's current work consists of speaking to youth in order to inform them about the nature of the Occupation, the largest part of which consists of controlling civilians both pointlessly and cruelly. In my interview with him, he noticed a significant change in Israeli society in the last 10 years.

> *Eva*: What do you see in young people? Or in the audiences you're talking to?
>
> *NW*: I joined the army fifteen years ago, and nobody had an iPhone, we had just started using digital cameras. Today, young people ... have access to a lot more information, and still the perception of Palestinians is like that. They claim they are murderers, that they educate their children for murder, they do not care that their children are killed, they use children and pregnant women as human shields. I come to preparatory military schools [*mechinot*] and talk about the policy of shooting in Gaza, and shooting artillery into crowded neighborhoods, and kids answer, "Yes, but you know that, under every rocket launcher, they intentionally put a kindergarten, and terrorists go with older Palestinians as a human shield." As if life for Palestinians is not something to be fought for. We sanctify life. They sanctify

death. And there's also the matter of a "dirty" Palestinian. There were two foreign guys with us in the team. A Jew from Brooklyn and a Jew from London. The one who came from the United States would call them "camel fuckers" and "towel heads." So he brought this American perception with him. But these are sentences that I hear today . . . You meet this a lot in *mechinot* and in American students who immigrated to Israel [made *Aliyah*] and stayed. And they call the Palestinians those names. Or American settlers cursing Palestinians like that. This stereotype of a simple Palestinian, a farmer or building worker who does not understand his life and is exploited, yesterday he wore an explosive belt on him and today he is given a stone to throw at soldiers. He does what he is told and has no self-thought. They [the Palestinians] are an entity. It's like fish swimming together or birds flying together. The teenagers we meet, when they talk about Palestinians or peace agreements, they are always using the concept of "We give to them, we know what should happen. They don't know, we have to figure out the way for them and decide what to do because they are immature."

Eva: You told me [earlier] that you saw a difference over the years [in the audience he addresses]. You see a difference?

NW: The difference is probably the extremity of the discourse. In the past, not everyone called me a traitor or cursed me, or blew up my lectures. Those blowing up lectures were Im Tirzu. They would come to the lecture, write every word that comes out of your mouth with a laptop, and then start screaming and blowing up the lecture. They were the "crazy ones." But today I come to do a lecture at a kibbutz and people close the electricity. Some kibbutz member comes and closes the electricity, or screams, "Who let them in here?" Even in a moshav [a type of small village] in the Galilee, they shut down the electricity or shut the doors and do not let the lecture happen. Or there are schools that the children want to hear us speak but the teachers are afraid of what would happen if the parents hear about it and call them later, so they cancel the lecture. It's self-censorship. They prefer not to discuss the issue, not to express their own opinion that will lead them to such a discussion. I understand their fear. But this is at the very top of the reduction of democratic space in Israel. The places where it is legitimate to voice an opinion that opposes the occupation regime are reduced. Or opinions that are perceived as leftist [are not welcome]. Miri Regev [a member of the Likud party, former minister of culture, and minister of transport in the current government] has done this very successfully in recent years. Everywhere we came, she closed it, the Barbur [art] Gallery in Jerusalem, [the community center] Beit Haam in Pardes Hana, a private gallery I spoke at in Haifa. . . . It started from the government level. Miri Regev says, "I will stop the funding for the Kiryat Ono Municipal Library," which is about to host us for the event, because it is a political event, so it's forbidden, even though Miri Regev herself made a toast there two weeks earlier on Rosh Hashana. And then that message seeps down so it triggers people on the extreme right, and then people who invite us to a house gathering find out that they have a demonstration outside the house. In one case, a far-right radical activist tried to break into a house that hosted us. Actually break in and scare the residents. Or they organize boycotts on businesses of people who invited us to their homes. So this is how it works. From the government level, it seeps down to the "crazy" people. Then Bibi [Netanyahu] doesn't have to give a direct order. It's the same in the education system. It starts with Bennett [at the time minister of education, from July 2021 until November 2022, alternating as prime minister] passing the law of "Breaking the Silence," which doesn't apply to us at all, it's all a media spin, but then teachers . . . It happened a few months ago that a school scheduled a tour with us in Hebron, and they also scheduled to meet the settlers. Then the settlers leaked it to Rafi Peretz, who was then minister of education [formerly the leader of the national religious party HaBayit HaYehudi]. And Rafi Peretz says, "There is the 'Breaking the Silence' law, you can't meet 'Breaking the Silence,'" which is a complete lie. I explained it to them, and the Civil Liberties Union wrote a professional opinion, but it's too late because teachers are afraid to lose school funding, or they fear what parents will do to them, and then they don't meet us and only meet settlers. So they [the right-wing politicians] narrow down the spaces where we are allowed to speak, and within those spaces the language has become much more violent. The word "traitor" is common. There are lots of personal curses. People collect personal information about me, and then they know how to curse me personally when I arrive, to really threaten violence. When the educational team doesn't really like "Breaking the Silence," then the "restrain me" attitude of some kids doesn't really work. People are actually throwing things at us. No one holds them back. Someone beating me up in Hebron is one thing, but I've been in situations . . . I was invited to one kibbutz, a group of leftists, to talk about operation "protective edge" [Tzuk Eitan, the 2014 Gaza operation]. And the kibbutz members needed to physically restrain someone who wanted to hit me. But the opinions which people voice are very extreme, especially kids before the army. A [population] transfer used to be an idea of messianic crazy people, Gandhi [the nickname of Rehavam Ze'ewi, founder of the Homeland party]. Kahane, when it was part of his platform, was kicked out of the Knesset. When he came to speak, they wouldn't hear him. Suddenly, children in preparatory military schools, in a political debate, give the transfer as a legitimate idea, as a legitimate position in a democratic society. And I explain to them that it's not. This is something that I stop a tour for. I stop in the middle of Hebron. It is impossible to continue the conversation now, as this is not a legitimate position. And if, a few years ago, most of the group would understand that deporting people from their home and taking their land

(and I tell them that's what they did to my grandfather in Poland – not the genocide part, but the part of taking the land and driving them out) [is illegitimate], *so today many more kids from the group will say that this is a legitimate position, and the counselors are really defending that position as well* [emphasis added]. They say, "He asked you a question that is legitimate and you will answer it, and there is nothing wrong with that." This shows some kind of moral decay. In *mechinot* you can understand where the wind is blowing in Israeli society. There are ideas that are really radical. There is also the idea that maybe democracy is not the best way to manage it.

What Nadav Weiman describes here is the result of a long process of disgust being spread throughout society, and he identifies some preparatory military schools as exemplifying this process. The reactions to his own organization (an ordinary civil rights organization) display the fear of contamination and the sense of threat to purity described above: Breaking the Silence is perceived as being close to or even conspiring with Palestinians. Therefore, the disgust felt towards Palestinians contaminates the NGO, making it illegitimate in the eyes of many in the Israeli public. His audience's reactions have grown in intensity precisely because disgust has taken hold of ordinary morality and has profoundly transformed mentalities. This happened because disgust has become intrinsic not only to the ideology of certain groups but is also embedded in the propaganda which the state diffuses through schools, media, culture, how history is told, how the "we" is constantly repeated against the "them." Contamination is an imagined fear which spreads through emotions, and the fear of contamination is activated through imagination. It plays a significant role in designating objects that should be expelled from the body politic.

Dr Hassan Jabareen, a lawyer and human rights activist,

founder and CEO of the Adalah Foundation, a human rights organization mostly run by Israeli Arabs, concurs with Nadav Weiman:

> Like in the "Knife Intifada" [a series of violent events in 2015–16], for example, the entire political system said, "If you suspect someone, shoot him, with the purpose of killing." In the past such a thing was forbidden, to execute someone without trial. But, as the right became hegemonic, they began to justify these things. The right succeeded in justification, and really succeeded in convincing that the Arab was an enemy. They managed to convince [others] in such a way that, even if [Benny] Gantz wins the election and can form a government, he does not dare because he has to talk a bit with Ayman Odeh [chairman of "Hadash," a socialist Arab party in the Israeli Knesset]. *So now we move on to disgust. At first we killed Arabs because they are an enemy, now the transition is . . . he [the Arab] becomes abominable. He is less human. That's why the loathing I see now rises, because of the right-wing hegemony. It's a very strong hegemony, you don't have to convince anyone that the Arabs are an enemy, you've already succeeded. And if you succeed, then killing an Arab does not require a trial, it is a matter of impunity* [emphasis added].

Disgust has direct consequences on the willingness of people to view other groups as equal to Jews. This is all the more crucial because 21 percent of the population, or nearly 2 million people, inside the green line is Arab, while those residing in the West Bank account for an additional 2.16 million, bringing the total to over 4 million Arabs living within the greater Israel. Disgust is thus an additional informal mechanism alongside the formal ones in order to keep at bay the option of true equal rights for Palestinians.

A 2010 survey conducted by the Harry Truman Institute at the Hebrew University of Jerusalem revealed that 44 percent of Jewish Israelis support rabbis' calls to refrain from renting apartments to Arabs in the town of Safed. Less than half – 48 percent – of Jews in the country oppose these calls[51] (it is more than likely that in the last decade the number of opposers has decreased). Another more recent survey conducted by the Israel Democracy Institute among the ultra-orthodox population found that three-quarters of respondents said they disapprove of friendship with an Arab person,[52] slightly less than the number who feel that way about Israelis from the former Soviet Union, who are not considered Jews according to Jewish law.[53] In addition, a staggering 93 percent of ultra-orthodox Jews in Israel say they have no confidence in the Supreme Court (the institution supposed to defend equality among human beings), while 76 percent say that Jewish citizens should have more rights than non-Jewish ones.[54]

In line with Nadav Weiman's personal assessment, it seems that Israeli youth are even more prone to overtly intolerant attitudes: in 2020, Jewish Israeli teenagers were asked about their attitudes towards Arabs – 24 percent of secular Jews, 42 percent of national-religious Jews, and 66 percent of ultra-orthodox Jews reported negative feelings such as hate. Following this sentiment, 49 percent of national-religious teenagers and 23 percent of secular teenagers supported the option of denying Arab citizens the right to vote (ultra-orthodox youth were not asked about this).[55] These numbers show clearly that Israeli youth do not perceive Arabs as equal citizens, and that this may be related to observance of a certain version of Jewish religion steeped in ultra-nationalism and a feeling among those inside Israel and living in the territories that the Arab population is a threat. This complex mixture of emotions translates as disgust and thus becomes more rigidly fixed in people's political attitudes.

Conclusion

The politics of fear and the politics of disgust are tightly intertwined. A politics of fear unites us against a common enemy, while a politics of disgust ensures that we remain separate and distant from it, that fear does not in fact acknowledge the equality or superiority of the threatening other. Disgust is the emotion that best suits political regimes based on the regulated separation of populations, political regimes which institute a geographical and legal separation between groups and need constantly to justify that separation by casting the other as abominable. According to Dr Jabareen,

> When domination has entered all aspects of life, when Palestinians are under domination, they [Jewish Israelis] cannot sustain it without racism. . . . Racism comes after domination. You need to control the Palestinians and maintain the checkpoints and explain to your child why it's justified that a pregnant Palestinian woman is standing for ten hours and you pass quickly. You don't treat her like a person. She looks like that, but you do not treat her like that.

Dr Jabareen flips here the connection between racism and domination and makes an interesting suggestion: racism did not motivate the Occupation but is an outcome of it. For him, it is not disgust that makes a soldier abusive but, rather, the opposite: abuse needs a justification and disgust provides that justification. The more domination becomes routine and entrenched in Israeli society, the more needed are justifications for it. Indeed, there is hardly any more powerful justification for domination than disgust. As researchers have argued, anger and hostility alone are not enough to provoke violence, but disgust from another group is.[56] The emotion of disgust emanates from the ongoing Occupation, which has tended to separate populations through an elaborate system of bureaucratic control.[57] The real threat to a democratic and pluralistic society is disgust, not only because it radicalizes all camps, but also because it is through disgust that political rivals become irreconcilable enemies: by casting the left as traitors or non-Jews as dangerous elements threatening the body collective, the extreme-right assigns an impure (evil) essence to the adversary and thereby creates the psychological conditions for violence.

Before I conclude, a few strong caveats need to be put in place: even if it has been quite influential, the extreme Kahanist version described here is highly unrepresentative of the many strands of humanist and tolerant forms of Judaism. Kahanism and its offshoots are exceptions rather than the rule, and Judaism, like other religions, has its own distortions and deviations which become operative when political and social circumstances make these aberrations relevant. It should also be added that Israel, while not allowing interfaith marriage within its territory, is less stringent on these issues than certain Muslim countries, such as Egypt, in which the marriage of Muslim women to non-Muslims is prohibited (Israel recognizes civil marriages performed in other countries).[58]

Another caveat is that we should distinguish between critiquing a religious belief and critiquing the import of that belief in the public sphere. When practiced in the private sphere, none of the injunctions to separation called for by Judaism have an inherently racist motivation. They aim to preserve a religion and a culture and have a theological meaning (for example, keeping the covenant with God). It is only when they move to the public sphere that such injunctions should be scrutinized and that the question of whether they conflict with the basic tenets of democratic societies should be asked. The same might be said, by the way, about evangelicals in the USA. What has made them a particularly dangerous group is precisely their relentless attempts to extricate religion from the private sphere and turn it into the arbiter of ideological conflict in the public sphere.⁵⁹ The third and final caveat is that extreme right-wing groups are not the only ones to express disgust in the public sphere. The liberal left does not lack targets. For example, people who express even mild transphobic, sexist, or racist views generate intense disgust. This often follows the same logic of contaminating chains evoked earlier: having been in touch with a sexist or a racist is enough to turn someone into an object of liberal disgust. But there is a fundamental difference: what we may call liberal disgust concerns opinions and not group members; nor does it directly threaten one of the founding organizational principles of liberal democracies, namely cultural pluralism. When disgust actually entrenches group separations and distinctions (because some groups are contaminating), it promotes a social order based on the capacity to subdue and contain the contaminating essence (we may wonder if that is not indeed the reason why a supremacist such as Bezalel Smotrich preferred the political wilderness to a government supported by an Arab party).⁶⁰ Disgust thus plays a powerful if unacknowledged role in creating and fostering enmity between social groups. It must not only be acknowledged as a political emotion but also be recognized as playing a key role in the polarization and radicalization of politics observed worldwide.⁶¹

3

Resentment, or The Hidden Eros of Nationalist Populism

To be in anger is impiety;
But who is man that is not angry?
        William Shakespeare, *Timon of Athens*, Act III, scene V

Resentment has probably always been present in organized polities (Aristotle mentions it in his *Politics*).[1] For Aristotle, even if leaders lead justly, they still can end up generating resentment. Resentment is as much an angry reaction to inequality as it is to leadership and even excellence. One of the most insistent questions raised by this emotion is how much it is an expression of a demand for justice or how much it is a variation on petty envy. Søren Kierkegaard expressed this ambivalence in his wry view that *ressentiment* (the French word was the one used by German philosophers) is the emotion that wants to "level."[2] *Ressentiment* is not a democratic emotion per se but, as Nietzsche averred, it is typically generated by democracies, because it is likely to be felt by members of groups who experience inferiority but who hold a norm of equality and who are unable, for legal, physical, or normative reasons, either to reach equality or to repair or avenge their sense of inferiority.

This was indeed also the view offered by Max Scheler in his book *Ressentiment*, written in 1912:

> Revenge, envy, the impulse to detract, spite, Schadenfreude, and malice lead to *ressentiment* only if there occurs neither a moral self-conquest (such as genuine forgiveness in the case of revenge) nor an act or some other adequate expression of emotion (such as verbal abuse or shaking one's fist), and if this restraint is caused by a pronounced awareness of impotence. There will be no *ressentiment* if he who thirsts for revenge really acts and avenges himself, if he who is consumed by hatred harms his enemy, gives him "a piece of his mind," or even merely vents his spleen in the presence of others.[3]

In Nietzsche and Scheler's view, *ressentiment* importantly differs from revolutionary protest, which actually aims to destroy and change the social order (and sometimes succeeds in doing so). For these thinkers, *ressentiment* is animated by a mob-like desire for revenge on leaders and elites without the capacity to act on that desire for revenge. To this extent, also, *ressentiment* is an emotion which activates imagination (imagining how the person who has harmed us will suffer) rather than action. It is not surprising then that *ressentiment* would have been imbued with negative connotations: it is a passive emotion, which claims equality without acting on that demand. It is the emotion which ruminates about and rehearses the wrong that has been done to us.

Ressentiment is a key emotional idiom of capitalist democracies because it is provoked by loss of power, real or imagined – a loss of power that is all the more unacceptable because it coexists with norms of equality. Thus, societies with high degrees of normative equality but which also include mechanisms of downward mobility (or of social stagnation) will be prone to *ressentiment*. *Ressentiment* is likely to be strong when competition with others and comparisons with them are dominant features of social relations. It takes the form of an incessant rumination over the lack or loss of privilege and contains the desire, implicit or explicit, to exact revenge on what we take to be the cause of our inferior status and privilege.

Nietzsche and his followers have indicted *ressentiment* for its mob-like properties and for being a degenerate way of establishing a relationship between elites and the people.[4] Such a view can be questioned on two counts: first, *ressentiment* often expresses an envious rejection of inequality that is difficult to separate from a legitimate denunciation of injustice.[5] Moreover, *ressentiment* is not historically fixed. It can and does change its meaning. While some scholars use *ressentiment* as if it was an unchanging and fixed emotion, I argue that, in the political arena, it has become the site of power struggles between various social and political groups. *Ressentiment* has profoundly changed its directionality in the sense that it no longer flows from the bottom to the top but flows in many directions in society. This multi-directionality explains, in part, the nature of nationalist populism. Following the tenet of the sociology of emotions, I suggest that, as a political emotion, *ressentiment* has a meaning and effect which depend on the social groups who use it and the goals they pursue. Such groups and goals vary, and it is the groups who promote *ressentiment* and the goals they pursue that form the proper sociological object of an analysis of *ressentiment*. Israel offers one outstanding example of the political populist uses of *ressentiment*.

*

Mizrahim are Jews who immigrated to Israel from Africa and Asia (Morocco, Iraq, Yemen, and many other countries), mostly in the 1940s and 1950s, and their descendants. It is now beyond dispute that these Jews were significantly discriminated against by what was then a socialist left-wing establishment[6] composed almost exclusively of Ashkenazim (Eastern- and

Western-European Jews),[7] who, like many of their non-Jewish European counterparts, held deeply orientalist views of Arabs and, by association, of Mizrahim as well.[8] They regarded them as primitive and inimical to the Western project that Israel was vying to implement in the Middle East.[9] The discrimination against Mizrahim took many forms: after the founding of the state in 1948, the Israeli government created transit camps to house the tide of incoming immigrants. In many cases, the camps included tents and shabby huts, with no electricity or running water. Ashkenazi immigrants were usually taken out of the camps fairly quickly and housed in what became urban centers and proper neighborhoods, while Mizrahi immigrants typically had to stay in the camps much longer, sometimes for several years, even organizing a new identity around them. In 1952, over 80 percent of people living in these transit camps, or *Ma'abarot*, were Mizrahim,[10] which generated a significant gap in the conditions of integration and mobility of the two ethnic groups. The education system in Israel favored Ashkenazim as well. Mizrahim were clearly at a disadvantage: in the 1970s, only 27 percent of Mizrahi boys attended high schools.[11] More glaringly, Mizrahi pupils were more likely to be steered towards vocational schools[12] and prevented from gaining a full high school diploma. Many of the towns dominated by Mizrahim did not have regular high schools, which, of course, *de facto* prevented them from entering the universities,[13] which after the 1970s throughout the world became the surest path to social mobility. The discrimination, orientalism, and unapologetic dismissal of Mizrahim by Ashkenazim are beyond doubt, despite the fact these have been sorely and vehemently contested.[14] Ashkenazim discriminated against Mizrahim to the same extent that whites discriminated against black people, or Christians against Jews, with the difference that they belonged to the same people and were supposed to be an integral part of the same political collective entity. This is why it offers us a particularly good case to reflect on the ways in which victims react to the injustices inflicted on them by members of the same national group. The reaction is all the more interesting in that Mizrahim were supposed to be the equals of the Ashkenazim who had preceded them and who presumably held socialist ideas. Loss of privilege is a contributing factor to the development of *ressentiment* and to the shift towards populist ideas. In the case of Mizrahim, it was the obvious and continuous discrepancy between the status of the two ethnic groups that contributed to the sentiment of injustice. As Jews in a Jewish state, Mizrahim should have been "first-class citizens." Instead, they were discriminated against in all domains of political, economic, religious and cultural life.[15]

It is therefore unsurprising that *ressentiment* became the leverage used by the right-wing competitor of the left-wing party (Mapai), the Herut party (which later morphed into the Likud party), to unseat the continual power of the left on political institutions. Menachem Begin, who headed the Herut party, managed to do just this – that is, to transform the real social experience of discrimination of Mizrahim into a long-lasting resentment against the Ashkenazim as an ethnic group. This in turn profoundly transformed Israeli politics: it created a powerful constituency for the right and enabled it to gain power almost continually since 1977.

Before the 1981 elections, things did not look good for Prime Minister Begin. After Likud had removed the left from power for the first time in Israel's history in 1977, the polls predicted a clear victory for the left camp in 1981. On 27 June, three days before the election, the well-known television presenter Dudu Topaz took the stage at a Labour Party event in Tel Aviv and insulted and denigrated Likud supporters, saying that "Metsudat Zeev," the Herut party headquarters (the predecessor of Likud), was full of riffraff (in Hebrew the highly derogatory and condescending term of *tshachtshachim*). The following day, at a Likud election rally at the very same venue,

Begin, in all his political cunning, seized the opportunity. With emphasis, he said:

> What I'm asking you to do is, tomorrow, from morning to evening, make phone calls. What you need to do, which is important, is to call all your acquaintances in Jerusalem and Haifa and Rishon Lezion and Ness Ziona and in Rehovot and Beer Sheva. Just tell them what Dudu Topaz said here, the whole people of Israel must know this, one sentence in all: "All the riff-raff are in Metzudat Zeev."[16]

This speech, followed by a victory for the Likud in elections, was a milestone in the political history of Israel, and it adequately revealed and denounced the real contempt in which Mizrahi voters were held. It became in a way the blueprint of the ways in which the Likud would now frame its relationship to Mizrahim, creating a long-lasting connection between a political party and an ethnic group, associating the left with Ashkenazi domination (which was and remains real), accentuating the ethnic divide at the same time that it denounced it, and keeping alive the memory of the discrimination of which Mizrahim had been victims. The right-wing Likud party assumed the vocation of representing Mizrahim not so much by implementing concrete policies to change their socio-economic condition as by invoking and keeping alive their resentment.[17] This strategy succeeded, as the Likud (and its predecessor the Herut) has led the government for roughly thirty out of the forty-six years since its first success in 1977. However, where Begin offered an example of what Dani Filc has dubbed inclusionary populism – a form of populism that could accommodate the left and aimed, at crucial historical junctures, to unite the people,[18] Netanyahu's Likud resorts to exclusionary populism, a form of nationalism which took the form of excluding most noticeably Arabs and left-wingers.[19] How did this shift come about? According to Filc, Israel

Beitenu, a far-right but non-religious party founded and led by Avigdor Lieberman, was a main factor in the transformation of the Likud and its adoption of exclusionary politics.[20] But the radicalization of the Likud towards exclusionary politics heavily based on *ressentiment* was also fueled by another party, the ultra-orthodox Shas, whose constituency has been almost exclusively Mizrahi.

The Shas party, which represents religious Mizrahi Jews, was founded in 1984. It has been in government coalitions for roughly thirty of the thirty-nine years since its foundation. More than any other party, it has entertained a very close relationship with the Likud. In fact, we cannot overestimate the role Shas played in shifting the politics of the Likud to an exclusionary style of populism. After the 2009 elections, the political messages of Shas started to express overtly anti-elite, anti-Ashkenazi sentiment, nationalism, and xenophobia, and the Likud followed suit shortly afterwards. Academia and the media, and anything that smacked of the old Ashkenazi elites, became their familiar targets. In 2012, under Netanyahu's second government, Aryeh Deri (head of the Shas party and one of its founders, who served as minister of the interior from 1988 to 1993 and again from 2016 to 2021, a known political ally of Netanyahu) published this post in his Facebook page:

> Today at midnight a series of new taxes will take effect. Among other things, water prices will rise by about 3.5% and property taxes will rise by about 2%. Seniors in the public sector will actually benefit from salary increases. This insolence knows no limits.
>
> This is a direct continuation of the ruthless policy of the Prime Minister and the Minister of Finance, a policy in which they take from the weak and give to the strong. A policy that worsens the situation of those who drink tap water with simple bread [the poor] in order to fund those who can deliber-

ate about the type of champagne that will accompany their caviar.

You will not be surprised to find that over 80% of the senior workers in the same public sector are Ashkenazi while the vast majority of the poor who from now on will think twice whether to drink another glass of water are Sephardim. This is how discrimination is perpetuated, this is how we are led to social disaster. Only a strong Shas will stop the discrimination and take care of the weak and take care of those who have nothing.[21]

Deri's post shows the political ambivalence of *ressentiment*: it denounces real injustices and inequalities, but it does so not by denouncing inequality as a matter of principle but by invoking and rehearsing the ethnic enmity between two groups. This post was published during the election campaign for the 19th Knesset. At the time, Shas was part of the government, holding the Ministry of the Interior, the Ministry of Construction and the Ministry of Religious Services. However, Deri himself was just returning to Shas after political exile, following his conviction in 1999 on corruption charges, for which he served twenty-two months in prison.

In a similar vein, during the campaign for the 2015 elections, Shas released a promotional video featuring Deri speaking, with short clips accompanying his words. Shas was supposed to represent the "invisible" people: children who go to school hungry, elderly people who wait in line for money from social security [*Bituach Leumi*] only to be refused payment, Mizrahim who can't break the glass ceiling that prevents them from becoming judges and professors – all justified objects of denunciation. In the clip, Deri introduces Shas's "rich tax" that will take money from the rich and powerful in order to give it to the "invisible" Israelis.[22]

From the standpoint of a progressive politics of equality, Deri's denunciation of these tax policies is undoubtedly right.

But here again we meet the ambivalence of *ressentiment*: first, it is ironic that Deri casts himself as the champion of the dispossessed and demands greater taxation when he himself has been convicted of tax evasion and other tax offenses;[23] second, and more importantly, in associating the struggle for greater distributive justice with the ethnic identity of the public officials whose salaries will increase and those who will have to pay indirect taxes, he is not so subtly translating an economic struggle for justice into an ethnic struggle, with resentment as the key emotion doing the work of translating one into the other. The difference between the two is crucial: a struggle for equality is universal, and it puts general principles at the center of the polity. An ethnic struggle is different: it organizes the struggle for justice around particular identities which, by definition, cannot be extended to non-members. In 2015, Deri also cast his political opponent, Yair Lapid, head of Yesh Atid, a centrist secularist party, in ethnic terms:

> The arrogance of the "Yairs" crosses every boundary of arrogance and racism towards the Sephardic [Mizrahi] public, its heritage and culture. About two weeks ago, it was Yair Lapid who, in a television confrontation, wanted to "rehabilitate" us, and the day before yesterday, Yair Garbuz [An Israeli artist of Ashkenazi descent], who mocks our culture and the "kissing of amulets" and "laying down on the graves of religious figures [*Tzadikim*]," which he sees as the root of evil in Israeli society. We are mocked and targeted for "rehabilitation" and no one speaks against it. Again and again the racists raise their heads. Again and again the arrogant group that represents white Israel, the evil old elite, receives a stage and support. We are here to stay, we are here with pride to preserve our culture and identity, an identity that respects its sages and its *Tzadikim*. A tradition that preserves and kisses its Torah that is thousands of years old and does not seek [inspiration] in foreign and non-Jewish cultural fields. We will fight with all our might against

the manifestations of racism, we will condemn them on every stage and remove them from the centers of influence.[24]

Interestingly, this claim intertwines left-wing themes (denunciations against racism, the right to cultural dignity, anti-elitism) with highly conservative ones (religious identity, preservation of tradition, rejection of foreigners). This hodgepodge is typical of populism.[25] Ironically, it also essentializes Ashkenazi and Mizrahi identity, thus deepening the ethnic divide while contesting it. Discrimination assigns the other to a fixed identity, and the act of reclaiming proudly that same identity actually contributes to solidify it, to ironically perpetuate the self-reification of the oppressive other. As Edward Said eloquently put it:

> For that is the main intellectual issue raised by Orientalism. Can one divide human reality, as indeed human reality seems to be, genuinely divided, into clearly different cultures, histories, traditions, societies, even races, and survive the consequences humanly? By surviving the consequences humanly, I mean to ask whether there is any way of avoiding the hostility expressed by the division, say, of men into "us" (Westerners) and "they" (Orientals).[26]

Edward Said was referring to the reification inflicted on people from Arab countries by Westerners. But the same logic certainly applies in the other direction as well, when the Orientalized can view themselves and the others only in the terms of the essence that has been ascribed to them, thus perpetuating the binary distinction.

It follows from the above that the use of resentment in politics does not aim at building bridges across competing groups towards the struggle for justice. A contrasting model would be that of Martin Luther King who, when denouncing the ravages of slavery and demanding equal rights, was also holding his hand open to the whites and invoking inclusionary principles, thereby effectively making the struggle for civil rights the concern of everyone for whom human rights mattered. Not so with the Mizrahi politics of Shas, geared not only to Jews but to Jews of descent from Arab countries (one should note that this has been reinforced by the stubborn refusal by the Ashkenazi elites of yore to recognize any past wrongdoing).

Because Shas represented the disenfranchised Mizrahim, its right-wing and reactionary character was not immediately perceptible. More than that, Shas was even enthusiastically endorsed by representatives of the left-wing multiculturalist movement known as HaKeshet Hamizrahit [The Mizrahi Rainbow/Arch]: for them, Shas represented all the disenfranchised and enabled them to retake pride in their cultural heritage. As in many countries around the world, the multiculturalist left neglected, here again, to stress that the struggle for equality must go through a universalist affirmation of the equal dignity and equality of all human beings.[27]

Three things are worth noticing: while Arabs have been, in many ways, far more discriminated against than the Mizrahi Jews (by the sheer fact they are not Jewish, they are significantly more excluded from the body politic), their social and political condition never translated into *ressentiment*, while this was indeed the case for Mizrahim, suggesting that *ressentiment* derives from the fundamental assumption of equality, an assumption Israeli Arabs cannot make. The second interesting fact is that, in terms of actual policy, the right actually did not close the inequality gaps between Mizrahim and Ashkenazim. In fact the opposite is true. While the salary gap between these two groups may have slightly diminished,[28] some studies have found that children of Ashkenazim are still 2.5 to three times more likely to attain higher education than children of Mizrahim.[29] In 2012, among the urban population of Israel, second-generation immigrants of Mizrahi descent earned salaries only slightly higher than the average Israeli salary (by 9 percent), while second-generation immigrants of Ashkenazi descent earned salaries which were 42 percent above the average,[30] suggesting that social and economic disparities between the two groups were not only present but may in fact have increased with time.[31] Furthermore, when one takes into account the overall assets of a household, even greater inequalities between Jewish people of Mizrahi descent and those of Ashkenazi descent are revealed than when income alone is considered.[32] Netanyahu's economic policies can be described as neo-liberal: lowering the rates of income tax and corporate tax and reducing government expenditures on various social services.[33] These policies benefit the highest echelons of society while disadvantaging the lower classes, such that, in 2016, 26.6 percent of Israeli households could be defined as living in poverty. Furthermore, 27.7 percent of first-generation immigrant Mizrahim are considered as living in poverty or close to it, as opposed to 17.8 percent of first-generation immigrant Ashkenazim,[34] suggesting that these policies don't benefit the electorate of the Likud. In parallel, over the past decade, Mizrahim have become even more likely to vote for right-wing parties than they were in the 1970s.[35]

Thus, if the right still represents the Mizrahim, it is mostly for symbolic reasons: it provides them with greater symbolic status, based on the incessant claim they have been victims of a historical discrimination – a claim which is ironically substantiated by the accentuation of inequalities to which the neo-liberal right of Netanyahu has contributed.[36] In other words, inequalities which should have long been the responsibility of the various right-wing policies of the last forty years are still credited to the long defunct rule of the left wing, illustrating how *ressentiment* is built around the memory of past injuries and is not able to take stock of present and persistent inequalities. We may wonder if, as Yascha Mounk has argued in a comparative international study, this is not one of the reasons why populist leaders last, on average, much longer than non-populist leaders.[37] Indeed, this longevity may be explained by the fact that they are able to activate and keep alive the memory of past traumas in a way which feeds into a form of collective wounded narcissism. Despite the fact that the Mizrahi constituency increasingly had massive access to political representation (through the Likud and Shas), the political discourse addressing Mizrahim in Israel still incessantly ruminates on feelings of exclusion. For example, in the days leading up to the election of April 2019, it was revealed that the Likud campaign had used bots on social media networks to promote their messages. This incident showed that the Likud would stop at nothing to gain votes. But, instead of distancing himself from this affair, Netanyahu embraced it and turned it around, hammering the idea that the mainstream media and the left-wing parties saw Likud supporters as "bots" and not as humans. Netanyahu released a propaganda video which listed insults that had historically been thrown at Likud supporters; it utilized the image of Mizrahim as primitive and simple (riff-raff, a herd of animals, undeveloped, etc.). To this, he added the new insult of "bots" and encouraged his supporters to vote Likud as a protest against their historic oppressors.[38] The past oppression was recast as a present one, and the accusation was turned around. On the Twitter page of Yediot Ahronot, an influential Israeli newspaper, a minister and coalition whip, Dudi Amsalem, a man of Moroccan descent, was quoted as saying in June 2020: "Some Ashkenazim wish that I would be a poodle, a pet. I say to Yair Lapidim [the plural for Yair Lapid, today the main political figure opposing the Likud], as far as you are concerned, I, David Amsalem, should have sold vegetables in the market, cleaned your apartment or been in prison."[39] Amselem refers here to his name and Mizrahi origins and casts his political conflict with Lapid not as an ideological one but as an ethnic one, based on his symbolic reenactment of their historical discrimination. Thus, despite their massive political representation and *de facto* domination of the political process for the last forty years, the initial wounds of discrimination become inscribed, rehearsed, and reinforced in the collective psyche of Mizrahim. This suggests that *memory* of past wounds is key to the political mobilization of *ressentiment* and that this memory can very well feed on itself, even when the present seems to contradict it. *Ressentiment* creates not only a memory but a ruminant one, which incessantly invokes and repeats the past, as if it had remained fixed and unchanged. This rumination becomes constitutive of the group and of its identity. Second and third generations of Mizrahim are able to appropriate the stories and the memory of the real collective humiliation of their parents and grandparents in order to forge their own social and political identity in their struggles to gain equal footing.

In the Israeli context, *ressentiment* has had far-reaching consequences and reorganized Mizrahi identity, thus securing enduring loyalty to Likud. We may ask just how it does this.

Ressentiment latches onto the social inferiority produced by *real* economic inequality, cultural expropriation, and racism, but instead of being translated into a politics of universal justice it focuses on wounds and on hostility against groups identified as elites; it does so by looking for historical guilt and by rehearsing symbolically the promise of revenge on these designated groups. This has three consequences. First, it discards the universalism which the cultural elites have historically defended (this universalism is both moral and social); in fact it even comes to view universalism as a characteristic of the elites, who are viewed as intending to eliminate cultural difference and dominate oppressed groups. In that sense, it misses what is properly emancipatory about universalism. Such elision in actual fact no longer demands that institutions represent the universalist standpoint, the two most notable being the law and education. The second consequence is that leaders of such movements almost invariably hold a discourse of victimhood (about those they represent or about themselves), which enables them to "weaponize victimhood,"[40] make the status of victim into a useful currency in the political arena, because it is bestowed with a moral glow. In this respect, *ressentiment* is a species of what Wendy Brown has called a *wounded attachment*, a form of political claim which organizes group identity around its weakness and its need to be protected.[41] We may add that it entitles one to seek revenge on and the defeat of the perpetrator of the historical wrong. It transforms political disagreement into a zero-sum struggle in which revenge comes to play a significant part. Finally, the desire for revenge and a sense of grievance become so powerful that they can make one ignore one's economic interests in order to repair the perceived historical injustice. *Ressentiment* plays a key role in flawed ideologies, since it makes citizens willingly disregard their own present self-interests in order to avenge or repair a past wound. The upshot of all this is that it prevents the building of universalist alliances with other oppressed groups, such as Ethiopian Jews, African refugees, or Arabs.

In fact, *ressentiment* creates a foundation for a flawed ideology: its main effect is to make the dispossessed rehearse their wounds and demand revenge rather than focus on changing the current state of affairs along with other groups. Groups become susceptible to manipulation by leaders who have an interest in making a historical injustice into an irreparable one. These leaders become the object of strong emotional investment because they become closely and intimately associated with individuals' wounded selves: the leader becomes the one who promises to avenge the past wounds and thus will become a father, a brother, someone who not only belongs to the group but protects it. Accordingly, as Ohad Cohen has documented, some Mizrahim view Netanyahu as a saint, as a protective figure who defends them from a mean world, akin to the saints venerated by some Jews of Moroccan descent.[42] It follows that *ressentiment* creates a political atmosphere in which avenging the group takes precedence over the overcoming of the sense of historical grievance.

Since 1977, there have been few left-wing governments in Israel. One reason for this is the institutionalization of neo-liberal policies, meaning that economic policies are no longer really the object of political struggles, as neo-liberalism successfully presents itself as the only possible and desirable way to conduct the economy.[43] The left failed to offer the Israeli public a significantly different economic policy. But another reason is the power of *ressentiment*: despite some rare attempts to issue apologies for its historical egregious "mistake," despite the fact that the Labor party nominated at its helm two Mizrahi leaders, the sense of grievance persisted. When grievance organizes and constitutes identity, it becomes difficult to repair it, because the aggrieved must relinquish an identity. *Ressentiment* justifies cultural wars whose aim is to find *symbolic* and token reparations for past discriminations. Miri Regev, the Likud culture minister in 2016, could declare that the Ashkenazim were people who think that "classical music is better than the Andalusian music" of Morocco, or that "Chekhov is more important than Maimonides."[44] Such declarations have no aim other than to declare a culture war and to affirm symbolically the status of an aggrieved group.[45] Perhaps most deleterious is the fact that a politics of resentment, focused on the rehearsal of wounds, does not enable the "guilty" side to genuinely start a process of self-examination. Instead of holding Ashkenazim accountable for the betrayal of their own political ideals, a grievance fed by *ressentiment* creates the sense of an irreparable injury, a sense of chasm that cannot be overcome. A politics of *ressentiment* generates a truncated political dialogue, one that cannot lead to alliances with other deprived or oppressed groups or to reconciliation with the initial perpetrators of the discrimination. *Ressentiment* provides a powerful glue to create cohesive boundaries within the group and is at the foundation of a politics of identity. Political affiliation comes to resemble clan-like forms of loyalty.[46] More: the party itself, here the Likud, becomes part of the personal identity of many Mizrahi voters. To betray the party is to betray one's tribe.

*

In his *The Politics of Resentment: A Genealogy*, Jeremy Engels, who studies the rhetorical foundations of democratic cultures, states that, "Though it might seem like our primary trouble today is the over-abundance of civic resentment, this is not the case. The problem with our weak democracy is not the quantity of resentment but *its directionality*."[47] Engels, contrary to many other authors, does not view resentment as an emotion that should be banned from the political bond. The problem, for him, as perhaps it was for Adorno, is the displacement in consciousness it operates.

> What I call the politics of resentment involves channeling civic resentment – engendered by economic exploitation, political alienation, and a legitimate sense of victimhood – into a hatred of our neighbors and fellow citizens. Rather than allow resentment to build up as the unifying emotion through which a demos becomes itself in opposition to an elite, the politics of resentment redirects resentment within the people, thereby taming the force of democracy to act as a path to justice.[48]

In this view, *ressentiment* is not intrinsically anti-democratic. Its impulse is to express democratic demands for repair and justice, but, when recuperated and used by populist leaders, it becomes a tool for social divisions rather than repair, precisely through entrenched and non-negotiable forms of identity.

For Nietzsche and Scheler, *ressentiment* flows from the bottom to the top, yet the history of the Likud and right-wing ideology in Israel shows that a great deal of contemporary populist *ressentiment* aims to attack and undermine other competing Ashkenazi elites. The *ressentiment* of excluded social groups has become the battleground for a struggle between competing elite factions.

Netanyahu inaugurated a very interesting political tactic to keep his hold on the Mizrahim: he may well be one of the first leaders to have incessantly attacked, while in office, the establishment he was supposed to lead and represent, accusing it of being full of old left-wing (a.k.a. Ashkenazi) elites.[49] He enthusiastically promoted the concept of the "deep state," the idea that state officials persecute a victimized leader, who is hounded by the media, the courts, and the police.[50] As Ami Pedahzur put it, the populist Israeli right is characterized by the view that "the media, the civil society, the university and especially the judiciary [are] institutions controlled by small, yet powerful left-wing elitist groups that manipulate the rest of society in accordance with their narrow interests."[51]

But Netanyahu actually did not entirely invent this tactic. He borrowed it from a famous precedent. In 1999, Aryeh Deri was convicted for bribery and breach of trust. This was the culmination of many years of vehement denial by his followers that he had committed any crime. As Pedahzur recounts: "The party's rabbis (that is, their rabbinical board) decided that Deri was innocent, thus giving the electorate a source of authority to replace that of the official court."[52] A tape was widely circulated among Mizrahim before elections, affirming his innocence.

> Ten days after the elections, Shas turned to pure incitement. Some of its illegal radio stations called for a rebellion against the secular population and the criminal justice system because the police intended to shut down some of these stations. In one case, the announcer said that there would be a holy war against the left and, according to this Shas activist, God would be on the side of the religious population and would help them to

take up knives and slaughter their challengers. He would also put to death all the High Court justices.[53]

Netanyahu curiously adopted the style of Shas and the wholesale idiom of victimhood: in a mirror effect, victimhood of Mizrahi Jews resonated with his own personal victimhood, much as Deri cast himself: he consistently portrayed himself as personally persecuted by the media, the establishment, the academics, the justice and court system, and of course mostly the left, thus attempting to create a continuity and parallel between him and his Mizrahi constituency. When charged with corruption, like Deri and his supporters, he engaged in a campaign of victimization, turning the police, the attorney general, the judge assigned to examine his case, and the newspapers into participants in a vast conspiracy to bring him down and persecute him.[54] This is entirely reminiscent of Trump's accusations against the FBI, which, in August 2022, raided his Florida home to retrieve evidence of wrongdoing and crimes.[55] Victimhood is a key element of *ressentiment*, and it is key to Netanyahu's presentation of self, both on the personal and on the national level. In this respect, Ohad Cohen presents here a very interesting finding: in his doctoral study of Likud voters, he shows that, the more Bibi presents himself as a persecuted victim, the more he is supported by Mizrahim, making victimhood a source of identification.[56] In the politics of resentment, victimhood is a way of forming a bond between voters and leaders, of replacing ideology with identification.

The victimizers are the elites: the very fact that the legal and police establishment hold norms of governance make them left wing, by simple logic of contamination.[57] This view, carefully maintained by the Likud for the last forty years, has deeply reshaped the political language used by ordinary social actors and citizens. This may be one of the most astonishing transformations of the political discourse of the last two decades. It is certainly prevalent in Israel and is present in other countries as well, namely the appropriation of the victimhood status by groups who enjoy various privileges.

Let me give a glaring example. I interviewed an orthodox rabbi who lives in one of the settlements in the West Bank. Before I quote him at some length, some background information is needed.

Israeli settlements are civilian communities, inhabited by Israeli Jewish citizens, built on lands occupied by Israel in the 1967 Six Day war. The legality of many of these settlements according to international law is questionable.[58] Based on figures given by the Israeli Central Bureau of Statistics for the end of 2018, the number of settlers was 427,800, an increase of 14,400 over the previous year, which in turn suggests that the enterprise is flourishing.[59] The presence and ongoing expansion of existing settlements by Israel and the construction of settlement outposts is frequently viewed as an obstacle to the peace process. The international community and the United Nations have repeatedly upheld the view that Israel's construction of settlements constitutes a violation of the Fourth Geneva Convention.[60] The United States, despite being a staunch supporter of Israel, has also considered the settlements to be "illegitimate" (the Trump administration changed decades-long American policy).[61]

Israeli soldiers search Palestinian houses in the middle of the night, often for no other reason than to remind the population of the military's presence,[62] stop sick people at roadblocks and prevent them from receiving treatment;[63] settlers assault Palestinians and prevent them from harvesting their fields and are rarely indicted by the legal system (in fact it is more likely that the victims will be held accountable);[64] houses are demolished as a punishment for any attempt to resist and revolt.[65] With this background in mind, let me quote the rabbi living in a West bank settlement. He has a highly articulate worldview of his enemies.

Eva: Would you say that your society, the community in which you live, how would you characterize its attitude towards Arabs? And is there a difference in relation to Israeli and Palestinian Arabs? Is it the same attitude?

Gabriel: I, for example, was a tutor of some boy, and this boy I once went with him to a zoo, and there were Arabs who came to visit, and he would harass them. It bothered me a lot. Harassing Arabs just because they are Arabs does not seem like a right thing to me. But, on the other hand, one has to understand the situation that these boys are going through. He's still a boy. Boys do not always act using their minds.

Eva: What does he believe? I think he does this because he thinks they are threatening him.

Gabriel: What he grew up and saw was that Arabs can do whatever they want and we Jews are limited. So, for him, every Arab he sees is an illustration of the discriminatory treatment he receives.

Eva: That's very interesting. Explain to me where the Arab can do what he wants and the Jew is more limited and discriminated against.

Gabriel: In Judea and Samaria, Arabs build where they want, as much as they want, and [the state] does not destroy anything.[66] And a Jew, if he even builds, it could be a settlement that has already been built, and his house will be demolished. It could be in a demonstration that Arabs could threaten and throw stones freely. There is an attempt to stop those who throw stones, but the proportion [of the actions] towards a Jewish stone thrower and an Arab stone thrower is completely different. I do not justify throwing stones, but the proportion of the severity is quite different.[67] ... The desire to keep things quiet in the area means that it is better to give the Arab the feeling that he is right. If a person [a Jew] goes and tries to just shoot in the air then they will confiscate his weapon. There is a feeling among many people that, because there is a desire to keep the quiet, and there is a fear that if there is aggressive action against Arabs then there will be more riots and more mess, so [the state] prefers to act more aggressively towards Jews than towards Arabs.

Eva: Very interesting. So why not direct your anger at the Israeli authorities? Suppose the army or courts? The injustice stems from there.

Gabriel: What happens is that the Arabs cause a provocation. *The police prefer to discriminate in favor of the Arabs* (emphasis added). So you can protest against the police, but it's easier for people to say, "I cannot trust the police to handle the problem, so I prefer to show the Arabs, without the mediation of the police, who is the boss." So there are all sorts of retaliatory actions that places do privately. In recent years the authorities have taken it more seriously and stopped it in all sorts of ways, but there are still people who independently go down to the village, burn some trees or catch an Arab and beat him up. For them it is a message that they convey to the Arabs, "Do not mess with us," because the police will not do it, so I have no choice but to do it myself.

Eva: So the reason there are these actions is that basically the Jews do not feel sufficiently protected in the territories? They feel there is a preference, that the authorities prefer the Arabs to maintain the quiet.

Gabriel: Yes. . . . A Palestinian who wants to sell land to a Jew is executed [by their Palestinian neighbors]. And no one is talking about it being immoral. Only we should be moral; they are not. The treatment of LGBT people in Arab society is a disgraceful treatment, much worse than what . . . Any religious rabbi who does conversion therapy, it is much better than how they are treated over there. And we do not hear statements against it. We have certain opinions, and if you hold a certain opinion I think you should be proud to say it, even if it's in front of people who want to make peace with us. If they do something wrong, then one has to go against it. It feels like we have to give up everything for them, even our opinions, just so that they will agree to sit with us in peace.... The things that seem to be most important to the left, when it comes to the Arabs, they are afraid to talk [about them] because maybe the Arabs will be hurt and [it's not] politically correct, it will not sound good, it is racism. Everything is crooked. There is no straight gauge between what Jews should do and what Arabs should do, and that is not right. Even according to what the left thinks, there should be equality and everything should be the same. It's not the same thing, from the beginning.

Ressentiment turns the victims into the perpetrators and thus creates a deep alienation from state authorities themselves.

According to Francis Fukuyama, the mixture of religion and nationalism throughout the world is due to the fact that democracies cannot, or, at least, have not, so far, resolved the problem of *thymos*.[68] Fukuyama explains the persistence of religion in contemporary society through resentment as a force in politics and defines it as the gap between legal equality and isothymia, being recognized and respected, and thus, like Nietzsche and Scheler, makes of resentment mostly an attribute that flows from the bottom to the top, an attribute of those who feel deprived and inferior, a sentiment which, for Fukuyama, in turn is compensated through national pride and religion. But Fukuyama's frame is ill equipped to grasp the fact that, in the example of this rabbi, *ressentiment* is expressed by a member of a group who enjoys enormous territorial, economic, and legal privileges and who appropriates the language of injustice – not in a consciously manipulative way, but because the causal frames have become distorted and inverted: Jewish settlers genuinely experience themselves as victims of the very minorities whose lands they expropriate and whose movements are tightly controlled. Note that the rabbi does not invoke his historical right to the land; nor does he invoke the

Israeli military supremacy enabling him to substitute might for right; instead he invokes the fact that the left is dominant, that it acts as an oppressor, and that his group is a victim of that group. Resonating with Netanyahu's theories of the deep state, the Jewish police and the legal apparatus are viewed as discriminating against the Jews; most interestingly, the rabbi invokes a repressive normative order he calls political correctness. Political correctness is not only a set of norms which prevent him from attacking a group under army surveillance and control – the Palestinians – but also the fact that this norm is publicly upheld and defended by the left and the establishment. This is why, for this rabbi, it is the left which confuses victims and perpetrators and inverts moral categories; it is the left that is dominant because it sets up norms of morality and speech. A survey undertaken by the Israeli Democracy Institute in 2019 found that only 7 percent of Israeli Jews identify with the left, thus suggesting that the rabbi's views are based on inaccurate and distorted empirical facts.[69] On the one hand, he excoriates the left for betraying the true culture of the Jews and Israel, for being an imitator of the non-Jews, and for failing to be authentically Jewish, but, on the other hand, he accuses it of not being left wing enough. Against the edicts of Jewish orthodoxy to which he subscribes, he denounces the left for not defending the rights of LGBTQ people in Arab nations. He indicts the left and Arabs for not upholding values of human rights that, normally, orthodox Judaism is happy only to dismiss and scoff at.

This rabbi's discourse is a fascinating hodge-podge: it is the self-victimizing discourse of the member of a group with many legal, territorial, and economic privileges, who denies basic human rights to another group, but who does this by pointing to their problematic human rights track record. He professes ideas that are at once democratic and supremacist. This contradiction stems from an appropriation of the language of rights by a right-wing and religious view.

An International Political Style

As the sociologist Rory McVeigh and others argue, *ressentiment* is at the heart of the appeal and rhetoric of fascist politics. In their book *The Politics of Losing*, McVeigh and Estep show how, in the 1920s, the Klan (KKK) capitalized on the anger and frustration of the middle class when significant changes in American society undermined their economic power, political influence, and social status.[70] In the early 1900s, millions of immigrants arrived on American shores, mostly Catholics and Jews from Central and Southern Europe. They provided the labor that fed the factories, and they fueled rising political constituencies and carried with them cultures, practices, and beliefs that set them apart from the native-born white Protestants who were predominant in America. To recruit members, the Klan used race, religion, and birth to cobble together a new constituency of those seeking redress for their lost power and scapegoated immigrants for their losses.[71] Millions embraced the Klan and took immigration as the chief cause for their state. The historian Nancy MacLean examined the financial records of Klansmen, and she found a "grim testimony to the toll the postwar recession and economic reorganization took of them: nearly half suffered economic losses between 1918 and 1927."[72] In other words, there seems to be rather significant historical evidence that economic loss and loss of status are connected with the embracing of radical ideologies that scapegoated other groups and reaffirmed the supremacy of one's own religious, racial, or ethnic identity. According to McVeigh and Estep, this is the same dynamic present in contemporary America with Trump. Almost a century later, Trump appealed to the resentments of a new segment of mostly white Americans, primarily those in towns bypassed by the global economy.[73] While the changing economy has been profitable to the better educated, jobs that paid well disappeared from the towns that didn't have the highly educated workforces to retain them. To quote

McVeigh and Estep: "Service-sector and retail jobs filled the vacuum, but they were a poor substitute for the jobs that once provided respectable wages and full-time hours. Immigration, which generated new Democratic constituencies and seemed to be slowly changing American culture, once again became a political whipping post."[74]

Much like Netanyahu, Trump capitalized on this and made *ressentiment* an overt political style. In an article published in NCA's *Quarterly Journal of Speech*, Casey Ryan Kelly analyzed Trump's speeches in light of the structure of *ressentiment*. Central to these speeches is white victimhood as well as argument for the need for revenge against political enemies.[75] Focusing on the language used in Trump's post-election rally speeches, Kelly argues that *ressentiment* captures "the paradoxical but mutually reinforcing relationship between virtue and victimhood."[76] Trump self-identifies as the chief victim of attacks. To take one example among many: "When addressing criticisms of his immigration policy, he notes: 'And think of it in terms of immigration. And you may love it, or you may say, isn't that terrible. Okay? And if you say isn't that terrible, who cares? Because the way they treat me – that's peanuts compared to the way they treat me. Okay?'"[77] In a recent poll, 75 percent of Republicans viewed conservatives as facing real discrimination in America; only 49 percent said the same thing of black people.[78] *Ressentiment* inscribes wounds inside the psyche; it typically rehearses a wound or trauma located in the past (sometimes the wound is real, often it is imaginary), but, in the case of the settler and of nationalist populists, the loss is located in an ambivalent time structure, in the past and in a feared future. Kelly suggests that the invocation of victimhood is actually key to Trump's emotional and rhetorical style, a style entirely informed by the emotion of *ressentiment*.

Trump describes the nation as tough and strong, strong enough to overcome the gangs of immigrants who want to flood it, and yet simultaneously as a fragile young woman whose vulnerable body will be senselessly tortured by immigrant foreigners. According to Kelly, this seeming incoherence of the message is unified by the perception of a hostile world,[79] a perception that is key to the political vision of the nation of Orbán, Erdoğan, or Netanyahu.[80] All of these leaders at once describe their nation and themselves both as victims and as strong, creating two conflicting images of the same object. More: similar to Trump, who frames his audience experience as vulnerability as if they themselves were experiencing structural oppression, even though white people in America have been, and continue to be, in command of the entire political and economic apparatus, it is the settlers, the right wing, who have been in power for almost forty years, who become the victims.[81] This rhetoric denies the fact that these groups hold great power, much in the same way that the settler rabbi denies the reality of the military occupation of the West Bank. The Israeli rabbi and the settlers he represents have won an incalculable amount of political victories: they are represented in the Knesset, they have powerful lobbyists, laws have been passed which reflect their worldview, yet the idiom of victimhood is persistent and even dominant. The roles of victim and oppressor can be so easily switched. More generally, as the online magazine *Politico* put it: "We've never had a president in the modern era who has actively cultivated an image of victimhood, a posture that once would have been considered whiny and weak, but that Trump has, through his personal alchemy, made into a kind of political strength."[82]

Interestingly enough, 54 percent of Trump voters believe that Christians are the most persecuted group in the United States.[83] To take another example of a country which veered towards populism, the turn to the extreme right in Poland was characterized by one key ingredient: it now portrays itself as a victim of Hitler and the Nazis, and not as a willing accomplice or perpetrator.[84] Victimhood has thus become an idiom of the rhetoric of populism, an idiom without which we cannot understand political polarization and antagonism.

Kelly argues that: "If being a victim is the price of entry to his political ethos, then Trump must continually ruminate on his injuries, invent new tormentors and resurrect old ones, pursue ill-conceived policy goals, and perpetually defer the resolution of their collective grievances."[85] The same might be largely said of the political ethos that has been instilled by Netanyahu's politics of resentment, which works on the rumination of the past injuries of Mizrahim.

Ressentiment described in this case does not derive from a sense of injustice that flows from the bottom to the top but, rather, is an affect of "aggrieved entitlement" – that is, the wound felt by groups who claim lost privilege or denounce the privilege held by others.[86] This form of *ressentiment* enables representatives of dominant groups (such as Trump or the settlers) to mimic and ventriloquize victimhood, and this in order to contest the power of other groups. Here *ressentiment* has changed its meaning and is no longer the emotion which contests the power of the powerful by the powerless (as is the case with the Mizrahim) but, rather, is used in the relationship between elites and other elites. It consists precisely of shifting responsibility from the right-wing neo-liberal elites that have vampirized the lower-middle class (Mizrahim in Israel) to the Ashkenazi cultural elites who have developed in cities, the media, and cultural industries and universities, and who, by and large, defend human rights and minorities. Much as Adorno described,[87] *ressentiment* enables a shift in the attribution of causes and blame. Such *ressentiment* is a weapon not only for mobilizing social groups but for waging a struggle against specific elites.

Why Is Victimhood So Successful?

In order to explain why the narrative of victimhood and *ressentiment* can be grasped so well and be plausible to so many, we must account at one and the same time for the supply side and the demand side of the political arena: the former is how elites manipulate *ressentiment* and the latter is the fact that people have a social experience that lends itself easily to such a sentiment. We need to explain the mechanism of resonance – that is, the "congruence between the content of the message and the predispositions of the audience."[88]

Because right-wing elite groups define themselves not only as representing the forgotten ones but as the forgotten ones themselves, they can efficiently attack the left-wing/liberal people perceived as intellectual and cultural elites. This seems supported by the fact that it is the same social groups whose power grew in the growing cities from the 1960s onward. In particular, it is their symbolic and cultural capital which was amply rewarded in such an expanding urban environment. In this way, members of highly elite groups as Trump or Netanyahu can efficiently hide their status and objective distance from those they purport to represent.

In the American context, Jeremy Engels locates the emergence of such politics of resentment with Nixon:

> Though the two master tropes of the politics of resentment – "the silent majority" and "the tyranny of the minority" – had circulated in American public discourse before the 1960s, Nixon pronounced them in a way that fundamentally rewrote ancient democratic practices. Rather than call on the poor to unite to battle the rich, Nixon arrayed the army of the silent majority for an internecine battle against tyrannizing minorities who disturbed the tranquility of traditional political hierarchies. We continue to fight such battles today – the silent majority is the rhetorical precursor to Karl Rove's "red states,"

Sarah Palin's "real America," and Paul Ryan's "makers." The tyrannizing minority is the racialized fear of "the takers" and "the 47 percent" derided in contemporary discourse.[89]

The sociologist Arlie Hochschild's study of Lake Charles, Louisiana, a red state, presents further illustration of how this process may have gelled in the last decades and reorganized consciousness.[90] Her interviewees[91] claim they feel distinctly both silent and silenced, and that women, blacks, Latinos, or gays made great progress but did so illegitimately, at the expense of white working-class men. The former groups are perceived, in Hochschild's words, as "line cutters," people who are cutting the line to get ahead of others. These are exactly the conditions described by Scheler for ressentiment:[92] these groups elicit envy and anger, but a powerless form of envy since, in the eyes of the "victims," the "line cutters" are protected by the legal apparatus and the liberal elites. This is exactly the kind of *ressentiment* Trump and Netanyahu have incessantly invoked, referring to a real inequality and channeling the social malaise it generates against social groups defined as "others," against social groups defined as elites and against the state itself. "The affirmation that the system is rigged against the people – rigged by corporations, rigged by the media, rigged by the political elite, rigged by special issues, rigged by donors – and that your anger is legitimate, that there is a truth to it. And, importantly, the affirmation that you are not alone in that anger – other people feel it."[93] Trump belongs to these elites, of course, but manages, as Netanyahu did, to convince masterfully that he belongs to the people, the lower-middle class or the Mizrahim.[94]

Netanyahu is very familiar with the Republican Party and its rhetoric. He has in fact a long relationship with the Republicans. In the 1980s, during Reagan's presidency, Netanyahu was the Israeli ambassador to the UN and promoted the idea that the Soviet Union was aiding Palestinian terror. Netanyahu was impressed with the neo-liberal practices of the Reagan administration and imported many of these practices into the Israeli economy in his later roles as prime minister and minister of finance. He grew acquainted with Republican strategic advisors and speech writers,[95] who helped create his unique rhetoric and later assisted in securing his first tenure as prime minister.[96]

Netanyahu learned his lesson from the Reagan-era Republican Party which had adopted its political rhetoric from Nixon, making elite *ressentiment* the hallmark of his politics, a *ressentiment* that was all the more confusing in that he pretended to represent the excluded. Netanyahu's and Nixon's politics of resentment has been a "perversion of the classical legacy of democracy as the political empowerment of the masses."[97] More than that: once Netanyahu's right appropriated the resentment of the masses, it could name the other camp as an enemy. The politics of resentment became central to American political life as it became central to Israel – which perhaps might be explained by the fact that, in the two countries, segments of the population came to build the story that they were victims of a left-wing minority.

Paradoxically, Nixon's and Netanyahu's rhetoric could bear long-lasting fruits because a culture of grievance and victimhood was increasingly made intelligible and plausible in the aftermath of the post-1970s democratization movements. I now suggest that, paradoxically, what made possible the continued plausibility of victimhood culture (which forms the backdrop of new *ressentiment*) is the very language that has been promoted by the left. Racial minorities and women who experienced real inequalities used a language of victimhood which was appropriated by white people and men.[98]

The rhetoric of victimhood has been, in a way, always a part of the left in the form of what Hannah Arendt dubbed the politics of pity.[99] In the politics of pity, it is not institutions and abstract rules of justice that are invoked but the singular plight of a singular person. Victimhood became a political claim which gained traction in the public sphere (because it managed to get attention in a field crowded by various people seeking attention); it bestowed moral status, in that it made victims morally superior; it gained traction in the legal sphere, as trauma and psychological injuries were increasingly recognized by courts and thus moved the intangible realm of psychological harm into an objective space; finally, it had an enormous politically performative power, as it helped organize both individuals and groups around their victim's identity, thus enabling a double process of individualization and group affiliation. In other words, the last thirty years have seen a process of increasing objectivation of the status of victim in the culture at large (that is, a large number of institutions contributed to create and objectivate the idea of victimhood), which in turn has made victimhood a resource in the political sphere. The political language of victimhood is now entering a new phase of its history: having been appropriated by the right in order to incriminate the old left as an oppressor, it can no longer be effectively used by liberals. *Ressentiment* becomes a weapon in an internecine war between elites, one representing business and neo-liberalism, the other representing the cultural vanguard. As McVeigh put it: "The politics of resentment works to capture popular resentment and direct it away from structures of oppression and towards neighbors and fellow citizens and thus leaves untouched the legitimate target of civic resentment."[100]

What this suggests is a profound crisis of the moral language of liberalism: our societies count real victims (refugees, poor people, victims of racism, children, and women casualties of daily violence). But if the key moral claims of liberalism are used and recuperated by the enemies of liberalism, it suggests that this language has become empty and can no longer effectively represent the downtrodden. One of the main effects of populism is precisely to blur the moral categories that are contained and implied by liberal political language. In this sense, populism's efficacy lies less in its ideological clarity than in the enormous moral and political confusion it generates. A politics of *ressentiment* blurs identity and justice, universalism and particularism, victims and oppressors.

Conclusion

Resentment has been a key aspect of the process of capturing the voice of the Mizrahim, who were discriminated against in a deep, wide, and persistent way. The process has been occurring in Israel for the last forty years, deeply affecting relationships between different social and ethnic groups. Politically, *ressentiment* is the most slippery of all emotions, for it contains genuinely democratic claims to equality, which can be easily hijacked and subverted by anti-democratic leaders in an atmosphere of particularism and revenge. Fear, disgust, and resentment thus form the powerful emotional matrix that draws strong boundaries between social groups and creates a strong attachment to a leader who becomes a caretaker for the group. What enables these emotions to ignore the divisiveness, hostility, and mistrust they actually sow is the fact that they are superseded by an emotion which binds people to an imaginary body collective. That feeling is love.

4

National Pride as Loyalty

Love your country. Your country is the land where your parents sleep, where is spoken that language in which the chosen of your heart, blushing, whispered the first word of love; it is the home that God has given you that by striving to perfect yourselves therein you may prepare to ascend to him.

Giuseppe Mazzini[1]

In his book *Humanity: A Moral History of the Twentieth century*, Jonathan Glover recounts how, during World War I, soldiers experienced the atrocities of the war in the trenches. Some of these soldiers went home, either because they were wounded or because they were on leave, and tried to tell their nations of the horrors. But their revelations were met only with hostility.

In *All Quiet on the Western Front*, Erich Maria Remarque described the strain of going back to Germany on leave. Attempts to say what the front was like simply made no impact on the confidence of patriotic civilians that things were *really* quite different. ... The same was true on the Allied side. ... The outer guards of the trap were civilians on both sides who believed what they read in the newspapers.[2]

This reminder of the often observed disparity between the first-hand experience of war and the blind nationalism displayed by those who were removed from it, far from the front, raises the possibility that nationalism feeds itself particularly well from the imagination, from the denial of what it actually means to defend a country with one's body. We may wonder if nationalism, like romantic love, is not all the more strong that it is oblivious to reality.

Nationalism and Community

A nation is, as Max Weber put it, "a community of sentiment."[3] Some scholars of nationalism view such sentiment as a pathology of modern history, as an expression of fear and hatred, yet others, such as Yoram Hazony or even Benedict Anderson, view it as a species of love.[4] I believe the latter thinkers are mostly right in the sense that nationalism is an expression of the deep attachment some groups feel towards the symbols, the values, and the history they come to see as defining their national community and their own sense of self as a member of that community.

This is also the reason why nationalism has proved to be an enduring collective emotion. It should have disappeared after the murderous form which nationalism took in the middle of the twentieth century, but it didn't. It should have disappeared in the subsequent era of globalization, but it didn't then either. Instead, it became a key dimension of populism which played the theme of nationalism in the background of class politics, separating groups who care about the nation from those who care also, and no less so, about international courts, immigrants, and refugees. Populism, more than most political ideologies, has played on the new divide generated by nationalism, becoming a field in which class distinctions and class conflicts[5] are played out.

*

Along with capitalism, nationalism has been the most momentous force shaping the nineteenth and the twentieth centuries. This is because it contained two powerful moral impulses: it was a liberating movement that freed people from colonizers or capricious rulers, and it enacted an equalitarian vision of the social bond as modern nations were defined by their claim that citizens belonging to a single nation are equal to each other.[6] In most parts of the world, nationalism inflamed the masses because it was about emancipation and brotherhood. After World War II in Europe and the Vietnam War, and after economic globalization broke down borders and boundaries, nationalism fell in disrepute. For many decades, globalization, the New Left and the post-World War II association of racism and nationalism discredited the latter. Yet, it is impossible not to see that, throughout the world, nationalism is back and is at the heart of the populist turn we have witnessed in the last decade or so. For example, the British media scholar Anne Graefer suggests that "the Brexit vote in June 2016 was an act of patriotism. Defending the nation against the bureaucrats in Brussels and 'taking back control' of Britain in order to tackle the issues of immigration and – by default – unemployment."[7] Arron Banks, an alt-right populist who funded UKIP's Brexit campaign with £8 million,[8] tweeted after the Westminster Palace attack in 2017 (killing six) and invoked this issue in his ideological platform: "We have a huge Islamic problem courtesy of mass immigration . . . we have communities who hate our country and way of life."[9] We may see clearly that, in European countries, the return to nationalism is intertwined with anti-immigrant policies as well as with the sense that the European Union has dispossessed nations of their sovereignty.

Nationalism identifies territory with a people and thus creates a powerful identification of the land with its (real or invented) history. The common ancestry on which nationalism is based implies that the members of the nation are kin or like kin, a kind of super family to which one has obligations.[10] This ancestry consequently becomes mythologized and sacralized, especially when it is viewed as one which has sacrificed itself for the heroic beginning of the nation. Sacrificial death thus becomes a debt we must repay in the form of love and remembrance. Writing about the French Revolution, the French historian Jules Michelet made it clear "that those whom he was exhuming were by no means a random assemblage of forgotten, anonymous dead."[11] Patriots and nationalists do the same: they regularly exhume the dead in order to sacralize the nation through them.

Such patriotic love has three characteristics: it contains the love of similar others – that is, of those who are a part of the nation; it is a form of self-love, since those I love resemble me; and it draws a boundary between the in-group and those who are not loved. Whether in the amorous relationship or in nationalism, love is an emotion that excludes and includes at one and the same time. Which of the two mechanisms prevails in each case leads to crucial differences between different forms of nationalism. The love of a nation can be either inclusive or exclusive – that is, it can be oriented towards the inclusion of foreign others (French or American revolutionary nationalism was inclusive, for example)[12] or it can be oriented towards exclusion, discrimination, and self-celebration. It can be geared to institutions (loving a country for its universalist constitution or democratic features) or it can be geared to the greatness and superiority of one's ethnic or religious group. It can be critical (or constructive) or blindly committed.

In this respect, it has become customary for liberal Israelis to make a distinction between the so-called inclusive patriotism of the early years of Zionism and the jingoistic exclusive nationalism of the right that ensued. The first type of nationalism is viewed as enlightened and democratic, while the second was (presumably) dark and based on declared superiority of one community over another. For although the early Zionists expelled Arab indigenous populations and established the legal, political, and economic supremacy of the Jewish people, there are some key differences between the early nationalism of the pioneers and its later populist version.

Israeli Nationalism

In contradistinction to Western European countries, nationalism and patriotism have remained a key element of Israeli national life, very long after its creation, and this because securitism and fear make the survival of Israel depend on citizens' will and love (see chapter 1). As Uzi Arad, a fellow at the Institute for National Security Studies who was an advisor to Netanyahu in the past, and Gal Alon, founder of the consulting company Insights, put it in a joint working paper, Israeli citizens have a high degree of patriotism when it is measured as willingness to fight for the country (85 percent) and the desire to remain in it (87 percent).[13] The authors even add that, "In comparison to other developed countries in the West, there is none that surpasses Israel in this declared readiness to fight for one's country."[14] Indeed, sacrifice has been made into a key element of Israeli social life through a long compulsory military service (thirty-two months for men, twenty-four months for women) and recurrent wars or military conflicts. We may also add that *ahavat Israel*, the love of the Jewish people, has long been a powerful motive of Jewish liturgy and memorial history.[15] Undoubtedly, Zionism morphed from a movement of emancipation into a nationalist ideology constantly present in the body politic, an ideology used by the state and the army to create historical continuity with the military feats of the early pioneers.

Zeev Sternhell has dubbed the type of nationalism that was promoted by the socialist establishment that came to rule the pre-nation Jewish community in Palestine [*Yishuv*] and the nation until 1977 *nationalist socialism*. Because this nationalism was supposed to assemble the nation, it denied any class or social conflict. In his words, it "refused to accept society as a theater of war."[16] It was also based on the principle that the individual was evaluated only according to the principle of what she or he was able to contribute to the collective. This nationalism, in contradistinction to the liberal nationalisms of Europe (France most notably) was a nationalism of blood and soil. Sternhell goes as far as to dub it a biological nationalism, based on biological filiation. That nationalism, Sternhell suggests, was not as brutal as some of its Eastern European counterparts, but was still set to conquer land and settle it.[17] But, where this nationalism succeeded in geopolitical and cultural terms, it failed in social terms in the sense that it was based on unacknowledged profound social divisions, most conspicuously between Jews of Eastern Europe and Jews of Arab countries and between Arabs and Jews (see previous chapter). So profound was its ideology of unity that nationalist socialism could never properly acknowledge these divisions (except in vague excuses that were pronounced much later by leaders of left parties).

A nationalism blind to the social divisions became the prime ideology, the moral and cultural framework of the incipient state. The *Histadrut*, which was the general organization of workers, was a key institution creating networks of loyalty and submissiveness reflecting and solidifying rather than overcoming these divisions but seemingly integrated them into a national labor framework. Moreover, this nationalism was no less intent on conquering land than its subsequent right-wing nemesis (the prominent Labor leader Igal Allon promoted the creation of the infamous settlement of Kiryat Arba,[18] which became a hotbed for extremists). As Sternhell once again put it: after 1967, nationalism remained what it had always been under the Mapai (left-wing party) rule. It was, says Sternhell, tribal, *volkisch*, and steeped in the myth of the heroic past, entirely convinced of the righteousness of its cause.[19] The "socialist" leadership was first and foremost nationalist, and it is as such that it provided all the sacred symbols which would later come to inflame the imaginary of the right-wing settlers. The proof that such nationalism was imbued with deep religious symbols is to be found in the fact that Israel does not recognize "being Israeli" as a valid nationality – thus standing apart from its Western European or American counterparts. Since 1948, the nationality of Jewish citizens has been registered as Jewish, that of Muslim or Christian Arabs as Arab, and non-Jews by their country of origin. "The Interior Ministry has compiled a list of more than 130 possible nationalities for Israeli citizens including Jewish, Arab, Druse, Circassian, Samarian, Hong Konger, German, Albanian and Lichtensteinian. 'Israeli' is not on the list."[20] A petition to the Tel Aviv District Court and later to the Supreme Court by a Jewish man in the 1970s had demanded to allow him to be registered as Israeli and not as a Jew. It was rejected by the judges on the grounds that there was no Israeli nation, only a Jewish one.[21]

This indicates clearly that Israeli nationalism has always relied on a primordial, quasi-religious definition of what a nation is, one that refers to the ancient past, to the supra-territorial entity of the Jewish people, rather than to a civic-republican one. And such primordial religious definition of the nation has been endorsed by the Israeli Supreme Court from the beginning of the state. Israeli patriotism runs very high, yet Israeliness is not recognized as the nationality of Israel, suggesting that such patriotism is premised on a state viewed as an ethnos, the Jewish people and Jewishness. The state then occupies a key function in shaping and maintaining a primordial identity based on an extra-territorial worldwide collectivity called the Jewish people and on a history which, for the most part, did not include any national existence.

Listen to Eliya, a young and articulate woman who lives in the West Bank and is a self-professed right-winger. She is a young settler living in the Occupied Territories but could have been a poster girl for the pioneers of early Zionism.

> My father came from a rather "dark" regime in Argentina to the Jewish state, which was a kind of a dream and a goal for both him and my grandparents, whose parents came from Poland and Germany. So this idea of the Jewish state was really my dad's dream, and I'll tell you more than that, I was also an officer in 8200 [an elite intelligence unit], and after I finished the officers' course, for my dad it was . . . He came from something that . . . and now he has children serving in the army of the state of Israel. It was a dream he grew up with. And from my mother's side, my mother's parents immigrated from Iraq; they fled because they were attacked and immigrated to Israel, so the Zionist dream is something that was very noticeable in my house. So the state of Israel is a place that I feel very, very connected to, and I also really care about what happens [to it]. . . .
>
> Here everything is very emotional and very heated, and I tried to understand why. It's a little funny because really we're all somehow connected, in this country, someone is a friend of your cousin, somehow we're all connected and we all know each other. And this place, because it's so small and intimate, it feels to me like we're a family, and maybe that's why our fights are so deep and so emotional. I think it's also because I was raised in the Jewish tradition, but we very much believe in the one and whole and special people of Israel, and in that we need to remember that always and from the dawn of history, whenever there were quarrels history led us to a bad place. Now it's part of what hurts me, because it seems like some ongoing quarrel between people living together in a small place, in a place that is very sensitive to everyone, and the goal that I'm sure is the same goal [for everyone], to keep the country safe. There may be some arguments and friction, but in the end we have

a common interest. When I look at the rest of the world, from what I know, I may be a little wrong here, the rest of the world is not the same. For an American living in New York, the great United States is something more abstract than the state of Israel for someone living in Kfar Saba. There really is a connection here, there is a connection to the country, to the territory, which I personally have not seen elsewhere. So for me, when I try to think about what the state of Israel is, then I really think we are a family here. And I think that's why people take it to very personal places, because it's very close to the heart and very close to home. For me, as part of the second generation or the third generation in total, who received this country, it is very close. The rest of the countries in the world are not so young . . . it's less in your flesh, or in the flesh of those close to you, that this country was established in blood. The state of Israel is a very, very small, intimate, explosive place, and when I try to liken it to something it feels a bit like quarrels within the family. . . .

Eva: Did you ever get excited when you saw the flag, or when you hear the anthem? What are the national events that move you?

Eliya: I have some. First of all, I am now in the process of returning to the army. So events that I saw and that were moving, say the first Memorial Day I was a soldier after Operation "Protective Edge" [*Zuk Eitan*, 2014 Gaza War]. My friends were in Gaza, my partner at the time was too, and after that, on Memorial Day, we went up to Mount Herzl. And my ex-boyfriend, there was someone who studied with him at the military boarding school who was killed at Zuk Eitan, so we went up to the grave, all the friends together. And suddenly hearing the anthem when you're in uniform and an officer, and you're looking at the grave of a person you knew, is something destabilizing. Suddenly you realize in a second, and we're talking about age nineteen, it's a very young age, suddenly you get an understanding that it's real, this thing that everyone described, it's real and it's happening.

Eva: What is this thing that everyone described?

Eliya: This feeling, all the time you are told that the country was built on blood, that the earth cries out with blood, you suddenly understand that. You suddenly feel, I at least felt a chill in my body. This is an event that I found very, very moving. When I went to Taglit [in the course of sponsored Taglit trips, foreign Jews have been able to get to know the country of Israel since 2000; soldiers such as Eliya sometimes accompany these programs], we went with them to the Western Wall, they saw the Western Wall for the first time, I felt the excitement and I was excited as well. The anthem specifically I do not think I ever heard it and got excited. But these events, Memorial Day, have since been etched for me as something moving.

Eva: I guess your excitement comes from a deep identification with something or someone. If so, can you formulate with whom or what you identify? Is it the dead?

Eliya: I think, through a personal story, I suddenly realized the great connection there is in the country of both bereaved families and people who have lost friends, whether it is in wars or terrorist attacks, and suddenly it happens to you and you understand what it means. Memorial Day, or bereaved families, is a concept that sits in the back of the mind; we do not really think about it and do not understand so much what it means, and, like everything in life, suddenly when you feel it in your own flesh then you understand the meaning. Then because I knew I was going to continue in the military, and because now I know that I'm going to continue in the military, I think about the fact that I know one story out of tens of thousands of stories and it shocked me. Both because I knew the guy whose life had been cut short, and also because I realized that there was a whole group of people here that this is the way they are feeling, and that it was not some kind of slogan. This thing is real.

Eva: You could have been so shocked by the death of someone you know that you say to yourself, I do not want this to happen to me, then walk away and try not to be a part of this thing. But that's not what happened. On the contrary. It actually produced commitment in you. It increased your commitment. Am I wrong?

Eliya: It totally increased my commitment, to the state, to the army, to the soldiers.

Eliya is a young settler, committed to a settler's ideology, but her patriotism is indistinguishable from the ordinary nationalism which the left implemented for so many decades in Israel. Eliya repeats here the key elements of Jewish love of the people and Israeli nationalism which was militantly promoted and implemented by the left: Jews were persecuted and dreamed of a land of their own – an idea, I must add, which is as legitimate as other forms of nationalism. But she goes on to state that the nation is an extension of the family; it connects and unites people. She invokes ancestral and sacred religious motifs (such as the Wailing Wall) as much as the self-sacrificial death of soldiers. This patriotism is based not only on the emancipation of the Jews from a history in which they were the objects of other people's whims but also on the love of the land and a binding commitment which entails self-sacrifice of the young. Note that she speaks of Israel as a "dream," much like the American Dream: the nation is an imagined project; it fulfills an ideal of emancipation and sovereignty for destitute Jews. It constitutes a community of meaning as well as a community of brotherhood. But it is also a religious project of reenactment of biblical history. As the conservative thinker Yoram Hazony has argued,[22] a nation is first and foremost a community built on loyalty. This is why, for him and other conservative thinkers, the nation assumes the character of the family and acts as an extended family, thus creating bonds of loyalty. It should be stressed, however, that historically (and perhaps ironically) it was the socialist left who built successfully this form of nationalism, based on religious symbolism and reference to the ethnic identity of the Jews.

*

Even though early Zionism relied heavily on religious symbols and was forcefully patriotic, it was also secular at least in the sense that it attempted to create a common culture based on *secularized religious symbols*. The populist ideology of Netanyahu continued this nationalism but profoundly changed its content, making it lean more literally on religious symbols, laws, and principles (and not on a secularized version of them), thus smoothly incorporating the biblical land of Israel with the modern Israeli state. It radicalized the definition of Jewishness and pitched it against its imaginary detractors who became at once not Jewish enough and unpatriotic.

As we have seen in chapter 2, Meir Kahane was a pioneer of this kind of populist politics and the type of nationalism which came to characterize the right embodied by the Likud.[23] Meir Kahane helped achieve this new nationalism in breaking key taboos, such as promoting the legal segregation of Arab Israeli citizens. Netanyahu operated in a similar fashion and broke a taboo of his own in July 1995, when he led a mock funeral procession featuring a coffin and hangman's noose at an anti-Rabin rally, where protesters chanted, "Death to Rabin," under the pretext that the Oslo negotiations endangered the state. Although Carmi Gilon, the then head of Israel's domestic intelligence service Shabak, alerted Netanyahu to a plot on Rabin's life, Netanyahu refused to moderate or tone down his rhetoric. This would be only the beginning of a long series of incitements which would ultimately successfully undermine the idea that the left could be patriotic and create a profound divide within Israeli society.

In 1997, a mere two years after the fateful slaying of the center-left prime minister, Netanyahu famously whispered in the ears of Rabbi Kaduri (a kabbalist rabbi and the spiritual eminence behind the Shas party): "The left have forgotten what it means to be Jews, they think our security will be put in the hands of Arabs, the Arabs will take care of us – they are given a part of the land and they will take care of us."[24] Netanyahu invoked survivalist fear to make his accusation against the allegedly un-Jewish founders of the state, claiming he was the only true caretaker of the nation.

Once nationalism leans on religion, it is easier to create exclusionary categories in designating groups of people who are presumably unaligned with the nation. In that sense, populist nationalism differed from left-wing nationalism, which was far more preoccupied with the real enemies outside of Israel's borders and which denied the profound class and ethnic conflicts at work in society. The religious nationalism promoted by Israeli populists nowadays is far more reminiscent of white Christian nationalism in the USA. White Christian nationalism "is a cultural framework ... that idealizes and advocates a fusion of Christianity with American civic life. But the 'Christianity' of Christian nationalism is of a particular sort ... it includes assumptions of nativism, white supremacy, patriarchy, and heteronormativity, along with divine sanction for authoritarian control and militarism. It is as ethnic and political as it is religious."[25] (A recent Pew survey found that 45 percent of Americans believe that the USA should be a Christian nation, with 31 percent of those believing that the federal government should stop enforcing the separation of church and state.)[26]

In the same manner, Israeli exclusionary nationalism views as unpatriotic anyone who doesn't adhere to its strict ideals and stipulations. This is why Netanyahu had no compunction vilifying the left as anti-nationalist, making it an inner enemy even though it was the same left which had sacrificed so many of its sons (and sometimes daughters) for the establishment of the country, had fought the British in the pre-nation community (Yishuv), built the key institutions of the state, won the war of independence, and created an entire country. Netanyahu's career was launched through a lie: he borrowed the bullying tactic and rhetoric of the radical wing of the American Republican Party and turned the left, who had built all the state institutions of Israel, into an unpatriotic inner enemy.[27] Indeed, as Jan Werner Müller put it, the characteristic of populism is not that it claims to represent the people, but that it claims to be the *only one* entrusted with the legitimacy of representing the people.[28] The strategy of the Big Lie succeeded, and Netanyahu lastingly undermined the deep connection between the Israeli left and nationalism and could offer a nationalism that was a source of pride and which connected it back to Judaism. Netanyahu associated the left with Arabs and *de facto* eliminated the tension that had existed between Jewishness and Israeliness by putting Jewish identity at the center of the polity, much as other populist leaders throughout the world have done: the Jews were on his side; the anti-patriotic Arab lovers were on the other side. A political issue was transformed into one of authentic identity. His own supporters were the true "Israelis." A single Facebook post published by Netanyahu exemplifies this perfectly: on 16 September 2019, one day before the elections for the 22nd Knesset, Netanyahu (known to lead an entirely secular lifestyle) posted a picture of himself at the Western Wall wearing a yarmulke and wrote: "Praying at the Western Wall for the success of the people of Israel."[29] The content of this post may seem innocuous, but its timing, one day before elections, leads to a more subtle interpretation: clearly, just before the elections, any Israeli political leader would be praying for the success of their own party and their supporters. Thus, when Netanyahu writes that he's praying for the success of the people of Israel, he's actually insinuating that the true people of Israel are his supporters, while other Israeli citizens are not part of the nation. This post also emphasizes the Jewish-religious identity of the "people of Israel" by featuring the Western Wall, the yarmulke, and Netanyahu's prayer.

Netanyahu also made it clear that the anti-patriotic Arab lovers were on the other side, separate from the true people of Israel. On February 24, 2020, Netanyahu tweeted:

"Shameful and disgraceful. While IDF soldiers and security forces maintain Israel's security, Gantz's [one of Netanyahu's opponents] partner in the Knesset condemns it. Gantz has no government without Ayman Odeh and Ahmad Tibi [two Arab lawmakers] and such a government would endanger the security of the state of Israel. Only a vote for the Likud will stop this disaster."[30] This tweet was a response to a quote by Ayman Odeh [the Arab leader of the Joint List party] on Channel 12: "We won't assist the existence of a government that attacks Gaza,"[31] and alone it captures the entire rhetorical strategy of Netanyahu: cast Israeli Arabs as enemies and any left-wing or center party that might collaborate with them as contaminated by the pollution and danger represented by the inner enemy (following the logic of contamination discussed in chapter 2).

Indeed, one of the most distinctive changes of Israel in the last few decades is the new prominence of Judaism and Jewishness in the public sphere as well as in culture, with Netanyahu (and other secular right-wing figures) leading this process. Israeli politicians have been going out of their way to prove their affiliation with religious ideas, regardless of their actual belief in Judaic principles, demonstrating the new-found importance of religious ideals to the Israeli polity. For example, Miri Regev, a former minister from the Likud party, has been known to brag about her pilgrimage to the tomb of Shimon Bar Yochai in Meron,[32] but she herself is not religious. Similarly, Ayelet Shaked, a secular minister from the Yamina (literally: "Rightward") party, most recently minister of the interior in the Bennett–Lapid cabinet, uploaded a picture of herself lighting candles on the evening of Sabbath, in accordance with Jewish law and customs.[33]

Since the 1990s, Netanyahu has successfully associated the secular left with anti-patriotism and thus has entirely redrawn the contours of national identity, passing in 2018 the infamous nation-state law which asserted the ethnic primacy of Jews in Israel. This technique has been used by numerous populist and authoritarian leaders, most conspicuously Jarosław Kaczyński, Orbán, and Modi, all three of whom have appealed to primordial and identitarian views of the nation.[34] This law asserted the authentic identity of Israel, grounded it in ethnicity and religion, and cast those who appealed to a civic definition of citizenship as traitors.

Gabriel, the rabbi living in a West Bank settlement, explains why Jewishness is so important to nationalism.

> *Eva*: Is the concept of love for Israel a concept you grew up with or one you acquired later? What is the importance of this concept in your education, and what is its importance today in your Judaism, in your political perception? Because I have a feeling that this concept connects both some of the religious commandments [mitzvos], and also the love of the state. That it's a kind of glue between things.
>
> *Gabriel*: You could say I grew up with it. I do not know if it's as much a matter of loving everyone as of helping anyone who needs help. I grew up with it more on the practical side, of opening my eyes, seeing a person in distress and helping him, no matter who he is. I think that's the basis. Also in the Torah it's stated: If you see the donkey of your hater collapsing under his load, you have a mitzvah to help him. What is the meaning of "your hater"? Someone who has done you an injustice, not necessarily a leftist who does an injustice to all the people of Israel, but someone who has done something to you privately, you have a mitzvah to help him when he is in distress. I think that's where the base is.

National Pride as Loyalty

When war comes, then we suddenly unite. So I would say it's a lot easier in an emergency. And in peace, all the swords of contention are sharpened and then it's harder. But personally today, when I look at what is happening, it is indeed not very simple... I have not experienced, I have not been in the deportation [the evacuation of Jewish settlements in Gaza in 2005], I have not been there or in Amona [a small illegal settlement that was evacuated and torn down several times]. But my friends got beaten up in Amona by cops. They felt like someone came to murder them. People saw it as hating them. So there are a lot of breaking points. But we need to find a way to transcend that.

Eva: Is there a priority to help a Jew over a non-Jew? I want to know what you think about those who think you should love everyone, and not just those from your group.

Gabriel: For me it is clear that, even among Jews, say within a mitzvah of charity, there is a mitzvah to help the people of your city first. This concerns another point that is more general: there is a certain desire of Jews to be like all the Gentiles. This may be the root of the controversy between us. I do not think I should be like all the Gentiles. In some ways they also say that we should not be like all the Gentiles, because they say that our morals should be higher and more special. Our morality is already higher. From the left side, they say, I want to be like all the Gentiles, but I still need to be better. So I say I should be better and expect myself to be better, but on the other hand I also think I should not be like everyone else. I have to take care of my people, and within that there is no reason not to take care of others, but if it's my blood and the blood of my brothers, or their blood then I'm sorry...

Eva: This is very interesting. So in your eyes the leftists do not care enough for their people? I think this is said in many countries about the left. It is a recurring complaint.

Gabriel: Makes sense. I think it's twisted. That you say I will be like everyone else and demand more of yourself, and then you are not like everyone else. You need to decide. If you demand more of yourself, you should also give yourself better treatment. But if you say "I am like all the Gentiles," then someone who says we are unlike all the Gentiles, then maybe for you he is not part of your people. Then there is no need for nationalism at all, because the whole world is one. So, you say, they [your people] should not be the people I support. But it is a fact that this is not happening, because they [the left] don't take care of Arab LGBT people. They should have been in "their people" and they should have cared for them more than they care about an Arab, who is against LGBT people.

Gabriel's response follows the logic of nationalism, which is to view fellow nationals as kin; you owe them more than you owe people outside the nation because they are members of your family. This in turn enables an ethic of mutual help and brotherliness which in turn reinforces identity, filiation, and membership. In other words, nationalism articulates here a hyper or double identity, one that is bound to a territory and the second that is defined by religion and history. The rabbi uses themes evoked in other countries whose democratic institutions have also been deeply transformed by populist leaders. In an article they published in the *Journal of Democracy*, the political scientists Ivan Krastev and Stephen Holmes[35] explain the turn to the extreme right of such nations as Hungary through a refusal to imitate Western nations. Eastern countries for the last thirty years have given many different names to imitation (liberalization, democratization, integration), but for them it remained an imitation. According to this rabbi, it is the same sin of which the Israeli left is guilty: it wants to imitate the rest of the world; it wants to give up the genuine and authentic identity of the Jews – a view that, according to Krastev and Holmes in their book *The Light That Failed*, has been at the center of the making of illiberalism in Eastern Europe.[36] Such imitation, they claim, creates frustration and a permanent feeling of inferiority in the imitator as they claim an authentic, primordial sense of collective identity. Not only does imitation entail a profound sense of moral inferiority, it also implicitly delegates to the object of imitation the right to evaluate the imitator. Gabriel's claims are reminiscent of the accusations of Kaczyński (the leader of the Polish Law and Justice party) that liberalism is "against the very notion of the nation,"[37] and of the claim by Mária Schmidt (a Hungarian historian who supports and advises Orbán) that "we are Hungarians, and we want to preserve our culture."[38] In that sense, we may say that nationalism – certainly of the populist kind – is deeply intertwined with assertive pride, an attempt to restore a wounded pride, to correct the perception of an inferior position, and to reaffirm the authenticity of one's culture. The sin of the Israeli left becomes clearer: the left displays a deficit in national (self-) pride. It is not only critical of its country according to standards of morality applied in other countries, it is also guilty of wanting to imitate Western democratic institutions and thus to discredit Israel by using international standards of justice. The left are the ones who want to follow international moral and legal norms – a cultural process increasingly contested by those who emphasize a proud Jewish identity. Thus, the political rival becomes an enemy, which, as Levitsky and Ziblatt argue, is the mark of declining democracies.[39] More: designating inner enemies becomes a substitute for politics.

*

What enabled this stupefying stigmatization of the very same groups that had been intimately involved with Israeli nationalism was a key feature: the fact that nationalism was injected with a healthy dose of Jewishness – that is, religiosity which delegitimized the secularity of the elites and of the state institutions.

The coalition of the Shas party with Likud played a significant role in changing the orientation of the Likud and making it promote Jewish-religious values. Netanyahu simultaneously and alternatively allied himself with the ultra-orthodox Mizrahi Shas party and with the national religious parties which have become increasingly dominant in Israeli life. Both parties and constituencies hold congruent views on nationalism as the expression of Jewish identity. Shas pushed forward simultaneously agendas of social welfare and distributive justice (aligning itself with the lower classes) and a proud form of religious and ethnic Jewish identity.[40] The Israeli political scientist Yoav Peled identified this duality in Shas's ideology as early as 1998, stating that "Shas seeks to replace secular Zionism with religious Judaism as the hegemonic ideology in Israeli society, and presents this as the remedy for both the socio-economic and the cultural grievances of its constituency."[41] It seems that the efforts of Shas have indeed come to fruition with regard to right-wing supporters, as the Israeli right today is very much aligned with religious values and practices. Thus, Likud voters are more likely than other Jewish Israelis to have the religious blessing of wine (Kidush) on Fridays (82 percent of Likud voters vs. 62 percent of Jewish Israelis in general) and to eat kosher food (68 percent vs. 57 percent).[42] Among orthodox (but not Haredi ultra-orthodox) kippa-wearing people, those who define themselves as more religious are more likely to be right-wing supporters; 36 percent of liberal religious people, 62 percent of "regular" religious people, and 71 percent of very religious people identify as right wing.[43] Clearly, then, being secular or religious helps predict how right wing and nationalist one is likely to be. Perhaps unsurprisingly, religiosity helps predict how willingly one will adopt the official national narrative and how accommodating one will be towards the infringement of human rights.

Both Shas and the Likud, as well as other parties claiming to represent the national religious constituency of the settlers (such as HaIchud HaLeumi-Tkuma and Otzma Yehudit), contributed to putting identity – ethnic, religious, and nationalist – at the center of Israeli nationalism with two effects: under the banner of a politics of identity, they further fragmented the polity and created deep divisions between social groups, between Mizrahim and Ashkenazim, between secular and religious, and between patriotic and anti-patriotic, and redefined Israeliness as religious Jewishness.[44] In addition they contributed to further sacralize nationalism, not only by referring to those who died for the country but also by enhancing the ritual symbols of Judaism.

This ideological context helped religious nationalism become a major player in Israeli politics and society, while until the 1990s it had been considered a fringe movement. Religious nationalism (advocated by religious nationalist parties as well as by an orthodox party such as Shas), argues Roger Friedland, contains four elements.[45] First, religious nationalism views the territory as a sacred space; the land becomes a main actor in the unfolding of a divine history still in the making. Second, religious nationalists direct the bulk of their attention to the bodies of women – covering, separating, and regulating their erotic flesh. Third, religious nationalists accord considerable symbolic importance to foreignness – that is, on excluding foreigners. And the fourth element is that religious nationalists, much like other non-nationalist religious people, submit to God and, in submitting to God, intermix the love of God and the love of the nation. They shroud the land and the nation in the same metaphysical grandeur and fiercely guarded sacredness as God. They bring nationalism to another level. Religious nationalism is an appropriation of the land, the people, and the history through frameworks which lend them cosmic meaning and purpose. While *de facto* fragmenting society, the invocation of a single Jewish people is the seeming solution to it. Ironically, once division is sown, nationalism – and especially of the religious kind – can be reclaimed as a way of healing the fractures it itself has sown through its hyper-identitarian logic. It helps posit Jewishness as the unifying element of collective life. Eliya, the young woman we met earlier, exemplifies this view:

> I think we all see that lately, instead of remembering that we are one people, we . . . I just do not know how to explain it. There is a civil war, people are attacking each other, not having a discussion at all, not having a conversation. . . . We are completely divided, we are only deepening the rift between ourselves. For me personally to see this, it's a shame. Seventy years ago, there were people here who came from all over the world to establish a state and live together. And they knew how to put the disputes aside for a second and unite for a greater purpose. And right now I do not see this. I'm a bit sorry, because in the end we all live here, and no one will leave any time soon, so it's time for . . . Okay there are always arguments, let's say the state of Israel is like one big family, so there are quarrels in the family, but we should be able to put things aside. Let's look each other in the eyes, let's talk to each other. These are things I do not feel are happening anymore.

Eliya is unknowingly commenting on the very situation that has been carefully created and caused by the leader of the party she supports. Once national disunity is sown and incessantly cultivated, Judaism and nationalism become the solutions to overcome the social malaise generated by deep social conflict resulting from the fact of casting social groups as enemies. In other words, populist leaders are able to do many things at once: divide, incite, and create fictional enemies presumed to undermine the nation; and also they can offer to repair the very collective entity they helped break by resorting to their brand of exclusive nationalism. So with Eliya we have an example of the ways in which this religiously shaped nationalism aims to recenter an authentic Israeli identity around land and Jewishness.

Tu BiShvat is a Jewish holiday. It is celebrated on the fifteenth day of the month of Shevat (in the winter season) and marks the beginning of the agricultural cycle for the purpose of biblical tithes. It is little known in diasporic communities but celebrated with much fanfare in Israel. It enchants children, who get to plant a tree, officials, who remind Israelis that the land is theirs, and fruit sellers, who offer dazzling assortments of dried fruits ritually eaten on that day.

Yossi Dagan, head of Samaria Regional Council since 2015 [located in the West Bank], planted, as is customary, a tree during *Tu BiShvat* in 2021 and for the occasion wrote the following post in his Facebook page:

> We have been privileged to live in a generation where we can be significant partners in building the country for future generations.
>
> To see the vineyards, of which the prophet Jeremiah prophesied, flourish and win international medals.
>
> The Land of Israel gives love back to its sons, despite the obstacles and barriers – settlement is being built on its own and Samaria agriculture is flourishing more than ever.
>
> Samarian products are marketed worldwide (including to the United Arab Emirates) and demand is only rising . . .
>
> We are privileged . . . I planted with great excitement with her [Rina's] father, Rabbi Eitan Shnerb from Lod, an orange tree in the land of Samaria.
>
> The chairman of the Yishuv committee, Moti Feldman, told me with excitement that exactly today – on Tu BiShvat 25 years ago – the grove of trees that is right next to us was planted. Those were the difficult days of the Oslo Accords and the fear was that the settlement would be uprooted. 25 years have passed, the settlement has not only not been displaced – but has tripled itself: 3 times as many residents (!)

And we are growing and expanding, and here near this grove we planted another grove today, new fruit trees in northern Samaria – in the heart of the state of Israel. Happy holiday to the Land of Israel.[46]

Rina Shnerb, a seventeen-year-old adolescent, had been killed in August 2019 in a terror attack in the West Bank, and it is to her Yossi Dagan pays tribute in his post. But he also uses the opportunity to pay tribute to the successful commercial enterprise of the West Bank settlements, and, in doing so, he more importantly pays tribute to the biblical land of Samaria itself, which indeed has "expanded," as Dagan euphemistically put it. The head of Samaria Regional Council, which oversees thirty-five settlements spread across 2,800 square kilometers with 25,000 people, invokes two key emotional motifs of the Israeli collective psyche: the grief for a victim of the Israeli–Palestinian conflict and the love for the land of Israel, replete with history and sacredness as well as with commercial success (tapping into the capitalist ethos that has been part of the legitimation of Netanyahu's power). Such love is an emotion which human beings bestow on the land and which, by the alchemy of metaphors, the land knows to give back. The land has a quasi-agentic power and forms a bond of mutuality with the people who live on it. The expansion of West Bank settlements, the increased volume of its agriculture, and flourishing exports are all expressions of the love which the land gives back to its people. In this very short post, Dagan encapsulates the double emotional power of religious nationalism which dominates Israel: people die for the land, and their death consecrates the sacredness of the biblical land presented here in economic terms as a land which expands by natural economic growth. The land rewards grief and death through flourishing enterprises: the land binds citizens to their history and true identity as well as to their economic success.

*

Netanyahu's nationalist populism, however, driven by ideology and manipulation, was made possible by key social and cultural transformations.

Nationalism started articulating a class and ethnic divide, making religion and identitarian nationalism into class markers. Such identitarian nationalism became the prerogative of the less educated middle and lower-middle class.[47] Sociological factors contributed to this change.

One was the fact that, after the 1980s, with the development of a global economy, elites started subscribing to a cosmopolitan outlook, getting jobs which demanded frequent travel, becoming involved in the global networks of the economy, speaking English, pursuing education in higher numbers both inside and outside Israel, and holding Israel increasingly accountable to international legal norms.[48]

Israeli cosmopolitan elites were also developing international professional networks; as a result perhaps they were increasingly deliberately cast by Netanyahu as un-Jewish and unpatriotic. Cultural and financial elites, busy with globalization, have benefited even more than before from the extension of higher education. In parallel to this process, the Mizrahi working classes, who made social and economic gains but remained far behind their Ashkenazi counterparts,[49] identified more closely with religious nationalism.[50] Shas and the Likud itself transformed nationalism from being an all-inclusive framework into being a part of the political and moral habitus of the lower-middle class. In other words, nationalism has come to be a class marker, as it has become the identity of those who stand diametrically opposed to what is often dubbed as the "cosmopolitan class," defined not only as a class which has international opportunities for work and the group most likely to live abroad but also the class most likely to want to adopt a core set of moral values derived from the constitutions of Western democracies. This class divide translates into deeply antagonistic moral views.

Indeed, a consistent finding in research on xenophobia and nationalism is that negative attitudes towards outside groups are inversely correlated with educational attainment: more highly educated people tend to report significantly less xenophobic and nationalist sentiments. This relationship has been established in empirical research across time as well as in different countries.[51] Although most studies focus solely on attitudes towards ethnic outgroups, there is also empirical evidence that people with higher education are less prone to in-group favoritism than are people with lower education.[52]

For the Ashkenazi elites who built the country, nation and nationalism were a way to claim dignity in the face of the pan-European state of subjection in which they lived and to have access to the material resources which the state afforded them. Nationalism also helped them shape institutions in a way that reflected their ideology and interests. More: the Ashkenazi elites were probably far more nationalist than their working-class Mizrahi counterparts, because the latter were much further from the core and center of the state. For example, Mizrahi Jews were severely under-represented in public-sector jobs as compared to their Ashkenazi counterparts, and especially in high-status public-sector jobs that hold influence over state affairs.[53]

But once these same elites become invested in global economic activity and in the global circulation of knowledge, they become less identified with the nation, both subjectively and objectively. It is the working classes who, becoming "stationary" – that is, they have nowhere to go to and have no regular contact with foreign countries – appropriate nationalism as a source of social affiliation and identity.

In a wide-scale comparative analysis of twenty-two countries, the economist Moses Shayo has found that working-class people are more likely to identify with the nation, such that there is a negative correlation between income and national identification. Even more remarkable is that, in highly industrialized economies, such lower-class people are less likely to support redistributive policies than are their fellow affluent citizens.[54] These groups resort to nationalism as a way of asserting pride and lost privilege while renouncing policies that could promote their economic interests. Inasmuch as nationalism provides a sense of brotherhood and equality, it seems to overcome the affronts to dignity often entailed by inequalities. It gives a group a social uplift because nationalism is supposed to be a community of equals. As the scholar of nationalism Liah Greenfeld argues, it thus affords a psychological gratification because national identity affirms "the experience of dignity within wide and ever widening sectors of humanity."[55] This is a very important insight. Nationalism affords a sense of fraternity, dignity, and worth. I would argue that this is because, through nationalism, as Anthony Smith argues, members of particular groups "feel alike in just those respects in which they differ from non-members outside the group."[56] This "alikeness" provides them with a feeling of worth. Moreover, nationalism – or patriotism, which is the emotional expression of nationalism – provides deep feelings of belonging, precisely that which socially and economically marginalized groups may feel less of. Nationalism provides membership and affiliation, and in that sense is a powerful anchor of identity. Finally, the love of country is often translated into an ethic of brotherly and mutual help to those identified with the national community. Nationalists subsequently become identified with the defenders of the people; they become entrusted with the mission of safeguarding frontiers and memory. Nationalism then drives a wedge between social groups and rearticulates class divisions based on educational attainment.

The rabbi who appeared earlier and who expresses a commonly held view about the left and the peace process:

Eva: Why are leftists bringing the country to doom?
Gabriel: For example, the people who were the architects of

Oslo [the peace process initiated in 1993], for many Jews, for example a family of victims of terrorism, who were murdered by Palestinian policemen who received weapons from us, I can understand why they hate people who say they do not regret what they did [in the Oslo Accords]. For them [the leftists] it is a just act. I do not know if I was in this situation that I would hate them.

Leftists betray the vocation of the land itself which it is incumbent on us to love and protect.

Thus nationalism becomes a venue for the expression of populism because, as Cas Mudde puts it, populism is "a thin-centred ideology that considers society to be ultimately separated into two homogeneous and antagonistic groups, 'the pure people' versus 'the corrupt elite.'"[57] Therefore, it can use nationalism both as a "thick" ideology with which to supplement populism and as the reasoning behind the difference between "the people" and "the elite." The less educated lower-middle class becomes the nation's protector against the well-educated cosmopolitan elite. Such an antagonistic view intensifies commitment to and love of the nation, but only at the price of demonizing those perceived as collaborating with those outside it. The history of Zionism thus offers an ultimate irony and powerful example of the spectacular inversion populists are able to operate: while the socialist leaders who established the country were adamantly and sometimes ferociously nationalist, they have been recast as enemies of the nation, precisely at the same time that society became rife with class and ethnic divides, with nationalism now redrawing class and ethnic relations, mixing class struggles with a far more dangerous and ominous threat of betrayal.

But this is not the end of this story. It has another powerful and ironic twist.

When Netanyahu chose to support Trump before and after the elections, some people could be legitimately astonished yet still give him the benefit of the doubt. Admittedly, Trump was surrounded by people such as Steve Bannon, the head of Breitbart news, who reeked of racism and antisemitism,[58] but no one was sure of the direction that the new presidency would take. Even if Trump refused to condemn his antisemitic electoral base or the Ku Klux Klan who had enthusiastically backed him, and even if it took him a long time to dissociate himself from the KKK "Grand Wizard" David Duke,[59] we were not yet certain of the presence of antisemitism in Trump's discourse and strategies (especially since his daughter Ivanka had converted to Judaism). But the events in Charlottesville in August 2017 no longer allowed any doubt. The neo-Nazi demonstrators committed violent acts against peaceful counter-protestors, killing one woman by ploughing through a crowd with a car (an act reminiscent through its technique of terrorist attacks in Europe). Not wanting to alienate his base, Trump reacted to the events by condemning both the neo-Nazis and Klansmen and their liberal opponents.[60] Both had presumably been guilty in the same way and to the same extent. The world was shocked by Trump's conflation of the two groups, but Netanyahu did not object.[61] Once again, the indulgent (or cynical) observer could have interpreted this silence as a reluctant agreement of a vassal towards his overlord (of all the countries in the world, Israel is the one which receives the most military aid from the United States).[62] One was entitled to think that Israel had no choice but to collaborate, despite the outward signs of antisemitism in the American leader.

This interpretation, however, is not plausible because, before and since Charlottesville, Netanyahu has courted other leaders who are either unbothered by antisemitism or straightforwardly sympathetic to it and upon whom he is not economically dependent. His concessions go as far as participating in a partial form of Holocaust denial.

Take the case of Hungary. Under Orbán's government, the country showed troubling signs of the legitimization of antisemitism.[63] For instance, in 2015 the Hungarian government announced its intention to erect a statue in honor and in memory of Bálint Hóman,[64] a minister who played a decisive role in deporting 600,000 Hungarian Jews. Far from being an isolated incident, only a few months later, in 2016, another statue was erected in tribute to György Donáth,[65] one of the architects of anti-Jewish legislation during World War II. It was thus unsurprising to hear Orbán use antisemitic tropes during his reelection campaign in 2018, especially against George Soros, the Jewish Hungarian millionaire who supports liberal causes and acts in favor of open borders and immigration.[66] Reanimating the antisemitic cliché about the power of Jews, Orbán accused Soros of harboring intentions to undermine Hungary.

Whom did Netanyahu choose to support? Not the anxious Hungarian Jewish community who protested bitterly against the antisemitic actions of Orbán's government, nor the liberal Jew Soros who defends humanitarian causes. Instead, he created new fault lines, preferring right-wing political allies to members of the tribe. He backed Orbán, the same who resurrects the memory of dark antisemites.[67] To my knowledge, the Israeli prime minister's cabinet never officially protested against Orbán's antisemitic inclinations and affinities. The opposite is true: not long before the Hungarian elections in 2018, Netanyahu went to the trouble of traveling to Hungary, thus exonerating Orbán of the opprobrium attached to the antisemitism of the Shoah.[68] When Netanyahu visited Budapest he was received in a glacial way by the Federation of the Jewish Communities,[69] while Orbán gave him a warm welcome. To further reinforce the touching friendship, Netanyahu invited Orbán on an official visit to Israel in July 2018.[70] During this trip, Orbán was offered a reception fit for the most devoted of Jewish allies.

The relationship with Poland is just as engrossing. As a reminder, Poland is governed by the nationalist party Law and

Justice (PiS), which has an uncompromising policy against African or Muslim refugees and has undermined judicial power through a series of reforms that allow the government to control the judiciary.[71] In 2016 the Law and Justice government eliminated the governmental body whose mission was to deal with problems of racial discrimination, xenophobia, and intolerance, arguing that their job had become "useless."[72] Encouraged by governmental declarations and policies, signs of nationalism multiplied within Polish society. In February 2018, President Andrzej Duda declared that he would sign a law making it illegal to accuse the Polish nation of having collaborated with the Nazis.[73] The law was later changed as a result of international pressure, but instead an older law which forbids any public insult to the nation or the republic of Poland is being used to persecute people who accuse the country of collusion in the Holocaust and other Nazi atrocities.[74] While Israel protested against these developments, in June 2018, Benjamin Netanyahu and the prime minister of Poland, Mateusz Morawiecki, signed an agreement exonerating the Polish state and the Polish nation from any and all crimes against the Jews and condemning the phrase "Polish concentration camp" as patently erroneous and a trivialization of German responsibility. In this same agreement, antisemitism was juxtaposed with anti-Polonism, and it was declared that only a handful of sad individuals were responsible for the darkest hours of Poland.[75] In July 2018, this declaration was roundly condemned by the Yad Vashem International Institute for Holocaust Research, as well as by a group of seventeen historians, members of the Academy of Sciences.[76] But the stupefying result remained. Netanyahu, the head of the Israeli government, gave his support to what amounts to a version of Holocaust denial. Netanyahu the history buff could not have ignored that, in the words of the Polish commentator Sławomir Sierakowski, "two-thirds of the 250,000 Jews who escaped during the Nazis' 'liquidation' of Jewish ghettos in

1942 had been killed by 1945, most of them by Poles or with Polish participation."[77] This constitutes a decisive turning point for Zionism, which places Netanyahu in an avant-garde of sorts:[78] inside Israel, he shifted Zionism to its Jewish core, rejected Israeli identity, and linked Israeliness to Jewishness, yet, at the same time, he provided symbolic support to antisemitic leaders. Strikingly, the return to Judaism goes hand in hand with an alliance with antisemitic leaders and with the trampling of the conservative and reform Jewish leaders,[79] thereby cutting off Israel from a significant part of world Jewry.

Netanyahu thus put the sensibility and interests of Jewish communities on the back burner. Israel and its Netanyahu government even desacralized the memory of the Shoah and made deals with overt or covert antisemites. This is fascinating and begs the question, why is that the case?

At the same time that Netanyahu promoted an aggressive form of religious nationalism at home, he defended a new vision of Zionism which is parting company with the values of most Jewish communities around the world, privileging the strategies and geopolitics of Israel itself. Netanyahu has a deep political affinity with populist-authoritarian leaders such as Trump, Orbán, Morawiecki, and Putin and little interest in the mostly liberal American Jewish community. Thus, the intensification of Jewishness inside Israel went hand in hand with an increasing disentanglement of Israel from the interests and the views of Jewish communities. This pattern, interestingly enough, continues. In August 2022, a memorandum by the Israeli embassy in Tirana, Albania, which also serves Bosnia and Herzegovina, was leaked to the media. The memorandum expressed support for an electoral reform proposal favored by the far-right Bosnian Croat political party, which aimed to create over-representation of Bosnian Croat voters at the expense of minorities.[80] The memorandum was sharply criticized by Jacob Finci, the head of the Bosnian Jewish community, because the electoral strategies of the extreme right-wing party, he claimed, would diminish Jewish political influence.[81] Israeli populism may feed on strident nationalism at home, yet ironically it ends up allying itself with antisemites and undermining Jewish communities around the world.

To take a final and glaring example: one of the great admirers of Victor Orbán is none other than Yishai Fleisher, the spokesperson for the Jewish community of Hebron, which is a hardline bastion of religious nationalism. In 2022 Fleisher tweeted a selfie with the Hungarian prime minister and referred to Orbán as "a modern hero of nationalism . . . and [an] ally of Israel."[82] Now, what did Orbán say which enraptured Fleisher so deeply? As he inaugurated the conference, Orbán claimed that Hungarians didn't want to become a people of mixed race,[83] a phrase that almost smacks of Nazi racial ideology. Faced with criticism, Fleisher retorted with arguments perfectly aligned with Netanyahu's policy: "I am not looking at Hungary as a Hungarian Jew or a Diaspora Jew, I'm looking at it as an Israeli Jew – a fellow sovereign. And, from this nationalist perspective, nation-states must unite against the globalist agenda which seeks to open borders & erase national identities."[84] Fleisher sums up my point admirably. It illustrates the uneasy alliance between Israel and a global far right that endorses its antisemitism and pro-Zionism simultaneously. The researcher Jelena Subotić argues that this is a profound and novel feature of far-right antisemitism, a transformation that the Israeli far right itself helps to legitimize.[85] State rationality, undergirded by identitarian nationalism, thus takes precedence over the struggle against antisemitism and shows how far and how deep the alliance between various populist movements has gone.

The reason is obvious. Populist leaders share a nativist vision of the nation,[86] which is to say that they strongly oppose the ethnic, religious, or racial dilution of their country by immigrants or universalist rights. Israel in fact has long pioneered the model to which these nations aspire: predicating citizenship on ethnic and religious affiliation (law of return), rendering difficult or impossible the marriage of Jews with people of different religions, opposing immigration and ethnic intermixing, yet wanting to conserve the title of democracy (in the international community, the name comes attached with privileges): like Poland or Hungary, Israel has claimed for decades that it is both democratic *and* Jewish. Ann Coulter, a well-known alt-right American pundit, and Richard Spencer, president of the National Policy Institute, a supremacist think tank, often cite Israel as a model state of ethnic supremacy to which they aspire[87] (in fact Israel is a long way from "ethnic purity," since Arabs make up roughly 20 percent of its population, a fact that the American alt-right conveniently ignores). Israel, the nation-state of the Jewish people (privileging Jewish citizens over non-Jewish ones) is a more explicit version of the ethnic model of democracy.

More generally, these countries today share a deep common political core: fear of foreigners who can be considered "other" at the borders (it must be specified, however, that Israelis' fears are less imaginary than those of Hungarians or Poles); references to the nation's pride untainted by a dubious past; casting critics as traitors to the nation; outlawing human rights organizations; and contesting an international order based on liberal principles. The Netanyahu–Trump–Putin triumvirate had a definite vision and a strategy: to create a political bloc that would undermine the current liberal international order and its key players (the fact that Trump has been voted out of office does not mean that this vision is now obsolete).

In an article about Trump in *Project Syndicate*, legal scholar Mark S. Weiner suggests that Trump's political vision and practice follows (unknowingly) the precepts of Carl Schmitt, the Nazi legal scholar who joined the party in 1933:

In place of normativity and universalism, Schmitt offers a theory of political identity based on a principle that Trump doubtless appreciates deeply from his pre-political career: land (which, for Trump means real estate).

For Schmitt, a political community forms when a group of people recognizes that they share some distinctive cultural trait that they believe is worth defending with their lives. This cultural basis of sovereignty is ultimately rooted in the distinctive geography – say, land-locked and oriented internally, or coastal and outward-looking – that a people inhabit.

At stake here are opposing positions about the relation between national identity and law. According to Schmitt, the community's 'nomos,' or sense of itself that grows from its geography, is the philosophical precondition for its law. For liberals, by contrast, the nation is defined first and foremost by its legal commitments, [and not by its geography]."[88]

Netanyahu and his ilk subscribe to this Schmittian vision of the political, making legal commitments subordinate to geography and ethnicity and transforming the very meaning of the role of Judaism inside Israeli nationalism. The country's Jewishness has been radicalized with the highly controversial Nationality Law passed in 2018. Playing buddy with antisemitic leaders may seem a contradiction with the nationality law. However, they are motivated by the same statist logic where the state no longer views itself as committed to represent the people as a whole but, rather, aims to expand territory, increase its power by designating enemies, define who belongs and who doesn't, narrow the definition of citizenship, harden the boundaries of the body collective, and undermine the international liberal order. The line connecting Netanyahu's endorsement of Orbán to the nationality law is the sheer and raw expansion of state power.

But what is most startling is the fact that, in order to promote his illiberal policies, Netanyahu was willing to snub and dismiss a significant part of the Jewish people, its most well-accepted rabbis and intellectuals, and the vast number of Jews who have supported through money or political action the state of Israel, suggesting a clear and undeniable shift from a politics based on the people to a politics based on land, territory, and religion. For the majority of Jews outside Israel, human rights and the struggle against antisemitism are at the center of their core values. Netanyahu's enthusiastic support for authoritarian antisemitic leaders is an expression of a deep shift in the identity of the state as a representative of the people to a state which aims to expand through land seizure, the violation of international law, exclusion, and discrimination. Populism, at its core, is not fascism but a preamble to it.

Conclusion

One of the many effects of religion on society is to drive beliefs through sacred symbols and objects. Once the land becomes sacred, the demand of loyalty to the nation becomes total. Such nationalism can easily become a form of "'predatory identity... based on claims about and on behalf of a threatened majority.' Such identity is claimed by groups which view themselves as majorities whose identity is bound with that of the nation."[89] In such cases, nationalism becomes the overall organizing frame for a group to assert its privileges over another group. Such nationalism is a form of flawed ideology, one that rearticulates class inequalities around issues of loyalty to the nation. To such a conception of nationalism we may offer here an alternative one.

The above is not to say that all forms of nationalism or, rather, patriotism are necessarily pernicious. Eyal Lewin offers a very useful distinction between blind and constructive patriotism.[90] While blind patriotism demands total loyalty, constructive patriotism is a moderate form of patriotism characterized by constant judgment.

> Blind patriotism is characterized by political disengagement and deliberate political ignorance whereas constructive patriotism correlates with gathering information, striving for social conclusions, and high levels of political involvement. Blind patriotism is strongly connected with nationalism and a sense that the national security – indeed, the national culture itself – is at risk; constructive patriotism, for its part, might put national identity aside and even dismiss feelings of national superiority. Blind patriotism defines social attachment by means of genealogy and primordial origins generated from the nation's history whereas constructive patriotism forms social boundaries through civic procedures and commonly shared political structures.[91]

This underlies another distinction – that between authoritarian patriotism and democratic patriotism. The first describes surrendering one's will to the authorities and conceding one's individual right of choice, whereas the latter reflects the love that brings a people together rather than being united because of misguided loyalty to the institutions that dominate their lives.[92] Democratic patriotism, based on what I would call a critical love of the nation, should be the moral and emotional framework channeling people's aspiration to form a community.

Conclusion: The Emotions of a Decent Society

The sentiments analyzed in this book have a few things in common: they are all the result of manipulation by politicians, of the harnessing of ordinary people's fear, mistrust, and anger, and of *ressentiment* to the goals and strategies of unscrupulous political actors. To be sure, such manipulations do not emerge *ex nihilo*. They tap into preexisting geography, historical traumas, and collective social experiences. These same social experiences become inscribed in the political psyche, a part of people's identity and emotional make-up when they are framed in narratives that are repeated and hammered home in the public sphere by various politicians and political marketers and relayed, unconsciously or consciously by print or visual media and social networks avid for attention-grabbing texts. The mixture of these emotions forms the matrix of populism because they generate antagonism between social groups inside society and alienation from the institutions that safeguard democracy, and because they are, in many ways, oblivious to something we might call reality. More exactly: populism lives as much in reality (naming ills that have transformed working-class lives) as in the imagination. Fear provides compelling motivation to repeatedly name enemies as well as invent them, to view such enemies as fixed and unchanging, to shift politics from conflict resolution to a state of permanent vigilance to threats, even at the price of suspending the rule of law. Israel's fear of its outer and inner enemies runs deeper in the state apparatus than other populist forms of fear (it has also a different history and geography), but it bears affinities with them, as they all express fear of a shifting balance of power between majority (racial, ethnic, religious) and minorities and has become existential, about the very existence of the nation. Trump, Orbán, Le Pen, Meloni, the Swedish Democrats, and Modi have focused on the minorities who allegedly threaten their nation. Disgust creates and maintains the dynamic of distancing between social groups through the fear of pollution and contamination: it helps separate ethnic or religious minorities and, by the logic of contamination, it also contributes towards separating the political groups who either support or oppose the minorities. *Ressentiment* is a key process in self-victimization; its rhetoric has become generalized, as all groups, majority and minority, invoke it to designate the relationship of the other to them; it redefines the political self in terms of its wounds. Trumpist voters or Israeli settlers are united in their common sense of self-victimization against left-wing elites. When all groups are victims of each other, it creates antagonism and changes ordinary notions of justice. It also creates fantasies of revenge. Finally, a particular form of exclusionary patriotism promises solidarity to the in-group at the expense of the others, who become redefined as superfluous or dangerous members of the nation. We should not underestimate the deep relationship that nationalism entertains today with religion and tradition. Trump's white supremacists, Giorgia Meloni, Orbán – all claim that their countries and nations must defend their Christianity against atheists and non-Christians. They also call for a return to traditional family values and oppose gender politics and reforms that would bring equality to homosexuals. This is congruent with Israel's defense of its ethnic and religious supremacy (with the difference, however, that Jews represent a tiny fraction of humanity and have only one country in which they are sovereign). All of these emotions, together, create large imaginary spaces impervious to the real; these spaces are filled by emotional projections and scenarios which become prone to a paranoid interpretation of social and political life. These emotional imaginary spaces energetically fuel conflict within society through unavenged wounds and enemies and aggrandize a supposedly primordial and authentic definition of the true people.

This book has proposed a grid to analyze Israeli populism, keeping in mind that populism must be understood in the plural mode: its expressions vary from country to country and do not always arise from the same reasons. Israel represents only one of its versions and inflections. However, beyond differences and variations, we may highlight what might be its core: it does not claim to subvert democracy (as does fascism) but seemingly wants to uphold it. Orbán's illiberal democracy might be illiberal, but it is still democracy. Yet democracy is a political doctrine and regime which places at its epicenter fair institutions, not a leader and not a people. Thus, in invoking democracy, populism actually usurps its claim to be democratic. Populism is masculinist, and when it occasionally puts women at the forefront (Meloni or Le Pen), it is more as genderwashing than as commitment to feminism. Most populists appeal to traditional family values and reject LGBTQ movements. This is stressed less by Netanyahu himself, but only because his religious political partners promote fiercely conservative messages. Populism, in Israel and in other countries, is anti-cosmopolitan, anti-globalist, and anti-European. This deep suspicion of outside cultural forces goes hand in hand with an affirmation of one's primordial cultural identity, which is antithetical to the supposed recourse to international law of "elites," courts and norms. This is also the reason why religion and nationalism play a key role in the affirmation of this primordial cultural and ethnic identity. Finally, and most curiously, we may say that populism embodies a discourse of rebellion. The left no longer holds the center of the discourse of protest. Rebellion and transgression have shifted to the right.

This book has suggested that such political views are cast into deep stories which activate four key emotions and that a sociology of affects and emotions may be a useful grid to understand the mechanism through which populist leaders make sense of the malaise experienced by many social groups through narratives which spread anti-democratic ideas and hold their grip on their followers. This grid can and should be modulated in different countries and is not, obviously, the only explanation of populism. Rather, it is only one way of understanding its complex and changing forms.

On the basis of the Israeli case, there is one dimension of populism I find most distinctive, namely the fact that leaders from the extreme right have successfully severed the traditional relationship of the left with the working classes and have cast it as representing the elites. If there is one process which the Israeli case illustrates most cogently, it is exactly this: the conflation of a left-wing agenda (based on universalism, human rights, redistributive justice, and cultural pluralism) with "elitism" and with the idea that the elites no longer care (or never cared) for their own people. Many elements converge and coalesce around this new perception of the left: the fact that the working classes and some of the middle classes have been dismantled by global capitalism; the new geographical and cultural sharp divide between large cities and small towns, rural areas, or what is bluntly called in Israel the "periphery," with the former having mostly benefited from globalization and the latter having been hurt or destroyed by it; the increasing chasm between groups attached to the traditional family and a left demanding change in the realm of reproduction, sexuality, and gender relations at a speed that other social groups cannot follow; the weakening and fragmentation of the left (in Israel and worldwide), as well as its division between a traditional and so-called progressive left – all of these constitute the social basis for the new structure of feeling that has helped the populist right recast the social democratic left as a new elite, which speaks a foreign language and represents the interests and points of view of agents inimical to the nation. Israel, Hungary, Poland, and Trump's America have offered cogent and powerful examples of this process. Israel offers a particularly crisp case study because the overt class and ethnic struggles between Ashkenazim and Mizrahim overlap to a great extent with the struggles between the left and right and help explain how Mizrahi working-class voters have consistently subscribed to the agenda of the right for the last three decades. Israel's relatively new techno-capitalist elites are deeply involved in the globalization of the economy and relatively uninvolved in mending the large socio-economic gap between them and the working class, which in turn only fuels the deepening political chasm capitalized on by the populist right.

The political affects and emotions analyzed in this book do not explain populism so much as aspire to provide a thick description of the ways in which voters grasp their social world and build their political identities around affects which are all the more powerful in that they are also moral. Indeed, a key insight concerning populism is that it appeals to moral affects, defined as strong responses to moral violations, such as how we define good or bad behavior, good or bad people, how worthy our group is, and how we protect it.[1] Populist leaders know to recode problems to be solved by experts (for example, how much immigration should or should not be encouraged for the economy) into moral ones (how much immigrants threaten our way of life). Trump, Orbán, Le Pen, or Netanyahu have done this very successfully. The progressive left has also entirely recoded social problems into moral struggles and economic policy into identity, a fact that explains why the political terrain has become so polarized[2] and why it is now played on the terrain of morality. Moral emotions such as fear, disgust, *ressentiment*, and love for the group create a morality of exclusion and self-celebration.

Objections will undoubtedly be raised, especially with regard to the Israeli case. Given the tragic history of the Jews, the geography of Israel, and the fact that Israel was founded on a religious definition of the people, could fear, disgust, *ressentiment*, and exclusionary love have been absent from the public sphere? Answering this question presupposes that we are able to name alternative emotions which could and should form the basis of the "decent" society.

The Emotions of a Decent Society

In her book *Political Emotions*, Martha Nussbaum argues that love and compassion should be the candidates for the formation of a good political bond.[3] I take issue with this view. Love cannot, in any way, be a candidate to form the basis of civil bonds. In her discussion of Augustine's notion of *agape* – that is, unconditional love – Hannah Arendt famously wrote against the role of love in political affairs.[4] If love was to play any such role in politics, she averred, we could never have the power to forgive or judge. Arendt went as far as suggesting that Augustine's love is "unconcerned to the point of total unworldliness"[5] with our particularities, reminiscent of the indifference of *agape*. Such love does not enable (or even allow) human beings to judge and evaluate and thus prevents people from making up their minds on their own and exercising justice and fairness. Moreover, love is particularist. It cannot possibly be extended to many others, otherwise its very nature threatens to dissolve. Finally, love is a very bad candidate for building bonds in civil society because love always contains some form of narcissistic component: I love the other who loves me in return. I love in another the very fact that they love me. In liberal societies, the political bond, I believe, starts from a different position: it starts with distance and strangeness as well as with conflict. This understanding of the realm of the political has been with us since Aristotle, Nietzsche, and Arendt, who all understood politics as *polemos*, a view of society as a site of conflict and even a theater of war. One of the key aims of liberalism is to extend rights to strangers or people who do not belong to the same group. Another aim is to regulate conflict and difference, given that its starting point is the recognition that the conflict of opinion and interests is irreducible to human life. The strangeness of others and the necessity of conflict are not only a matter for institutions to regulate. Many philosophers, such as Jürgen Habermas,[6] understood that these questions must also be addressed in civil society, in how we communicate with one another and the kind of moral assumptions we make in such communication. Habermas neglected to discuss explicitly the role of emotions in such civil society. Civil society must include minimal respect, and such respect is necessarily underlain by specific types of emotions which allow us to acknowledge each other properly as citizens and as fellow human beings.[7] This is why we may say that good civil societies should encourage certain emotional dispositions or habitus.

For obvious reasons, fear, disgust, resentment, and blind patriotism are not good candidates for this, because they fuel conflict and claim to want to eliminate difference altogether through an imagined community of similar people and therefore cannot regulate either conflict or difference. Compassion and fraternity are far better candidates to be the emotions constitutive of the good civil society, because both emotions presuppose the radical strangeness and diversity of those they have as their objects.

From Solidarity to Fraternity

A common observation is that the tighter the community, the more solidarity there will be.[8] Solidarity here is based on the capacity to identify with others and to view them as "family" rather than recognizing them on universal principles. Even though the proper word for solidarity did not exist, Aristotle, using a proxy term for the notion, discussed solidarity as "the will to live together."[9] The philosopher Charles Taylor has suggested that patriotism and republican solidarity may be a remedy against the fragmenting individualism of democracies. "'Republics', in Taylor's sense of the word, differ from liberal societies in that their inhabitants see themselves as a community borne by common values and bound by a common destiny, prepared to defend this polity as a 'directly common good.'"[10] As in a family, an individual develops a sense that they are a member of whatever befalls them. But if we think of liberal societies as families, we cannot explain why people should be willing to allow new members to join in. To allow for this, there needs to be another moral element present in civil society.

Social democracies can embrace solidarity despite displaying high forms of individualism. As Ulrich Preuss rightly observes, solidarity is a modern concept.[11] It accompanies precisely the rise of the welfare state and is rooted not in *Gemeinschaft* but in *Gesellschaft*. Solidarity is the set of obligations we feel towards those that share with us a territory or history, towards those whom we view as similar to ourselves.

Ultra-orthodox and secular, right-wing patriots and universalist cosmopolitans, supremacists, and people who defend international law, Jews and Arabs, Mizrahim and Ashkenazim: dissensions and fractures in Israeli society run along several lines. In Israeli society, as in others divided by such sharp social distinctions, solidarity may not extend far enough to foster social cooperation. When social groups are unable to agree on the very principles of the society itself, on its higher goods, whether it should be Jewish or Israeli, democratic or illiberal, based on international law or Jewish religion, within clear or fuzzy borders, it is because they have not been able to create universalist covenants, which form the moral core of modern constitutions. Solidarity that extends only to the in-group will not be a remedy for this. Fraternity may be a better candidate.

Fraternity should not be confused with solidarity. At face value, both solidarity and fraternity constitute obligations and mutual support between people. They both "share a commitment to mutual aid and social responsibility."[12] But there is an important difference between them: solidarity is based on mutual agreement,[13] it is "always expressed through particular visions of human purposes and moral concerns."[14] In contrast, fraternity is based not on agreement or on a sentimental attachment to the other, but on a moral and judicial idea of justice within the political community.[15] Additionally, the two should be kept separate because, while solidarity can be present in a society, the same society may be highly deficient in fraternity. Israel is high on solidarity and low on fraternity. High levels of solidarity are apparent within different social groups, for instance feelings of solidarity towards missing soldiers and their families among Jewish Israelis.[16] On the other hand, low levels of fraternity are indicated by the fact that 42 percent of Jewish Israeli citizens support the claim that Jewish citizens should have more rights than non-Jewish citizens,[17] demonstrating low levels of commitment to the idea of justice within society.

Fraternity was and remains one of three cardinal principles of the French Revolution, even if, as John Rawls has remarked, "In comparison with liberty and equality, the idea of fraternity has had a lesser place in democratic theory. It is thought to be less specifically a political concept, not in itself defining any of the democratic rights . . ."[18] Indeed, of the three elements of the French Revolution motto, fraternity has been the most neglected.

Fraternity is the place where theology meets politics and may be the area where religion may play an active role in civil society (but not in its institutions). Fraternity was first affirmed as a political principle during the French Revolution, through the need to help the destitute (either by giving them labor or supporting them if they cannot work). It was viewed as a holy duty and in that sense was probably a secularized translation of a Christian imperative to help the poor.

The theologian Wolfgang Palaver views religion as having much to contribute to political fraternity.[19] Drawing a contrast between static and dynamic religions, he argues that the latter contain the possibility of universal fraternity. Universal fraternity is necessary to prevent democracy from succumbing to its populist temptations. It protects the rights of minorities against the dominating majority. Internationally, it prevents nationalist closures and forces a country to respect universal human rights.[20] For Palaver, dynamic religion is important for sustaining the fraternal spirit in democratic societies. Churches and religious communities play an important role in this regard in civil society.[21]

According to Palaver, it was the Catholic philosopher Jacques Maritain who worked out best the theme of sanctity through fraternity. "The common task, according to Maritain, is the 'realization of a fraternal community' and not the 'medieval idea of God's empire to be built on earth, and still less would it be the myth of Class or Race, Nation or State.'"[22] This stream in Catholicism helped pave the way to Catholic modernity – that is, to ideological pluralism, democracy, and human rights. Robert Schuman, perhaps the dominant figure in the founding of the European Union, "followed Bergson and Maritain by emphasizing Christian brotherhood to overcome hatred and to strengthen solidarity in Europe. Out of this fraternal attitude he understood the importance to 'counter the narrow-mindedness of political nationalism, autarkic protectionism, and of cultural isolationism', replacing them with the 'notion of solidarity' and 'accepting the interdependency of all.'"[23] Pope Francis is another striking example of such fraternity. He frequently mentions the importance of fraternity in his speeches and writings. The 2019 Declaration between Pope Francis and the Grand Imam Ahmad Mohammad Al-Tayyeb signed in 2019 was a document declaring

> the firm conviction that authentic teachings of religions invite us to remain rooted in the values of peace; to defend the values of mutual understanding, *human fraternity* and harmonious coexistence; to re-establish wisdom, justice and love; and to reawaken religious awareness among young people so that future generations may be protected from the realm of materialistic thinking and from dangerous policies of unbridled greed and indifference that are based on the law of force and not on the force of law.[24]

Dialogue, tolerance, justice, and full citizenship are all contained in the notion of fraternity: they are all paths to human fraternity, against terrorism and political extremism.

Let me provide a powerful example of fraternity deployed in the political sphere. In 1990, in the old Jewish cemetery of Carpentras, thirty-four Jewish tombs were profaned in a particularly gory way, which provoked an outcry in France.[25] The French minister of the interior flew to the site in a helicopter and denounced forcefully racism, antisemitism, and intolerance.[26] Many public personalities from the entire spectrum, both right and left, similarly went to the site and visited the Jewish community. Mass demonstrations followed to protest against racism and antisemitism. Perhaps most remarkable was the fact that it was the first time that a French president, François Mitterrand, had participated in a demonstration – very unusual for a serving president – a forceful reminder that human fraternity transcended partisan politics.[27]

As Munoz-Dardé suggests, although they are often opposed, justice and fraternity need not be so;[28] rather, invoking some nineteenth-century and post-revolutionary views, we may well view fraternity as emanating from a legal and moral framework. In that sense, it should be radically distinguished and differentiated from sentimental charity. Indeed, some have objected to fraternity on the grounds that it is subjective, too fuzzy and amorphous to constitute a viable political sentiment likely to be translated into any recognizable political form of action. The French philosopher Étienne Vacherot warned sternly in the nineteenth century against fraternity: "Liberty and equality are principles, whereas fraternity is only a sentiment. Now a sentiment, as powerful, as deep, as general as it may be, is not a right; it is impossible to make it a basis for justice. Politicians trying to establish it as a principle are making the same mistake as moralists who ground moral laws on love."[29] Yet, in practice, fraternity derives from legal and moral frameworks which extend rights to powerless others, from viewing the state as guaranteeing the rights of everyone and not only specific groups. I would add that it also derives from holding on to a firm conception of universalism, viewing all human beings as equal and defending such a view through institutions. Such a view is to be found in the philosophy of John Rawls, for whom the "principle of difference" amounts to a natural meaning of fraternity – that is, not wanting to have more than others who are less well off.[30]

Let me make an additional and important point: as a sentiment, fraternity needs to be connected to some key notion of what human beings are. Emotions cannot be activated without a key definition of the object they address. Fraternity is the sentiment that transforms universalism into an affect. It cannot take place if it is not connected to a universal conception of human beings. Perhaps, for that reason, Israel is an example of solidarity without fraternity, precisely because it has a weak and uncertain universalist political culture.

Fraternity and Universalism

The metaphors of the family are often invoked to refer both to solidarity and to fraternity. Yet, if anything, this book gives reasons to doubt whether this metaphor is the right one. If the metaphor of the family is to be pursued, we might say that Israeli society compels its citizens to support and participate in a family that feels like a coerced one or from whom one has long felt alienated. In fact, I would go further: it is probably when the metaphors of the family are the strongest that the feeling of human fraternity is the least likely to emerge.

Fraternity does not presuppose familiarity, closeness, and membership of the same primary group. Some people speak of fraternity in terms of cooperation and as a sense of shared responsibility.[31] But fraternity is first and foremost a benevolent emotional orientation towards others who are not necessarily members of one's primary group. This is why it necessarily contains a universalist component. Fraternity includes compassion, as a feeling typically elicited by strangers, but extends beyond it. It implies the capacity to feel benevolent, or at least not mistrustful towards foreign others, as well as concerned by what happens to people who are not from one's primary group, much as in the case of Carpentras. Only a deeply ingrained universalist conception of human beings, entrenched in the law and in moral culture, enables such deployment of fraternity. In an interview with the German weekly *Die Zeit*, Pope Francis underlined the fraternal beginnings of the European Union that were shaped by great politicians of the postwar period, such as Schuman or Adenauer, who dreamed of the unity of Europe. "They were not preoccupied with anything populist, but with the fraternalizing of Europe, from the Atlantic to the

Urals."[32] Their vision overcame the profound enmity between the Allied powers and Germany.

Universalism should be distinguished from universalization, the action of exporting one's belief to countries and groups. Universalism departs from La Boétie's observation that nature "has made us all in the same form and, so it seems, in the same mould, so that we all recognize each other as companions, or rather as brothers."[33] We may call this anthropological universalism. Formal universalism, entrenched in law and constitution, wins assent precisely through its capacity to tap into one's intuitive understanding that other human beings are brothers. It cannot be imposed. It should thus also be distinguished from an imperial desire to make all countries and cultures enter in a common time, space, and culture. Universalism has been developed by Kantianism, a philosophy which views universalism as a moral solution to evil and to political institutions. As understood by Kant, universalism contains three aspects: practical universalism (or the concern for the equal freedom and dignity of each and every person), autonomy (a demand for individual and collective self-legislation), and a state of "perpetual peace" in a republic.[34] Universalism is different from cosmopolitanism but is closely related to it. Cosmopolitanism is the fact of being or feeling or wanting to be a citizen of the world.[35] This is possible only if we assume the oneness of humankind and the desirability of such oneness. And, as the political philosopher James D. Ingram acutely observes, since all of us are still closely embedded in a country, a place, a language, a culture, the meaning of such membership is not straightforward. Indeed, as the Israeli case demonstrates, the very fact of orienting ourselves to humanity as a whole is a political act. Ingram invokes the notion of cosmopolitics to refer to "the politics of a common world," which is understood as "a reorientation of political actions conducted within various public spaces yet aiming at the world."[36] The question of what we want to extend to the rest of the world is a matter of discussion. It is a political issue that can and should be resolved locally: rights, citizenship, benevolence, help, charity, and respect, but cosmopolitanism is the horizon of such discussions.

Jews and Universalism

Since the eighteenth century, Jews have played a decisive role in the promotion of universalism, because universalism is deeply ingrained in the moral views of several strands and commandments of Judaism and because it promised Jews redemption from their political subjection. Jews participated *en masse* in the great universalist movements of emancipation. Through universalism, Jews could, in principle, be free and equal to those who dominated them: in a universalist community, membership of a religious minority should not influence one's political status. This may be one of the reasons why Jews participated in disproportionate numbers in communist or socialist causes.[37] This is also why Jews were model citizens of such countries with universalist constitutions as France or the United States.[38] This history of Jews as promoters of the Enlightenment and universalist values is drawing to a close. We are the stunned witnesses of new alliances between Israel, ultra-orthodox factions of religious Judaism throughout the world, and the new global populism, in which ethnocentrism and even racism hold an undeniable place. A whopping 53.59 percent of French Jews living in Israel voted for the extreme-right candidate Éric Zemmour for the French presidency;[39] AIPAC (American Israel Public Affairs Committee), a powerful but traditionally non-partisan lobby, supported Trump enthusiastically,[40] and, in a 2019 survey, 81 percent of orthodox Jewish Americans approved of Trump.[41] These numbers speak loud and clear. If the Jews and the working class were once what Marx called universal classes – they represented the point of view of the destitute for whom emancipation would occur through universalism – they now represent groups largely affected by the ideology and the politics of the extreme right.

This is due, no doubt, to the ways in which the Israeli right has preferred to ally itself with populist leaders (who are less likely to give Israel a hard time in international organizations that adhere to international norms and laws). And it is no less due to the fact that the religion that has been institutionalized in Israel refuses to be a dynamic religion. It is in fact highly static and anti-modernist. Israel has enabled the formation and expansion of stringent forms of ultra-orthodoxy which feed into rigid and binary conceptions of identity and extreme religious nationalism. These oppose liberal civil society in the sense that, while they may foster a great solidarity between their own members, they do not foster and even dismiss what is conventionally thought of as fraternal relationship between different human groups.

It is the universalism of the Jews which must be renewed through an alliance between liberalism and dynamic Jewish religion, today represented mostly by conservative and reform Judaism and some strands of orthodox Judaism, all equally mindful of the universalist vocation of Judaism. Universalism is not a foolproof safeguard against the failures of democracy, but it is certainly one of the strongest buffers against the nativist claims of populism. The renewal of Israeli civil society will emerge only from an energetic dialogue between a dynamic Jewish religion which taps into the universalist dimension of Judaism and a more radically universalist political culture which extends full human rights to non-Jewish minorities. This is, undoubtedly, the true and only spirit of Zionism and of the civil religion it tried to implement in the land of Israel. Whether or not it will succeed remains a tragically open question.

Notes

Introduction

1 Theodor W Adorno, *Aspects of the New Right-Wing Extremism* (Medford, MA: Polity, 2020), p. 2.
2 Peter E. Gordon, Espen Hammer, and Axel Honneth, *The Routledge Companion to the Frankfurt School* (Abingdon: Routledge, 2018), p. xvi.
3 Seymour Martin Lipset, *Political Man: The Social Basis of Politics* (New York: Doubleday, 1960); Daniel Bell, *The Radical Right* (3rd edn, New Brunswick, NJ: Transaction, [1955] 2002).
4 Among people who make under $30,000 a year, 53 percent voted for Clinton and 40 percent for Trump; $30,000–50,000: 51 percent Clinton, 42 percent Trump; $50,000–100,000: 46 percent Clinton; 50 percent Trump; $100,000–200.000: 47 percent Clinton; 48 percent Trump; $200,000–250,000: 48 percent Clinton; 49 percent Trump; above $250,000: 46 percent Clinton and 48 percent Trump. Statista Research Department, "Exit Polls of the 2016 Presidential Elections in the United States on November 9, 2016, Percentage of Votes by Income," November 9, 2016, www.statista.com/statistics/631244/voter-turnout-of-the-exit-polls-of-the-2016-elections-by-income/.

5 Jason Stanley, *How Propaganda Works* (Princeton, NJ: Princeton University Press, 2015).
6 Ibid., p. 5.
7 Bruno Latour, "Why Has Critique Run Out of Steam? From Matters of Fact to Matters of Concern," *Critical Inquiry*, 30/2 (2004): 225–48.
8 D. M. Lazer, M. A. Baum, Y. Benkler, et al., "The Science of Fake News," *Science*, 359/6380 (2018): 1094–6.
9 Jerome J. McGann, "Romanticism and its Ideologies," *Studies in Romanticism*, 21/4 (1982): 573–99.
10 David Scott Bell and Byron Criddle, *The French Communist Party in the Fifth Republic* (Oxford: Oxford University Press, 1994).
11 Steven Levitsky and Daniel Ziblatt, *How Democracies Die* (London: Penguin, 2018).
12 Jan-Werner Müller, *What Is Populism?* (Philadelphia: University of Pennsylvania Press, 2016); Ronald F. Inglehart and Pippa Norris, *Trump, Brexit, and the Rise of Populism: Economic Have-Nots and Cultural Backlash*, Harvard Kennedy School Working Paper RWP16-026 (2016); Noam Gidron and Peter A. Hall, "The Politics of Social Status: Economic and Cultural Roots of the Populist Right," *British Journal of Sociology*, 68 (2017): S57–84; Dani Rodrik, "Populism and the Economics of Globalization," *Journal of International Business Policy*, 1/1 (2018): 12–33.
13 Brian McCulloch, "Who Owns France's Media and What Are Their Political Leanings?," *The Connexion*, January 19, 2022, www.connexionfrance.com/article/French-news/Who-owns-France-s-media-and-what-are-their-political-leanings.
14 Liam Stack, "6 Takeaways from The Times's Investigation into Rupert Murdoch and His Family," *New York Times*, April 3, 2019, https://web.archive.org/web/20200812014550/https://www.nytimes.com/interactive/2019/04/03/magazine/murdoch-family-investigation.html.
15 Rodrik, "Populism and the Economics of Globalization."
16 Erica Etelson, "How Liberals Left the White Working Class

Behind," *Yes! Magazine*, December 16, 2019, www.yesmagazine.org/democracy/2019/12/16/book-politics-divide.
17 Patrick J. Deneen, *Why Liberalism Failed* (New Haven, CT: Yale University Press).
18 Helena Flam, "Emotions' Map: A Research Agenda," in *Emotions and Social Movements*, ed. Helena Flam and Debra King (Hoboken, NJ: Taylor & Francis, 2005), p. 19. For another cogent macro-political approach, see Ute Frevert, *The Politics of Humiliation: A Modern History* (Oxford: Oxford University Press, 2020).
19 Raymond Williams, *Marxism and Literature* (Oxford: Oxford University Press, 1977); Paul Filmer, "Structures of Feeling and Socio-Cultural Formations: The Significance of Literature and Experience to Raymond Williams's Sociology of Culture," *British Journal of Sociology*, 54/2 (2003): 199–219.
20 Tony Bennett, *Popular Culture: Themes and Issues (2), Unit 3: Popular Culture: History and Theory* (Milton Keynes: Open University Press, 1981).
21 Kevin Hetherington, *Expressions of Identity: Space, Performance, Politics* (London: Sage, 1998).
22 Mabel Berezin, "Secure States: Towards a Political Sociology of Emotion," *Sociological Review*, 50/2 suppl. (2002): 33–52; Filmer, "Structures of Feeling and Socio-cultural Formations."
23 For example, Maéva Clément, Thomas Lindemann, and Eric Sangar, "The 'Hero-Protector Narrative': Manufacturing Emotional Consent for the Use of Force," *Political Psychology*, 38/6 (2017): 991–1008; Cristopher Cepernich and Roberta Bracciale, "Digital Hyperleaders: Communication Strategies on Social Networks at the 2019 European Elections," *Italian Political Science*, 14/2 (2019).
24 Vonnie C. McLoyd et al., "Marital Processes and Parental Socialization in Families of Color: A Decade Review of Research," *Journal of Marriage and Family*, 62/4 (2000): 1070–93.
25 Jack M. Barbalet, "A Macro Sociology of Emotion: Class Resentment," *Sociological Theory*, 10/2 (1992): 150–63; Madan

M. Pillutla and J. Keith Murnighan, "Unfairness, Anger, and Spite: Emotional Rejections of Ultimatum Offers," *Organizational Behavior and Human Decision Processes*, 68/3 (1996): 208–24.

26 John Garry, "Emotions and Voting in EU Referendums," *European Union Politics*, 15/2 (2014): 235–54; Ted Brader, "Striking a Responsive Chord: How Political Ads Motivate and Persuade Voters by Appealing to Emotions," *American Journal of Political Science*, 49/2 (2005): 388–405.

27 Larissa Z .Tiedens and Colin Wayne Leach, eds, *The Social Life of Emotions* (Cambridge: Cambridge University Press, 2004).

28 Mabel Berezin, "Emotions and Political Identity: Mobilizing Affection for the Polity," in *Passionate Politics: Emotions and Social Movements*, ed. Jeff Goddwin, James M. Jasper, and Francesca Polletta (Chicago: University of Chicago Press, 2001), pp. 83–98.

29 Berezin, "Secure States."

30 Kennet Lynggaard, "Methodological Challenges in the Study of Emotions in Politics and How to Deal with Them," *Political Psychology*, 40/6 (2019): 1201–15.

31 Arlie R. Hochschild, *Strangers in Their Own Land: Anger and Mourning on the American Right*. (New York: New Press, 2018).

32 "Trump Support Remains Unmoved by Investigations, Poll Finds," www.nytimes.com/2022/09/22/upshot/donald-trump-approval-poll.html.

33 Williams, *Marxism and Literature*.

34 Joseph Epstein, *Envy: The Seven Deadly Sins* (Oxford: Oxford University Press, 2003).

35 Quoted in Jason Stanley, *How Propaganda Works* (Princeton, NJ: Princeton University Press, 2015), p. 48.

36 A report published by the UN in 2020 named 112 business enterprises worldwide with ties to the settlements. Of these 112 companies, 94 are Israeli, including leading Israeli banks and communications companies, and another 18 are international companies such as Airbnb and Booking.com. See "UN Rights Office Issues Report on Business Activities Related to Settlements

in the Occupied Palestinian Territory," February 12, 2020, www.ohchr.org/en/press-releases/2020/02/un-rights-office-issues-report-business-activities-related-settlements?LangID=E&NewsID=25542.

37 Dani Filc, "Political Radicalization in Israel: From a Populist Habitus to Radical Right Populism in Government," in *Expressions of Radicalization: Global Politics, Processes and Practices*, ed. Kristian Steiner and Andreas Önnerfors (London: Palgrave Macmillan, 2018), p. 122; https://doi.org/10.1007/978-3-319-65566-6_5.

38 This also could well be the effect of the use of common marketing strategists. Netanyahu's 1996 victory against Peres had been significantly aided by Arthur Finkelstein, the advisor and pollster of Ronald Reagan and numerous other Republican candidates and nominees. Indeed, there is a political style which, either through formal channels of political advice or through unconscious imitation and informal networks, has spread throughout the world.

39 Julius Maximilian Rogenhofer and Ayala Panievsky, "Antidemocratic Populism in Power: Comparing Erdoğan's Turkey with Modi's India and Netanyahu's Israel," *Democratization*, 27/8 (2020): 1394–1412; Kathleen Hall Jamieson and Doron Taussig, "Disruption, Demonization, Deliverance, and Norm Destruction: The Rhetorical Signature of Donald J. Trump," *Political Science Quarterly*, 132/4 (2017): 619–51; Andrew Arato, "Populism, Constitutional Courts and Civil Society," in *Judicial Power: How Constitutional Courts Affect Political Transformations*, ed. Christine Landfried (Cambridge: Cambridge University Press, 2019), pp. 318–41; Federico Neiburg and Omar Ribeiro Thomaz, "Ethnographic Views of Brazil's (New) Authoritarian Turn," *HAU: Journal of Ethnographic Theory*, 10/1 (2020): 7–11.

40 Isidore Abramowitz et al., "To the Editors of the New York Times," *New York Times*, December 2, 1948, www.marxists.org/reference/archive/einstein/1948/12/02.htm.

41 Yonatan Levi and Shai Agmon, "Beyond Culture and Economy: Israel's Security-Driven Populism," *Contemporary Politics*, 27/3 (2021): 292–315, at p. 293.
42 Ibid.
43 Ibid.
44 Dani Filc, *The Political Right in Israel: Different Faces of Jewish Populism* (London: Routledge, 2009).
45 Zev Stub, "Israeli Home Prices Rose 346% in a Decade, Fastest in the World," *Jerusalem Post*, September 1, 2021, www.jpost.com/israel-news/israeli-home-prices-rose-346-percent-in-a-decade-fastest-in-the-world-678028.
46 Jan-Werner Müller, *Liberté, égalité, incertitude: puissance de la démocratie* (Paris: Premier Parallèle, 2022).
47 Filc, *The Political Right in Israel*. It should be noted that the phrase "conservative nationalism" can be used with different meanings. In this case, it means a xenophobic view that ties national belonging to ethnic identity, along with anti-elite sentiment against any force (such as the left wing in politics) that is perceived as siding with "the other."
48 Mikko Salmela and Christian Von Scheve, "Emotional Roots of Right-Wing Political Populism," *Social Science Information*, 56/4 (2017): 567–95.
49 "Aristotle: Politics," Internet Encyclopedia of Philosophy, n.d., https://iep.utm.edu/aris-pol/#H2.
50 Martha C. Nussbaum, *Political Emotions* (Cambridge, MA: Harvard University Press, 2013), pp. 23, 384–7.
51 Pierre Bourdieu, *Distinction: A Social Critique of the Judgement of Taste*, trans. Richard Nice (Cambridge, MA: Harvard University Press, 1984).
52 Müller, *What Is Populism?*, p. 20.

Chapter 1 Securitist Democracy and Fear

1 Niccolò Machiavelli, *The Prince* (Harmondsworth: Penguin, 2003).
2 Mikko Jakonen, "Thomas Hobbes on Fear, *Mimesis, Aisthesis*

and Politics," *Distinktion: Journal of Social Theory*, 12/2 (2011): 157–76; Andrew Alexandra, "'All Men Agree on This ...': Hobbes on the Fear of Death and the Way to Peace," *History of Philosophy Quarterly*, 6/1 (1989): 37–55.

3 Judith N. Shklar, "The Liberalism of Fear," in *Liberalism and the Moral Life*, ed. Nancy L. Rosenblum (Cambridge, MA: Harvard University Press, 2013), pp. 21–38; https://doi.org/doi:10.4159/harvard.9780674864443.c2.

4 Alex Schulman, "Hobbes, Thomas (1588–1679)," *The Encyclopedia of Political Thought*, ed. Michael T. Gibbons et al. (Wiley, 2014), pp. 1675–86.

5 Zeev Jabotinsky, "The Iron Wall," November 4, 1923, Jabotinsky Institute in Israel, http://en.jabotinsky.org/media/9747/the-iron-wall.pdf.

6 Carl Schmitt, *The Concept of the Political* (expanded edn, Chicago: University of Chicago Press, 2007).

7 Quoted in Ronen Bergman, *Rise and Kill First: The Secret History of Israel's Targeted Assassinations* (London: John Murray, 2018), p. 49.

8 Even the Supreme Court, the institution entrusted with protecting the rights of citizens, has tended to side with the requests of the army and the secret police whenever these threatened any risk to "national security," sacrificing civil rights many times to gain security. Gad Barzilai, Ephraim Yuchtman-Yaar, and Zeev Segal, *The Supreme Court as Viewed by Israeli Society* (Tel Aviv: Papyrus, 1994) [in Hebrew].

9 Quoted in David Israel, "Watch: The Six Day War," June 5, 2017, www.jewishpress.com/news/israel/watch-the-six-day-war/2017/06/05/; emphasis added.

10 Dan Meridor and Ron Eldadi, "Israel's National Security Doctrine: The Report of the Committee on the Formulation of the National Security Doctrine (Meridor Committee)" (Tel Aviv: Institute for National Security Studies, 2019), p. 11; www.inss.org.il/wp-content/uploads/2019/02/Memo187_11.pdf.

11 Jeffrey C. Alexander, "The Social Construction of Moral

Universals," in *Remembering the Holocaust: A Debate* (New York: Oxford University Press, 2009), pp. 3–104.
12 Idith Zertal, *Israel's Holocaust and the Politics of Nationhood*, trans. Chaya Galai (Cambridge: Cambridge University Press, 2005).
13 Quoted in Guy Harpaz, "The Role of Dialogue in Reflecting and Constituting International Relations: The Causes and Consequences of a Deficient European–Israeli Dialogue," *Review of International Studies*, 37/4 (2011): 1857–83, at p. 1865.
14 Baruch Kimmerling, "Patterns of Militarism in Israel," in *Handbook of Israel: Major Debates*, ed. Eliezer Ben-Rafael et al. (Berlin: De Gruyter Oldenbourg, 2016), pp. 609–36; https://doi.org/doi:10.1515/9783110351637-046.
15 Bergman, *Rise and Kill First*.
16 Samara Asmir, "Introduction: In the Name of Security," *Adalah Notebooks*, no. 4 (April 2004): 2–9 [in Hebrew].
17 William Bloss, "Escalating US Police Surveillance after 9/11: An Examination of Causes and Effects," *Surveillance & Society*, 4/3 (2007).
18 Uriel Abulof, "Deep Securitization and Israel's 'Demographic Demon,'" *International Political Sociology*, 8/4 (2014): 396–415.
19 World Bank, "Military Expenditure (% of GDP)," 2020, https://data.worldbank.org/indicator/MS.MIL.XPND.GD.ZS?most_recent_value_desc=true.
20 Jonathan Cook, "Israeli Spyware Technology, Tested on Palestinians, Now Operating in a City Near You," *Washington Report on Middle East Affairs*, 2020, www.wrmea.org/2020-january-february/israeli-spyware-technology-tested-on-palestinians-now-operating-in-a-city-near-you.html.
21 Yuval Shany and Amir Cahane, "Under the Radar Screen?," Israel Democracy Institute, April 1, 2017, https://en.idi.org.il/articles/14247.
22 Josh Breiner, "Police Want Facial Recognition Systems Installed Across Israel," *Haaretz*, July 10, 2021, https://www.haaretz.com/israel-news/.premium-despite-concerns-police-want-facial-recognition-systems-installed-across-isreal-1.9988314.

23 Ilana Hammerman, "The Zionist Left Has Paved the Way to the Rise of the Extreme Right," *Haaretz*, January 26, 2020, www.haaretz.com/opinion/.premium-the-zionist-left-has-paved-the-way-to-the-rise-of-the-extreme-right-1.8443635.

24 The NGO Freedom House, which measures freedom and democracy in different countries, has rated the Philippines as "partly free," while Israel is rated as "free." See https://freedomhouse.org/country/philippines; and https://freedomhouse.org/country/israel.

25 Nicole Curato, "Politics of Anxiety, Politics of Hope: Penal Populism and Duterte's Rise to Power," *Journal of Current Southeast Asian Affairs*, 35/3 (2016): 91–109; https://doi.org/10.1177/186810341603500305.

26 Peter Beinart, "Sorry, Bibi: Iran Is Bad, but it Is No Amalek, Haman or Even Nazi Germany," *Haaretz*, March 4, 2015, www.haaretz.com/opinion/.premium-sorry-bibi-iran-is-bad-but-it-is-no-nazi-germany-1.5332277.

27 Binyamin Netanyahu, *A Durable Peace: Israel and its Place among the Nations* (New York: Warner Books, 2000).

28 "Benjamin Netanyahu Testifies about Iraq to Congress," CNN, September 12, 2002, http://edition.cnn.com/TRANSCRIPTS/0209/12/se.07.html.

29 Peter Hirschberg, "Netanyahu: It's 1938 and Iran Is Germany; Ahmadinejad Is Preparing Another Holocaust," *Haaretz*, November 14, 2006, https://www.haaretz.com/1.4931862.

30 "Bibi's Holocaust Remembrance Day Warning Message," *Australian Jewish Times*, January 28, 2010, https://ajn.timesofisrael.com/bibi's-holocaust-remembrance-day-warning-message/.

31 J. P. O'Malley, "Netanyahu Lambasted for Incitement in Insider's Rabin Biography," *Times of Israel*, March 19, 2017, www.timesofisrael.com/netanyahu-lambasted-for-incitement-in-insiders-rabin-biography/.

32 "Netanyahu Defends Comparison of Iran, Nazi Holocaust," Reuters, April 18, 2012, www.reuters.com/article/us-israel-iran-netanyahu-idUSBRE83H1EF20120418.

33 Adiv Sterman and Raphael Ahren, "Netanyahu Blames Jerusalem Mufti for Holocaust, Is Accused of 'Absolving Hitler,'" *Times of Israel*, October 21, 2015, www.timesofisrael.com/netanyahu-accused-of-absolving-hitler-for-holocaust/.

34 "PM Netanyahu Addresses Munich Security Conference," Israel Ministry of Foreign Affairs, 2018, www.gov.il/en/departments/news/pm-netanyahu-addresses-munich-security-conference-18-february-2018.

35 Herb Keinon, "In Holocaust Remembrance Speech, Netanyahu Responds to Iranian Threats of Retaliation," *Jerusalem Post*, April 11, 2018, www.jpost.com/israel-news/pm-netanyahu-responds-to-iranian-threats-of-retaliation-549548.

36 "Netanyahu Addresses Congress on Iran," *New York Times*, March 3, 2015, www.nytimes.com/live/netanyahu-address/jewish-people-will-defend-themselves-netanyahu-says/.

37 Dahlia Scheindlin, "The Dangerous Politics of Playing the Victim," *Foreign Policy*, July 4, 2019, https://foreignpolicy.com/2019/07/04/dangerous-politics-of-playing-the-victim-israel-netanyahu-serbia-vucic/.

38 Binyamin Netanyahu, "The Right-Wing Government Is in Danger – We Must Go Out and Vote Mahal," 2015, https://www.youtube.com/watch?v=Q2cUoglR1yk [in Hebrew].

39 TOI Staff, "Likud Says Herzog 'Crossed Red Lines' at Munich Summit," *Times of Israel*, February 8, 2015, www.timesofisrael.com/likud-says-herzog-crossed-red-lines-at-munich-summit/.

40 Dov Waxman, "It Wasn't Just Politics That Led to Netanyahu's Ouster – It Was Fear of His Demagoguery," *The Conversation*, June 15, 2021, https://theconversation.com/it-wasnt-just-politics-that-led-to-netanyahus-ouster-it-was-fear-of-his-demagoguery-162547.

41 Quoted in Israel Shahak and Norton Mezvinsky, *Jewish Fundamentalism in Israel*, new ed. (London; Ann Arbor, Michigan: Pluto Press, 2004), 12.

42 Ibid.

43 Benny Gantz, "1364 Terrorists Killed – 3.5 Years of Quiet in

the South," 2019, www.youtube.com/watch?v=PEUQId3oTNo&list=PLzT23Np5hqT3hFo-6tAc-3zxLO748e1Lu&index=3 [in Hebrew].

44 For example, Seth J. Frantzman, "Ten Takeaways from Nasrallah's Speech," *Jerusalem Post*, July 14, 2019, www.jpost.com/middle-east/ten-takeaways-from-nasrallahs-speech-595519; Louis Charbonneau, "In New York, Defiant Ahmadinejad Says Israel Will Be 'Eliminated,'" Reuters, September 24, 2012, www.reuters.com/article/us-un-assembly-ahmadinejad-idUSBRE88N0HF20120924.

45 Rym Momtaz, "How France Pivoted to the Right," *Politico*, December 6, 2021, www.politico.eu/article/how-france-pivoted-to-the-right/.

46 Matthew Goodwin and Caitlin Milazzo, *UKIP: Inside the Campaign to Redraw the Map of British Politics* (Oxford: Oxford University Press, 2015).

47 Hervé Le Bras, *Il n'y a pas de "grand remplacement"* (Paris: Bernard Grasset, 2022).

48 Sigmund Freud, "Beyond the Pleasure Principle," in *The Standard Edition of the Complete Psychological Works of Sigmund Freud*, Vol. XVIII: *(1920–1922): Beyond the Pleasure Principle, Group Psychology and Other Works* (London: Hogarth Press, 1955), pp. 1–64.

49 Corey Robin, *Fear: The History of a Political Idea* (Oxford: Oxford University Press, 2004).

50 Jonathan Renshon, Julia J. Lee, and Dustin Tingley, "Physiological Arousal and Political Beliefs," *Political Psychology*, 36/5 (2015): 569–85; Douglas R. Oxley et al., "Political Attitudes Vary with Physiological Traits," *Science*, 321/5896 (2008): 1667–70.

51 Carl Schmitt, "Definition of Sovereignty," in *Political Theology* (Chicago: University of Chicago Press, 2010), pp. 5–15.

52 "Declaring a State of Emergency," https://m.knesset.gov.il/en/about/lexicon/pages/declaringstateemergency.aspx.

53 Legal staff of the Foreign Affairs and Defense Committee, "Discussion of the Government's Request to Extend the State of Emergency" (Israeli Knesset, May 31, 2020), https://m.knesset.gov.il/Activity/committees/ForeignAffairs/LegislationDocs23/bit020620-4.pdf [in Hebrew].
54 Additionally, in intellectual history, fear is more congruent with the counter-Enlightenment movement, which tended to view human nature as in need of control and human beings as inherently hostile to one another and in a state of perpetual strife with one another.
55 Brian Michael Jenkins, "An Incremental Tyranny," in Gillian Duncan et al., eds, *State Terrorism and Human Rights: International Responses Since the End of the Cold War* (New York: Routledge, 2013), pp. 32–41.
56 "Size of the Security Services Market Worldwide from 2011 to 2020, by Region," Statista, July 6, 2022, www.statista.com/statistics/323113/distribution-of-the-security-services-market-worldwide/.
57 Rosa Brooks, *How Everything Became War and the Military Became Everything: Tales from the Pentagon* (New York: Simon & Schuster, 2016).
58 Ibid.
59 Rory McCarthy, "Gaza Doctors Say Patients Suffering Mystery Injuries after Israeli Attacks," *The Guardian*, October 17, 2006, www.theguardian.com/world/2006/oct/17/israel1.
60 The official report of the United Nations fact-finding mission following the conflicts in Gaza wasn't able to determine with certainty that such attacks had occurred, but several doctors who treated patients in Gaza described injuries consistent with the use of DIME weapons: *Human Rights in Palestine and Other Occupied Arab Territories: Report of the United Nations Fact-Finding Mission on the Gaza Conflict*, September 25, 2009, https://www2.ohchr.org/english/bodies/hrcouncil/docs/12session/a-hrc-12-48.pdf.

61 "Fatalities after 'Cast Lead,'" B'Tselem, www.btselem.org/hebrew/statistics/fatalities/after-cast-lead/by-date-of-event [in Hebrew].
62 Ibid.
63 Asaf Shtull-Trauring, "Report: 44% of Israeli Jews Support Rabbis' Edict Forbidding Rentals to Arabs in Safed," *Haaretz*, December 28, 2010, www.haaretz.com/1.5100368.
64 Quoted in Jason Stanley, *How Fascism Works: The Politics of Us and Them* (New York: Random House, 2020), p. 65.

Chapter 2 Disgust and Identity

1 Martha C. Nussbaum, *From Disgust to Humanity: Sexual Orientation and Constitutional Law* (Oxford: Oxford University Press, 2010).
2 TOI Staff, "Ohio Governor Pans 'Vile, Disgusting' Anti-Semitic Sign at Anti-Lockdown Rally," *Times of Israel*, April 23, 2020, www.timesofisrael.com/ohio-governor-pans-vile-disgusting-anti-semitic-sign-at-anti-lockdown-rally/.
3 Joshua M. Tybur et al., "Disgust: Evolved Function and Structure," *Psychological Review*, 120/1 (2013): 65–84; Paul Rozin, Jonathan Haidt, and Clark R. McCauley, "Disgust," in *Handbook of Emotions*, ed. Lisa Feldman Barrett, Michael Lewis, and Jeannette M. Haviland-Jones (4th edn, New York: Guilford Press, 2010), pp. 815–34.
4 Paul Rozin and April E. Fallon, "A Perspective on Disgust," *Psychological Review*, 94/1 (1987): 23–41, at p. 24.
5 Mary Douglas, *Purity and Danger: An Analysis of Concepts of Pollution and Taboo* (London: Routledge, 2003).
6 Ibid.
7 Ibid.
8 Bunmi O. Olatunji and Craig N. Sawchuk, "Disgust: Characteristic Features, Social Manifestations, and Clinical Implications," *Journal of Social and Clinical Psychology*, 24/7 (2005): 932–62.
9 Rozin et al., "Disgust."
10 See Kenneth Friedman, "What Is Kosher Wine?," July 20, 2021,

www.kosherwine.com/discover/what-is-kosher-wine#:~:text =In%20short%2C%20for%20wine%20to,or%20additives%20m ay%20be%20included. To be sure, Judaism isn't unique in this. Observant Muslims treat pork as a contaminant – in interfaith friendships between Christians and Muslims, a Christian who sells pork will not be welcomed in the Muslim community and is treated as contaminating. See Rashida Alhassan Adum-Atta, "The Politics of Purity, Disgust, and Contamination: Communal Identity of Trotter (Pig) Sellers in Madina Zongo (Accra)," *Religions*, 11/8 (2020): 421.

11 Thomas M. Leonard, ed., *Encyclopedia of the Developing World* (London: Routledge, 2013).
12 Ibid., p. 1640.
13 "Black People Disgust Me," Reddit, 2014, www.reddit.com /r/changemyview/comments/2kcvle/cmv_black_people_disgust _me/. All errors of spelling and grammar appear in the source.
14 Anna Bagaini, "The Origins of Right-Wing Populism in Israel: Peace Process and Collective Identities' Struggle," in European Consortium for Political Research, General Conference, Wrocław, September 4–7, 2019, https://ecpr.eu/Events/Event /PaperDetails/47201.
15 "Meir Kahane," *New World Encyclopedia*, www.newworldency clopedia.org/entry/Meir_Kahane.
16 James Q. Whitman, *Hitler's American Model: The United States and the Making of Nazi Race Law* (Princeton, NJ: Princeton University Press, 2017).
17 "Lehava: Preventing Assimilation in the Holy Land," www.leava .co.il/blog/ [in Hebrew].
18 "About the Im Tirzu Movement," https://imti.org.il/about-us /movement/?gclid=Cj0KCQjwpdqDBhCSARIsAEUJ0hOY9RgL 600FvOs_ldGn3T-JnqQ0ThQjRpATaZQa7Llz5pBqfQ_GOyAa AojWEALw_wcB.
19 "Israel Election Final Results: Netanyahu, Jewish Far Right Win Power, Fiasco for Left," *Haaretz*, November 3, 2022, www.haa retz.com/israel-news/elections/2022-11-03/ty-article/israel-elec

tion-final-results-netanyahu-jewish-far-right-win-power-fiasco-forleft/00000184-3e80-daf1-abc4-7f9a53f40000.
20 Arik Bender, "The Knesset Avoided a 'Racist Law,'" *Maariv*, December 1, 2004, www.makorrishon.co.il/nrg/online/1/ART/830/340.html [in Hebrew].
21 "In U.S., Far More Support Than Oppose Separation of Church and State" (Pew Research Center, October 28, 2021), www.pewresearch.org/religion/2021/10/28/in-u-s-far-more-support-than-oppose-separation-of-church-and-state/.
22 Lara Whyte, "Has Trump's White House 'Resurrected' Army of God Anti-Abortion Extremists?," Open Democracy, February 5, 2018, www.opendemocracy.net/en/5050/army-of-god-anti-abortion-terrorists-emboldened-under-trump/.
23 Chinki Sinha, "India's Interfaith Couples on Edge after New Law," March 15, 2021, www.bbc.com/news/world-asia-india-56330206.
24 Bezalel Smotrich, Twitter, 2016, https://twitter.com/bezalelsm/status/717220377483735040?lang=he [in Hebrew].
25 Yair Altman, "Public Invited to Inform on Those Renting to Arabs," December 12, 2010, www.ynetnews.com/articles/0,7340,L-3998121,00.html.
26 "Lehava: State-Sponsored Incitement," Institute for Middle East Understanding, September 10, 2012, https://imeu.org/article/lehava-state-sponsored-incitement.
27 Yagil Levy, "The Military as a Split Labor Market: The Case of Women and Religious Soldiers in the Israel Defense Forces," *International Journal of Politics, Culture, and Society*, 26/4 (2013): 393–414.
28 Matthew Zagor, "'I Am the Law!' – Perspectives of Legality and Illegality in the Israeli Army," *Israel Law Review*, 43/3 (2010): 551–89.
29 Yair Nehorai, "The Venom of the Snake," Facebook, 2018, www.facebook.com/yairnehorai1/videos/665854170422612/?v=665854170422612 [no longer available].
30 Yair Nehorai, "Garbage," Facebook, 2018, www.facebook.com/

yairnehorai1/videos/647591272248902/?v=647591272248902 [no longer available].

31 Guy Ezra, "Rabbi Tau: Coronavirus Outbreak – Due to Man Acting as Beast," 2020, www.srugim.co.il/438497-הרב-טאו-הקור- ונה-בגלל-התנהגות-האדם-כבה. [in Hebrew].

32 Yair Nehorai, "Rabbi Eliezer Kashtiel: 'The Jewish Supremacy Is Genetic, the Arabs May Be Our Slaves,'" Haaretz, 2019, www.haaretz.co.il/blogs/yairnehorai/BLOG-1.7644613 [in Hebrew].

33 Avishai Ben-Haim, "Ovadia Yosef: The Arabs Should Be Destroyed," 2001, www.ynet.co.il/articles/0,7340,L-654389,00.html [in Hebrew].

34 Shabtay Bendet, "Arab Communities Support Shas," January 3, 2013, https://news.walla.co.il/item/2603160 [in Hebrew].

35 Shimon Dotan, dir., *The Settlers*, 2016.

36 Ibid.

37 William Ian Miller, *The Anatomy of Disgust* (Cambridge, MA: Harvard University Press, 1998).

38 Shas Party, "Dial 'Asterisk-Giur' and Get a Certificate," January 8, 2013, https://www.youtube.com/watch?v=Y5wCALTOhCU [in Hebrew].

39 "NGOs: Eli Ishai Is Inciting against the Refugees," May 16, 2012, www.ynet.co.il/articles/0,7340,L-4229971,00.html [in Hebrew].

40 Suzanne Gamboa, "Donald Trump Announces Presidential Bid by Trashing Mexico, Mexicans," June 16, 2015, www.nbcnews.com/news/latino/donald-trump-announces-presidential-bid-trashing-mexico-mexicans-n376521.

41 Robin McKie, "Far-Right Leader Geert Wilders Calls Moroccan Migrants 'Scum,'" *The Guardian*, February 18, 2017, www.theguardian.com/world/2017/feb/18/geert-wilders-netherlands-describes-immigrants-scum-holland.

42 Jon Stone, "'Completely Dehumanising': Nigel Farage Describes Group of Children and Adults Landing in Kent as 'Invasion,'" *The Independent*, August 6, 2020, www.independent.co.uk/news/uk/politics/nigel-farage-kent-beach-invasion-video-anti-migrant-immigration-a9658246.html.

43 Bagaini, "The Origins of Right-Wing Populism in Israel: Peace Process and Collective Identities' Struggle," p. 5.
44 Ibid.
45 Ibid.
46 Jason Stanley, *How Fascism Works: The Politics of Us and Them* (New York: Random House, 2020).
47 Ibid.
48 Roee Kibrik, "The Real Reasons Israel Showed Solidarity with Lebanon after the Beirut Blast," *Haaretz*, September 8, 2020, www.haaretz.com/israel-news/.premium-the-real-reasons-israel-showed-solidarity-with-lebanon-after-the-beirut-blast-1.9132489.
49 Wolfgang Palaver, "Fraternity versus Parochialism: On Religion and Populism," *Religions*, 11/7 (2020): 319.
50 As Palaver put it: "Donald Trump . . . was supported by 81% of white evangelical Christians and 60% of white Catholics in the U.S. presidential elections in 2016. . . . Narendra Modi's Hindu nationalist policy in India also illustrates a problematic amalgamation of populism and religion. In Europe, many rightwing populist parties have begun to embrace Christianity to convince people that they have to defend their nations against an 'Islamization'." Ibid. For the numbers, see Jessica Martínez and Gregory A. Smith, "How the Faithful Voted: A Preliminary 2016 Analysis," November 9, 2016, www.pewresearch.org/fact-tank/2016/11/09/how-the-faithful-voted-a-preliminary-2016-analysis/.
51 Asaf Shtull-Trauring, "Report: 44% of Israeli Jews Support Rabbis' Edict Forbidding Rentals to Arabs in Safed," *Haaretz*, December 28, 2010, www.haaretz.com/1.5100368
52 Or Kashti, "Ultra-Orthodox Are Proud Israelis Who Don't Feel Oppressed, Survey Shows," *Haaretz*, July 17, 2020, www.haaretz.com/israel-news/.premium-ultra-orthodox-are-proud-israelis-who-don-t-feel-oppressed-survey-shows-1.8999412.
53 Israeli law allows anyone with at least one Jewish grandparent to gain Israeli citizenship, but, according to Jewish law, to be

considered Jewish one's mother must be Jewish. This causes a discrepancy between the number of people allowed to gain Israeli citizenship and those considered Jewish.

54 Kashti, "Ultra-Orthodox Are Proud Israelis Who Don't Feel Oppressed, Survey Shows."

55 Or Kashti, "Survey: Ultra-Orthodox Teenagers Hate Arabs, National-Religious Want to Deny Them Rights," *Haaretz*, February 19, 2021, www.haaretz.co.il/news/education/.premium-1.9551329 [in Hebrew].

56 Jacquelien van Stekelenburg, "Radicalization and Violent Emotions," *PS: Political Science & Politics*, 50/4 (2017): 936–9.

57 Yael Berda, "Managing Dangerous Populations: Colonial Legacies of Security and Surveillance," *Sociological Forum*, 28/3 (2013): 627–30.

58 Ali Gamal, "Egypt: The Forbidden Love of Interfaith Romances," November 24, 2014, www.bbc.com/news/world-middle-east-29932094; "Civil Marriage in Israel – Difficulties and Solutions," www.israel-visa.co.il/%D7%A0%D7%99%D7%A9%D7%95%D7%90%D7%99%D7%9D-%D7%90%D7%96%D7%A8%D7%97%D7%99%D7%99%D7%9D-%D7%91%D7%99%D7%A9%D7%A8%D7%90%D7%9C/ [in Hebrew].

59 Philip S. Gorski and Samuel L. Perry, *The Flag and the Cross: White Christian Nationalism and the Threat to American Democracy* (Oxford: Oxford University Press, 2022).

60 In 2021, Smotrich refused to join Netanyahu's proposed coalition because it would include an Arab party. This made possible the Bennett–Lapid government, during which Smotrich was part of the opposition. Tovah Lazaroff, "Smotrich: Arab Parties Are the Enemy, No Government Can Depend on Them," *Jerusalem Post*, April 15, 2021, www.jpost.com/israel-news/smotrich-arab-parties-are-the-enemy-no-government-can-depend-on-them-665296.

61 Natalie J. Shook, Benjamin Oosterhoff, and Barış Sevi, "From Disease to Democracy: How Disgust Shapes Western Politics," in Philip A. Powell and Nathan S. Consedine, eds, *The Handbook*

of Disgust Research (Cham: Springer, 2021), pp. 243–58; David Matsumoto, Mark G. Frank, and Hyisung C. Hwang, "The Role of Intergroup Emotions in Political Violence," *Current Directions in Psychological Science*, 24/5 (2015): 369–73; https://doi.org/10.1177/0963721415595023.

Chapter 3 Resentment, or The Hidden Eros of Nationalist Populism

1 Aristotle, *The Politics* (Oxford: Oxford University Press, 1998).
2 Søren Kierkegaard, "Two Ages: The Age of Revolution and the Present Age: A Literary Review (March 30, 1846)," in *The Essential Kierkegaard*, ed. Howard V. Hong and Edna H. Hong (Princeton, NJ: Princeton University Press, 2013), pp. 252–68; https://doi.org/doi:10.1515/9781400847198-018.
3 Max Scheler, *Ressentiment* (Milwaukee: Marquette University Press, 2007), p. 31.
4 Bernard N. Meltzer and Gil Richard Musolf, "Resentment and Ressentiment," *Sociological Inquiry*, 72/2 (2002): 240–55.
5 Guillem Rico, Marc Guinjoan, and Eva Anduiza, "The Emotional Underpinnings of Populism: How Anger and Fear Affect Populist Attitudes," *Swiss Political Science Review* 23, no. 4 (2017): 444–61, https://doi.org/10.1111/spsr.12261.
6 Sammy Smooha, "The Mass Immigrations to Israel: A Comparison of the Failure of the Mizrahi Immigrants of the 1950s with the Success of the Russian Immigrants of the 1990s," *Journal of Israeli History*, 27/1 (2008): 1–27; Shlomo Svirski and Dvora Bernstein, "Who Had Which Occupation, for Whom Did They Work, and for What?," in *Israeli Society: Critical Aspects* (Tel Aviv: Breirot, 1993), pp. 120–47 [in Hebrew]; Yinon Cohen, "Socioeconomic Gaps between Mizrachim and Ashkenazim, 1975–1995," *Israeli Sociology*, 1 (1998): 115–34 [in Hebrew].
7 Svirski and Bernstein, "Who Had Which Occupation, for Whom Did They Work, and for What?"
8 Aziza Khazzoom, "Western Culture, Stigma, and Social Closure: The Origins of Ethnic Inequality among Jews in Israel," *Israeli*

Sociology, 2 (1999): 385–428 [in Hebrew]; Yehouda Shenhav, "How Did the Mizrahim 'Become' Religious and Zionist? Zionism, Colonialism and the Religionization of the Arab Jew," Israel Studies Forum, 19/1 (2003): 73–87.

9 Ella Shohat, "Sephardim in Israel: Zionism from the Standpoint of Its Jewish Victims," Social Text, nos. 19/20 (1988): 1–35.

10 Sami Shalom-Chetrit, *The Mizrahi Struggle in Israel: Between Oppression and Freedom, Between Identification and Alternative: 1948–2003* (Tel Aviv: Am Oved, 2004), pp. 73–4 [in Hebrew].

11 Ibid., pp. 122–3.

12 Hanna Ayalon et al., *Educational Inequality in Israel: From Research to Policy* (Jerusalem: Taub Center, 2019).

13 Shlomo Svirski, Etti Connor-Attias, and Emma Rapoport, "Social Snapshot 2014," Adva Center, January 2015, https://adva.org/wp-content/uploads/2015/02/social-2014-11.pdf#page=28 [in Hebrew].

14 Svirski and Bernstein, "Who Had Which Occupation, for Whom Did They Work, and for What?"; Shlomo Svirski, "Mass 'Aliyah': On the Arrival of Iraqi Jews in the 1950s," in *Seeds of Inequality* (Tel Aviv: Breirot, 1995), pp. 9–70 [in Hebrew].

15 Nissim Mizrachi and Hanna Herzog, "Participatory Destigmatization Strategies among Palestinian Citizens, Ethiopian Jews and Mizrahi Jews in Israel," in Michèle Lamont and Nissim Mizrachi, eds, *Responses to Stigmatization in Comparative Perspective* (Abingdon: Routledge, 2013), pp. 66–83; Nissim Leon, "The Ne'emanei Ha-Torah Movement, 1962–1971: An Early Version of Shas?," *Journal of Israeli History*, 38/1 (2020): 213–32; Shohat, "Sephardim in Israel"; Shalom-Chetrit, *The Mizrahi Struggle in Israel*.

16 Ofra Ofer Oren, "Dudu Topaz Spoke of Tshachtshachim – Thanks to Him, Menachem Begin Won the Election," 2018, https://xnet.ynet.co.il/articles/0,7340,L-5422306,00.html [in Hebrew].

17 In fact, inequality in Israel has increased in recent years: in 1986, the Gini index for the country was 36.5. By 2016, it had risen to 39. An international comparison reveals that Israel has relatively

high levels of inequality. For instance, in 2016, Canada's Gini index was 32.7, while that of Germany and France was 31.9. This is perhaps not surprising, considering that Israel has significantly reduced government spending in the last two decades: in 1995, Israel, France, and Germany registered similar levels of government spending: roughly 55 percent of each country's GDP. By 2016, Israel had reduced its spending to 38.7 percent of GDP, while Germany spent 44.4 percent and France spent 56.7 percent. "Gini Index (World Bank Estimate) – Israel, France, Germany, Canada," https://data.worldbank.org/indicator/SI.POV.GINI?contextual=default&locations=IL-FR-DE-CA; "General Government Spending," https://data.oecd.org/gga/general-government-spending.htm.

18 Dani Filc, "We Are the People (and You Aren't!) – Inclusionary and Exclusionary Populism in Israel," *Studies on the Revival of Israel: An Anthology of the Problems of Zionism, the Yishuv and the State of Israel*, 20 (2010), pp. 28–48 [in Hebrew].

19 Ibid.; Dani Filc, "Political Radicalization in Israel: From a Populist Habitus to Radical Right Populism in Government," in *Expressions of Radicalization: Global Politics, Processes and Practices*, ed. Kristian Steiner and Andreas Önnerfors (London: Palgrave Macmillan, 2018), pp. 121–45; https://doi.org/10.1007/978-3-319-65566-6_5.

20 Ibid.

21 Arye Deri, "Today at Midnight," December 31, 2012, www.facebook.com/DeryArye/posts/442161212504022 [in Hebrew].

22 Shy Sulman, "Arye Machluf Deri in a Commercial against the White Askenazis and Discrimination," February 21, 2015, https://www.youtube.com/watch?v=Ui_vAmX4-1A [in Hebrew].

23 Yonah Jeremy Bob, "Shas Head Arye Deri Admits to, and Is Convicted of, Tax Crimes," *Jerusalem Post*, January 25, 2022, www.jpost.com/breaking-news/article-694482.

24 Arye Deri, "Yair and Arrogant," March 9, 2015, www.facebook.com/DeryArye/photos/a.433118606741616/785963514790455/?type=3&theater [in Hebrew].

25 In their seminal paper about the roots of populism, Inglehart and Norris explained this aptly: "Previous analyses of parties in Western Europe have often associated populism with the right, using terms such as 'radical right', 'far right', or 'extremist right' parties. But it is increasingly recognized that this fails to capture certain core features of populist parties around the world, such as in the Americas, Eastern Europe, and Asia, where populist parties often favor economic left-wing policies." For this reason, in their study, Inglehart and Norris viewed "the new cultural cleavage dividing Populists and Cosmopolitan Liberals ... as orthogonal to the classic economic class cleavage, which dominated West European party competition during post-war decades." Ronald F. Inglehart and Pippa Norris, *Trump, Brexit, and the Rise of Populism: Economic Have-Nots and Cultural Backlash*, Harvard Kennedy School Working Paper RWP16-026 (2016), p. 8.

26 Edward W. Said, *Orientalism*. (New York: Vintage Books, 1979), p. 45.

27 Susan Neiman, *Left is Not Woke* (Cambridge: Polity, 2023).

28 Momi Dahan, "How Successful Was the Melting Pot in the Economic Field?," *Israel Economic Review*, 14/1 (2016).

29 Or Kashti, "Even after a Generation in the Country, the Ethnic Gap in Higher Education Remains," Haaretz, 2015, www.haaretz.co.il/news/education/1.2770238 [in Hebrew].

30 Avital Lahav and Omri Efraim, "Ashkenazis, Mizrahis and Arabs: Report Exposes Gap," 2014, www.ynet.co.il/articles/0,7340,L-4482291,00.html [in Hebrew].

31 Ironically, the opening up of academic colleges (lesser versions of universities) which have played a massive role in enabling Mizrahim to gain an education is credited to an Ashkenazi and left-wing man, Amnon Rubinstein; see Omri Zarhovitch, "There Was a University Cartel That Was Deeply Damaging Society," 2018, www.globes.co.il/news/article.aspx?did=1001255943 [in Hebrew].

32 A 2019 study found that the average overall value of assets in

Ashkenazi households was 2.4 million shekels and for Mizrahi households only 1.8 million. Maor Milgrom and Gilad Bar-Levav, "Inequality in Israel: How Is Wealth Divided?," *Economic Quarterly*, 63/1 (2019): 35.

33 Dahlia Scheindlin, "Ten Years with Netanyahu: Maintaining Israel, the Conflict – and Himself," Berlin: Friedrich Ebert, 2017; https://library.fes.de/pdf-files/iez/13126.pdf.

34 "Risk of Poverty, Chance of Joining the Middle Class," Adva Center, 2019, https://adva.org/wp-content/uploads/2019/03/Near-Poverty-HE-2.pdf [in Hebrew].

35 Yonatan Berman, "Inequality, Identity, and the Long-Run Evolution of Political Cleavages in Israel 1949–2019," World Inequality Database, August 2020, https://wid.world/document/inequality-identity-and-the-long-run-evolution-of-political-cleavages-in-israel-1949-2019-world-inequality-lab-wp-2020-17/.

36 In addition to the neo-liberal policies cited above, in his roles as prime minister and as minister of finance, Netanyahu made employees in the public sector easier to fire, decreased government spending on health care, made the collection of unemployment benefits more difficult, and reduced child allowances significantly. These policies clearly favor higher socioeconomic sectors over lower ones. Dani Filc, *The Political Right in Israel: Different Faces of Jewish Populism* (London: Routledge, 2009).

37 Yascha Mounk, "International Patterns Show Why Trump Is So Hard to Beat," *The Atlantic*, October 1, 2020, www.theatlantic.com/ideas/archive/2020/10/its-really-really-hard-to-get-rid-of-a-populist/616551/.

38 Binyamin Netanyahu, "Go out and Vote and Stop a Left-Wing Government," 2019, www.facebook.com/Netanyahu/posts/10156276738122076 [in Hebrew].

39 Yediot Ahronot, "Minister Dudi Amsalem in '7 Days,'" 2020, https://twitter.com/YediotAhronot/status/1273873150162489345?cxt=HKwWgsC-xa-42q0jAAAA [in Hebrew].

40 Lee Bebout, "Weaponizing Victimhood," *News on the Right:*

Studying Conservative News Cultures, ed. A. J. Bauer (Oxford: Oxford University Press, 2019), p. 64.
41 Wendy Brown, *States of Injury: Power and Freedom in Late Modernity* (Princeton, NJ: Princeton University Press, 2020).
42 Ohad Cohen, "Likud Country: The Likud as a Political Home for Mizrahim? On Intersections and Regimes of Justification," PhD research proposal, 2021.
43 Daniel Maman and Zeev Rosenhek, "The Reconfigured Institutional Architecture of the State," in *Neoliberalism as a State Project: Changing the Political Economy of Israel*, ed. Michael Shalev and Asa Maron (Oxford: Oxford University Press, 2017), pp. 60–73; Joseph Zeira, *The Israeli Economy: A Story of Success and Costs* (Princeton, NJ: Princeton University Press, 2021).
44 Ruth Margalit, "Miri Regev's Culture War," *New York Times*, October 23, 2016, www.nytimes.com/2016/10/23/magazine/miri-regevs-culture-war.html.
45 These accusations usually go unanswered because the left has been awash in cultural relativism and has been unable to explain why Chekov matters more to the culture of Enlightenment than the Hallachic edicts of a Sephardic rabbi.
46 Leonie Huddy and Alexa Bankert, "Political Partisanship as a Social Identity," in *Oxford Research Encyclopedia of Politics*, 2017, https://calgara.github.io/Pol157_Spring2019/Huddy%20&%20Bankert%202017.pdf; Leonie Huddy, Alexa Bankert, and Caitlin Davies, "Expressive versus Instrumental Partisanship in Multiparty European Systems," *Political Psychology*, 39 (2018): 173–99; Shanto Iyengar and Masha Krupenkin, "Partisanship as Social Identity: Implications for the Study of Party Polarization," *The Forum*, 16/1 (2018): 23–45.
47 Jeremy Engels, *The Politics of Resentment: A Genealogy* (Philadelphia: Pennsylvania State University Press, 2015), p. 12 (emphasis added).
48 Ibid., pp. 12–13.

49 According to a 1996 article by Dani Filc, Netanyahu had these tendencies from the very beginning. It seems that they grew so gradually that it's impossible to pinpoint when it became as intense as it is today. Dani Filc, "Post-Populism in Israel: The South American Model of Netanyahu, '96," *Theory and Criticism*, 9/2 (1996): 217–32.

50 His most notable use of this rhetoric was to claim that the criminal charges against him were fabricated for political persecution. For example, Binyamin Netanyahu, "Livestream," 2021, www.facebook.com/Netanyahu/videos/1424596971209300/?t=117 [in Hebrew].

51 Ami Pedahzur, *The Triumph of Israel's Radical Right* (Oxford: Oxford University Press, 2012), p. 7.

52 Ami Pedahzur, "Supporting Conditions for the Survival of Extreme Right-Wing Parties in Israel," *Mediterranean Politics*, 5/3 (2000), p. 6.

53 Ibid., pp. 6–7.

54 For example, Barak Ravid, "Israel's Split Screen: Netanyahu on Trial as Post-Election Consultations Start," April 5, 2021, www.axios.com/netanyahu-trial-israel-election-consultations-25f90ee0-6642-40f0-8e92-82f735c483ad.html; TOI Staff, "Netanyahu's Lawyers to Court: The Charges Are Fabricated; Cancel Them," *Times of Israel*, November 29, 2020, www.timesofisrael.com/netanyahus-lawyers-to-court-cancel-invented-criminal-charges-against-pm/.

55 Stephen Collinson, "Trump Looks to Seize on Feud with FBI as Critical Court Hearing Looms," August 18, 2022, www.cnn.com/2022/08/18/politics/trump-fbi-court-hearing-analysis/index.html.

56 Cohen, "Likud Country."

57 Ilan Peleg, ed., *Victimhood Discourse in Contemporary Israel* (Lanham, MD: Lexington Books, 2019).

58 The transfer by an occupying power of its civilian population into the territory it occupies is a war crime.

59 Peace Now, "Population Data in Israel and the Occupied

Territories," October 2, 2019, https://peacenow.org.il/en/popul ation-data-in-israel-and-in-the-west-bank.
60 United Nations Security Council, "Israel's Settlements Have No Legal Validity, Constitute Flagrant Violation of International Law, Security Council Reaffirms," December 23, 2016, www.un .org/press/en/2016/sc12657.doc.htm.
61 Lara Jakes and David M. Halbfinger, "In Shift, U.S. Says Israeli Settlements in West Bank Do Not Violate International Law," *New York Times*, November 18, 2019, www.nytimes.com/2019 /11/18/world/middleeast/trump-israel-west-bank-settlements .html.
62 "Text Testimonies – Mapping, Arresting, Threatening," www .breakingthesilence.org.il/testimonies/database/297662.
63 "Text Testimonies – At the Roadblocks, Many Times, Ambulances Weren't Allowed to Pass," www.breakingthesilence .org.il/testimonies/database/644650.
64 "Text Testimonies – They Hung up a Sign, 'Mohammad's a Pig' and Vandalized a Few Olive Trees," www.breakingthesilence.org .il/testimonies/database/363474.
65 "House Demolitions: Demolition of Houses as Punishment," https://statistics.btselem.org/en/demolitions/demolition-as-pun ishment?tab=lists&demoScopeSensor=%22false%22.
66 This statement is misleading to say the least. Israel has direct control only on building regulations in area C of the West Bank (not areas A and B, which are regulated by the Palestinian authority). However, since areas A and B are "islands" surrounded by C territories, any expansion for building purposes needs to be approved by Israel. According to a report by B'Tselem, written in February 2019, any Palestinian building activity is severely limited by the bureaucracy of the Occupation. For example, planning permission is granted according to regulations drawn up by the British mandate, which doesn't take into account the massive population growth of the last seventy-two years. So Palestinians are at a disadvantage from the outset – they are much less likely to be granted planning permission (from 2000

to 2016, only 4 percent of Palestinian requests were approved). Yael Stein, "Fake Justice: The Responsibility of Supreme Court Justices for the Destruction of Palestinian Houses and for Their Dispossession," February 2019, www.btselem.org/sites/default/files/publications/201902_fake_justice_heb.pdf [in Hebrew].

According to B'Tselem, from 2006 to 2021, at least 3,942 Palestinian houses were destroyed on the pretext of unlawful construction. "House Demolitions: Demolition on the Pretext of Unlawful Construction," https://statistics.btselem.org/en/demolitions/pretext-unlawful-construction?tab=overview&stateSensor=%22west-bank%22&demoScopeSensor=%22false%22. As of 2012, the vast majority of criminal charges regarding unlawful buildings in C territories were against Palestinians (Palestinians are three times more likely than Jews to be charged), despite the fact that the Jewish settlers are the majority in that area. Akiva Eldar, "Most Cases of Unlawful Building in C Areas – Against Palestinians," *Haaretz*, May 26, 2012, www.haaretz.co.il/news/politics/1.1716365 [in Hebrew].

67 This statement also needs to be given context. There isn't enough documentation on the specific issue of throwing stones. However, there are important differences between the Jewish and the Palestinian populations in the West Bank. First, Palestinians are under the jurisdiction of the army, while Jewish settlers are handled by the police. As a starting point, this means that law enforcement of Jews is more highly regulated and monitored (they are citizens). Second, people who are suspected of terrorist activity can be held in administrative detention. This means that they can be held indefinitely (in some cases for several years), with no access to a lawyer and without having been indicted. This is used almost exclusively against Palestinians, because, in Israel, Jews are rarely considered terrorists, as may be seen in the following article, which describes the administrative detention of a Jew for the first time in a long period: Itai Blumental and Tova Tzimuki, "Suspicion of Jewish Terror: 18 Year Old Detained for Six Months without Trial," August 5, 2015, www.ynet.co.il

/articles/0,7340,L-4687596,00.html [in Hebrew]. According to B'Tselem, since 2001, Israel has used administrative detention against thousands of Palestinians (if not tens of thousands), and in September 2020 at least 376 Palestinians were held in administrative detention. "Data about Administrative Detention in the Occupied Territories," November 24, 2021, www.btselem.org/hebrew/administrative_detention/statistics [in Hebrew].
68 Francis Fukuyama, *Identity: The Demand for Dignity and the Politics of Resentment* (New York: Farrar, Straus & Giroux, 2018).
69 Tamar Hermann and Or Anabi, "Special Elections Survey," Israeli Democracy Institute, February 4, 2019, https://en.idi.org.il/articles/25848.
70 Rory McVeigh and Kevin Estep, *The Politics of Losing: Trump, the Klan, and the Mainstreaming of Resentment* (New York: Columbia University Press, 2019).
71 Ibid.
72 Quoted ibid., pp. 72–3.
73 However, as stated earlier, it would be wrong to assume that most of Trump's supporters were from the lowest-earning groups in American society. Rather, the highest level of support came from people with middle levels of income and those with very high income. See www.statista.com/statistics/631244/voter-turnout-of-the-exit-polls-of-the-2016-elections-by-income/.
74 McVeigh and Estep, *The Politics of Losing*, p. 8.
75 Casey Ryan Kelly, "Donald J. Trump and the Rhetoric of Ressentiment," *Quarterly Journal of Speech*, 106/1 (2020): 2–24.
76 Ibid., p. 8.
77 Quoted ibid., p. 13.
78 Charlie Tyson, "Why Are We So Spiteful?," *The Atlantic*, May 13, 2021, www.theatlantic.com/culture/archive/2021/05/why-are-we-so-spiteful/618865/.
79 Kelly, "Donald J. Trump and the Rhetoric of Ressentiment."
80 Dahlia Scheindlin, "The Dangerous Politics of Playing the Victim," *Foreign Policy*, July 4, 2019, https://foreignpolicy.com/2019/07/04/dangerous-politics-of-playing-the-victim-israel-netanya

hu-serbia-vucic/; Omar Al-Ghazzi, "We Will Be Great Again: Historical Victimhood in Populist Discourse," *European Journal of Cultural Studies*, 24/1 (2021): 45–59, https://doi.org/10.11 77/1367549420985851; James Traub, "Hungary's 500-Year-Old Victim Complex," *Foreign Policy*, October 28, 2015, https://fore ignpolicy.com/2015/10/28/hungarys-500-year-old-victim-comp lex-nazis-habsburgs/.
81 Kelly, "Donald J. Trump and the Rhetoric of Ressentiment," p. 3.
82 Rich Lowry, "The Victim President," Politico, December 18, 2019, www.politico.com/news/magazine/2019/12/18/trump-im peachment-victim-087534.
83 Jason Stanley, *How Fascism Works: The Politics of Us and Them* (New York: Random House, 2020), p. 94.
84 Rivkah Brown, "Poland Is in Denial about its Role in the Holocaust: It Was Both Victim and Perpetrator," *The Independent*, January 22, 2020, www.independent.co.uk/voices/poland-holocaust-de nial-antisemitism-ambassador-arkady-rzegocki-a9297106.html.
85 Kelly, "Donald J. Trump and the Rhetoric of Ressentiment," p. 6.
86 Michael Kimmel, quoted in Lee Bebout, "Weaponizing Victimhood," p. 68.
87 Theodor W. Adorno, *Aspects of the New Right-Wing Extremism* (Medford, MA: Polity, 2020).
88 Bart Bonikowski, "Ethno-Nationalist Populism and the Mobilization of Collective Resentment," *British Journal of Sociology*, 68 (2017): S181–213, https://doi.org/10.1111/1468-44 46.12325, at p. S192.
89 Engels, *The Politics of Resentment*, pp. 20–1.
90 Arlie Russell Hochschild, *Strangers in Their Own Land: Anger and Mourning on the American Right* (New York: New Press, 2018).
91 Hochschild interviewed right-wing supporters from Lake Charles, Louisiana. The median income of people in the town was $36,000 a year, and 23 percent of people in town had a BA. Most of her interviewees were lower-middle class, but some were also better off.

92 Scheler, *Ressentiment*.
93 Ben Anderson, "We Will Win Again. We Will Win a Lot": The Affective Styles of Donald Trump," *Society & Space*, February 28, 2017, www.societyandspace.org/articles/we-will-win-again-we-will-win-a-lot-the-affective-styles-of-donald-trump.
94 Bradley Campbell and Jason Manning, *The Rise of Victimhood Culture: Microaggressions, Safe Spaces, and the New Culture Wars* (London: Palgrave Macmillan, 2018), p. xix.
95 For example, Arthur Finkelstein, a political consultant for right-wing politicians such as Nixon, who later became Netanyahu's advisor in the elections of 1996.
96 Tal Shalev, "The Republican," 2016, https://theliberal.co.il/כך-נו /צר-והתפתח-הרומן-של-נתניהו-עם-המפלג/ [in Hebrew].
97 Engels, *The Politics of Resentment*, p. 74.
98 Campbell and Manning, *The Rise of Victimhood Culture*.
99 Hannah Arendt, *On Revolution* (New York: Penguin Books, 1990).
100 McVeigh and Estep, *The Politics of Losing*, p. 73.

Chapter 4 National Pride as Loyalty

1 Quoted in Eyal Lewin, *Patriotism: Insights from Israel* (Amherst, NY: Cambria Press, 2010), p. 45.
2 Jonathan Glover, *Humanity: A Moral History of the Twentieth Century* (New Haven, CT: Yale University Press, 2012), p. 164.
3 Quoted in Anthony D. Smith, *Nationalism and Modernism: A Critical Survey of Recent Theories of Nations and Nationalism* (Abingdon: Routledge, 2013), p. 14.
4 Maurizio Viroli, *For Love of Country: An Essay on Patriotism and Nationalism* (Oxford: Clarendon Press, 1995).
5 Philip J. Howe, Edina Szöcsik, and Christina I. Zuber, "Nationalism, Class, and Status: How Nationalists Use Policy Offers and Group Appeals to Attract a New Electorate," *Comparative Political Studies*, 55/5 (2021): 832–68; Mac Mckenna, "Income Inequality and Political Nationalism," 2016, https://ssrn.com/abstract=2994583.

6 Smith, *Nationalism and Modernism*.
7 Anne Graefer, "Patriotism and Populism," Birmingham City University, www.bcu.ac.uk/centre-for-brexit-studies/projects/patriotism-and-populism.
8 Adam Ramsay, "We Need to Talk about Where Brexit Funder Arron Banks Gets His Money," April 17, 2018, www.opendemocracy.net/en/opendemocracyuk/we-need-to-talk-about-arron/.
9 Quoted in Graefer, "Patriotism and Populism."
10 Anthony D. Smith, *National Identity* (Reno: University of Nevada Press, 1991).
11 Benedict Anderson, *Imagined Communities: Reflections on the Origin and Spread of Nationalism* (rev. edn, New York: Verso, 2006), p. 198.
12 This may seem historically inaccurate, as the American body politic did not include "others" such as native Americans and black people who had been brought to the country as slaves, and French nationalism excluded the populations of its colonies. However, the American Constitution and the French Declaration of the Rights of Man and of the Citizen created a strong foundation for the equal rights of all citizens, irrespective of ethnicity, race, or religion. They allowed for the gradual emancipation of diverse groups within France and the USA. For example, the slavery of African Americans was outlawed in the 13th amendment to the American Constitution in 1865, and segregation was outlawed based on the constitution as well. Thus, these countries allow for equal citizenship of different groups but, in practice, have not yet been able to create true equality. In contrast, the definition of Israel as a Jewish state means that any other ethnic groups will always be excluded to some extent.
13 Uzi Arad and Gal Alon, *Patriotism and Israel's National Security*, Lauder School of Government, Diplomacy and Strategy, Institute for Policy and Strategy, working paper, 2006.
14 Ibid.
15 The principle of *ahavat Israel* is considered a mitzvah and can

be traced back to the passage "love thy neighbor as thyself" in the book of Leviticus. It is said that Hillel the Elder (a prominent Jewish sage and leader who lived from 110 BCE to 10 CE) referred to this idea as the most important one in the Jewish faith. Maimonides (1138–1204) also referred to this mitzvah as an important one. See "Ahavat Israel," www.hamichlol.org.il/%D7%90%D7%94%D7%91%D7%AA_%D7%99%D7%A9%D7%A8%D7%90%D7%9C.

16 Zeev Sternhell, *The Founding Myths of Israel: Nationalism, Socialism, and the Making of the Jewish State* (Princeton, NJ: Princeton University Press, 2009), p. 9.
17 Sternhell, *The Founding Myths of Israel*.
18 "We Knew That If We Steped Foot in Hebron – They Wouldn't Take Us Out," Channel 7, November 29, 2018, www.inn.co.il/news/387834 [in Hebrew].
19 Sternhell, *The Founding Myths of Israel*, p. 332.
20 Dan Izenberg, "Supreme Court to Decide if There Is an 'Israeli Nation'," *Jerusalem Post*, March 7, 2010, www.jpost.com/Israel/Supreme-Court-to-decide-if-there-is-an-Israeli-nation.
21 *Tamarin v. State of Israel*, C.A. 630/70, 1972.
22 Yoram Hazony, *The Virtue of Nationalism* (New York: Basic Books, 2018).
23 Anna Bagaini, "The Origins of Right-Wing Populism in Israel: Peace Process and Collective Identities' Struggle," in European Consortium for Political Research, General Conference, Wrocław, September 4–7, 2019, https://ecpr.eu/Events/Event/PaperDetails/47201.
24 Kan News, "Netanyhau to Rabbi Kaduri: 'The Left Forgot What it Means to Be Jews,'" 2018, www.youtube.com/watch?v=N_5rVMDUI18 [in Hebrew].
25 Andrew L. Whitehead and Samuel L Perry, *Taking America Back for God: Christian Nationalism in the United States* (New York: Oxford University Press, 2020), p. 10.
26 Pew Research Center, "45% of Americans Say U.S. Should Be a 'Christian Nation,'" October 27, 2022, www.pewresearch.org/

religion/2022/10/27/45-of-americans-say-u-s-should-be-a-christian-nation/.
27 It should be noted that Ben-Gurion used a similar tactic towards the Israeli communist party (MAKI), which he dubbed as anti-Zionist and as a fifth column within the state. However, Ben-Gurion did not base these accusations on the fact that MAKI included Arab members of the Knesset, or that the party had ties with Israeli-Arab communities. Rather, it was the party's unconditional support of the USSR that he portrayed as threatening the state and the people of Israel. See Shlomo Nakdimon, "If We Have to – We Will Shoot!," *Haaretz*, November 11, 2011, www.haaretz.co.il/magazine/1.1563189 [in Hebrew]. Thus, Netanyahu may not have been the first Israeli leader to portray rival political actors as enemies, but he was the first to base these claims on the perceived closeness of said political actors to Palestinian citizens of Israel.
28 Jan Werner Müller, *What Is Populism?* (Philadelphia: University of Pennsylvania Press, 2016). Jan Werner Müller, *Liberté, Égalité, Incertitudes-Puissance de La Démocratie* (Premier Parallèle, 2022).
29 Binyamin Netanyahu, "Praying at the Western Wall for the Success of the People of Israel," September 16, 2019, https://m.facebook.com/Netanyahu/photos/a.10151681566507076/10156649002087076/?type=3 [in Hebrew].
30 Binyamin Netanyahu, "Shameful," February 24, 2020, https://twitter.com/netanyahu/status/1231946237223587841 [in Hebrew].
31 Ibid.
32 Srugim News, "Regev at Meron: 'Not Ashamed to Worship at the Graces of Saints,'" August 22, 2019, www.srugim.co.il/.
33 Ayelet Shaked, "Shabbat Shalom," December 4, 2020, www.facebook.com/ayelet.benshaul.shaked/posts/3430615497056852/ [in Hebrew].
34 Maya Tudor, "India's Nationalism in Historical Perspective: The Democratic Dangers of Ascendant Nativism," *India Politics and*

Policy, 1/1 (2018): 107–30; Richard C. M. Mole, Agnieszka Golec de Zavala, and Mahmut Murat Ardag, "Homophobia and National Collective Narcissism in Populist Poland," *European Journal of Sociology/Archives Européennes de Sociologie*, 62/1 (2021): 37–70; Christian Lamour, "Orbán Urbi et Orbi: Christianity as a Nodal Point of Radical-Right Populism," *Politics and Religion*, 15/2 (2022): 317–43.

35 Ivan Krastev and Stephen Holmes, "Explaining Eastern Europe: Imitation and Its Discontents," *Journal of Democracy*, 29/3 (2018): 117–28.

36 Ivan Krastev and Stephen Holmes, *The Light That Failed: A Reckoning* (London: Allen Lane, 2019).

37 Quoted in Krastev and Holmes, "Explaining Eastern Europe," p. 119.

38 Quoted ibid.

39 Steven Levitsky and Daniel Ziblatt, *How Democracies Die* (London: Penguin, 2018).

40 For examples of these two agendas, see Arye Deri, "Shas – The Revolution Returns," February 4, 2015, www.facebook.com/DeryArye/videos/772237692829704/; "Slaves," February 13, 2015, www.facebook.com/DeryArye/posts/776052929114847; "140 Fired," February 5, 2015, www.facebook.com/DeryArye/photos/a.540702515983224/772811562772317/?type=3&theater; "Visiting Families Facing Eviction," February 6, 2015, www.facebook.com/DeryArye/photos/a.540702515983224/773127839407356/?type=3&theater [all in Hebrew].

41 Yoav Peled, "Towards a Redefinition of Jewish Nationalism in Israel? The Enigma of Shas," *Ethnic and Racial Studies*, 21/4 (1998): 703–27.

42 "According to Polls, One Million Israelis Will Vote for the Likud: Who Are They, and What Do They Want?," Jewish People Policy Institute, February 19, 2019, https://ij.jppi.org.il/he/Press/article?likud-voters [in Hebrew].

43 Maya Mizrahi, "When They Say There Is a Struggle between

Left and Right, What Is This Struggle? It's a Struggle between an Elephant and a Fly. It's Not a Real Struggle," Jewish People Policy Institute, December 19, 2019, https://ij.jppi.org.il/he/Press/article?epochtimes [in Hebrew].

44 Michael Menkin, "Two Conceptions of Judaism and Israeliness," *Hazman Hazeh (These Times)*, September 2021, https://hazmanhazeh.org.il/israeli-judaism/ [in Hebrew].

45 Roger Friedland, "Money, Sex, and God: The Erotic Logic of Religious Nationalism," *Sociological Theory*, 20/3 (2002): 381–425.

46 Yossi Dagan, "Planting in Samaria," 2021, www.facebook.com/permalink.php?story_fbid=2840380296209385&id=1619338854980208 [in Hebrew].

47 There is evidence for higher nationalist sentiment among the lower-middle class and less educated people in several countries around the world. See Mikael Hjerm, "Education, Xenophobia and Nationalism: A Comparative Analysis," *Journal of Ethnic and Migration Studies*, 27/1 (2001): 37–60; Marcel Coenders and Peer Scheepers, "The Effect of Education on Nationalism and Ethnic Exclusionism: An International Comparison," *Political Psychology*, 24/2 (2003): 313–43. In Israel, there has not been a study attempting to link the two directly, but there is indirect evidence on the matter: religious Jews are more likely than non-religious Jews to view national identity in Israel as tied to ethnic and religious identity and excluding minority groups. For instance, when asked if Jews should receive preferential treatment in Israel, 97 percent of Haredim, 96 percent of religious orthodox (Dati) and 85 percent of traditional (Masorti) people answered yes, while only 69 percent of secular Jews answered in the affirmative ("Israel's Religiously Divided Society," Pew Research Center, March 8, 2016, www.pewforum.org/2016/03/08/israels-religiously-divided-society/).

Additionally, secular Jews in Israel are significantly more affluent than their religious counterparts: in 2018, secular households earned 1.3 times more than religious orthodox and masorti households and 1.7 times more than ultra-orthodox households. See "Family Day – Families and Households in Israel," Central Bureau of Statistics, February 10, 2021, www.cbs.gov.il/he/medi arelease/DocLib/2021/047/11_21_047b.pdf [in Hebrew].

48 For a careful documentation of this process, see Joseph Zeira, *The Israeli Economy* (Princeton, NJ: Princeton University Press, 2021).

49 Yinon Cohen et al., "Economic and Educational Gaps between Second- and Third-Generation Immigrants from Mizrahi, Ashkenazi, and Mixed Descent," National Insurance Institute, June 2021, www.btl.gov.il/Publications/research/Documents/mechkar%20-135-h.pdf [in Hebrew].

50 Uri Ram, "Why Secularism Fails? Secular Nationalism and Religious Revivalism in Israel," *International Journal of Politics, Culture, and Society*, 21/1 (2008): 57–73.

51 Coenders and Scheepers, "The Effect of Education on Nationalism and Ethnic Exclusionism"; Hjerm, "Education, Xenophobia and Nationalism."

52 Ibid.

53 Shlomo Svirski and Dvora Bernstein, "Who Had Which Occupation, for Whom Did They Work, and for What?," in *Israeli Society: Critical Aspects* (Tel-Aviv: Breirot, 1993), pp. 120–47 [in Hebrew]. Furthermore, many Mizrahi Jews who made Aliyah in the 1950s didn't necessarily identify as Zionists but chose to come to Israel because it was one of the only viable options available to them. Shlomo Svirski, "Mass 'Aliyah': On the Arrival of Iraqi Jews in the 1950s," in *Seeds of Inequality* (Tel Aviv: Breirot, 1995), pp. 9–70 [in Hebrew].

54 Moses Shayo, "A Model of Social Identity with an Application to Political Economy: Nation, Class, and Redistribution," *American Political Science Review*, 103/2 (2009): 147–74. It should be noted that Shayo's study did not refer to Israel, and that an Israel-based study found contradictory results, such that lower social-economic status was linked to more support for socialist policies. See Gilad Be'ery, "The Relationship Between Religiosity

and the Preferred Economic Regime in Israel," Israeli Democracy Institute, 2014, www.idi.org.il/media/4648/religiosit_and_pre ferred_economic_regime.pdf [in Hebrew]. However, this discrepancy can also be explained by the different phrasing of the questions in each study: Shayo's data were based on questions that measure the support for redistributive policies in an indirect manner (for instance, whether "we need larger income differences as incentives for individual effort"). In contrast, the Israeli study asked respondents directly whether they prefer a socialist or capitalist economic regime. Voting patterns in Israel are more consistent with Shayo's study, as higher-earning individuals are more likely to vote for the left, while the lower-middle classes are more likely to vote for the right. See Yaron Hoffman-Dishon, "The Elections for the 21st Knesset," Adva Center, April 14, 2019, https://adva.org/wp-content/uploads/2019/04/bchirot2019-socioeconomic-1.pdf [in Hebrew].

55 Liah Greenfeld, "Transcending the Nation's Worth," *Daedalus*, 122/3 (1993): 47–62, at p. 49.
56 Smith, *National Identity*, p. 75.
57 Cas Mudde, "The Populist Zeitgeist," *Government and Opposition*, 39/4 (2014): 541–63, https://doi.org/10.1111/j.1477-7053.2004.00135.x; Cas Mudde and Cristóbal Rovira Kaltwasser, "Exclusionary vs. Inclusionary Populism: Comparing Contemporary Europe and Latin America," *Government and Opposition*, 48/2 (2013): 147–74.
58 Graham Vyse, "Steve Bannon Is Absolutely Culpable for Breitbart's Racism, Sexism, and Anti-Semitism," *New Republic*, November 14, 2016, https://newrepublic.com/article/138723/steve-bannon-absolutely-culpable-breitbarts-racism-sexism-anti-semitism.
59 Melissa Chan, "Donald Trump Refuses to Condemn KKK, Disavow David Duke Endorsement," *Time*, February 28, 2016, https://time.com/4240268/donald-trump-kkk-david-duke/.
60 Dan Merica, "Trump Says Both Sides to Blame amid Charlottesville

Backlash," CNN, August 16, 2017, https://edition.cnn.com/2017/08/15/politics/trump-charlottesville-delay/index.html.
61 "Anger over Netanyahu Silence on Trump and Charlottesville," BBC, August 17, 2017, https://www.bbc.com/news/world-middle-east-40966720.
62 Katharina Buchholz, "Where U.S. Military Aid Is Going," January 20, 2022, www.statista.com/chart/26641/us-military-aid-obligations-by-country/.
63 William Echikson, "Viktor Orbán's Anti-Semitism Problem," Politico, May 13, 2019, www.politico.eu/article/viktor-orban-anti-semitism-problem-hungary-jews/.
64 "Stop Bálint Homan Statue, Ronald Lauder Urges Hungarian PM Orbán," World Jewish Congress, December 3, 2015, www.worldjewishcongress.org/en/news/stop-balint-homan-statue-ronald-lauder-urges-hungarian-pm-orban-12-4-2015.
65 "Statue to Anti-Semitic Hungarian Wartime Politician to Be Unveiled near Holocaust Memorial Center," *Budapest Beacon*, February 23, 2016, https://budapestbeacon.com/statue-to-anti-semitic-hungarian-wartime-politician-to-be-unveiled-near-holocaust-memorial-center/.
66 Shaun Walker, "George Soros: Orbán Turns to Familiar Scapegoat as Hungary Rows with EU," *The Guardian*, December 5, 2020, www.theguardian.com/world/2020/dec/05/george-soros-orban-turns-to-familiar-scapegoat-as-hungary-rows-with-eu.
67 Marton Dunai, "Orban Admits Hungary Wartime 'Crimes' Against Jews in Meeting with Netanyahu," Forward, July 18, 2017, https://forward.com/news/breaking-news/377270/orban-admits-hungary-wartime-crimes-against-jews-in-meeting-with-netanyahu/.
68 Andrew Byrne and Naomi Zeveloff, "Netanyahu Hails Orban's Hungary as an Ally of Israel," *Financial Times*, July 18, 2017, www.ft.com/content/1652bef2-6bb4-11e7-bfeb-33fe0c5b7eaa; TOI Staff, "Netanyahu Congratulates Orban on Reelection, Invites Him to Israel," *Times of Israel*, April 9, 2018, www.times

ofisrael.com/netanyahu-congratulates-orban-on-reelection-invites-him-to-israel/.
69. Raphael Ahren, "With Netanyahu in Town, Hungary's Jews Lament Israel 'Deserting' Them," *Times of Israel*, July 17, 2017, www.timesofisrael.com/with-netanyahu-in-town-hungarys-jews-lament-israel-deserting-them/.
70. TOI Staff, "Netanyahu Congratulates Orban on Reelection, Invites Him to Israel."
71. Andrew Arato, "Populism, Constitutional Courts and Civil Society," in *Judicial Power: How Constitutional Courts Affect Political Transformations*, ed. Christine Landfried (Cambridge: Cambridge University Press, 2019), pp. 318–41.
72. Zoya Sheftalovich, "Poland's PiS Abolishes Anti-Racism Body," Politico, May 5, 2016, www.politico.eu/article/polands-pis-lae-and-justice-party-abolishes-anti-racism-body/.
73. Rick Noack, "Polish President Signs Holocaust Bill, Drawing Rare U.S. Rebuke," *Washington Post*, February 6, 2018, www.washingtonpost.com/news/worldviews/wp/2018/02/06/polish-president-to-sign-holocaust-bill-despite-international-concerns/.
74. Tomasz Tadeusz Koncewicz, "From Captured State to Captive Mind," April 3, 2021, https://verfassungsblog.de/from-captured-state-to-captive-mind/.
75. Raoul Wootlif, "Amid Criticism of Poland Holocaust Deal, PM Says He'll 'Listen to Historians,'" *Times of Israel*, July 8, 2018, www.timesofisrael.com/pm-says-hell-listen-to-historians-in-polish-holocaust-bill-controversy/; Noa Landau and Ofer Aderet, "Netanyahu on Softening of Polish Holocaust Law: We Fulfilled Our Duty to Safeguard Historical Truth," *Haaretz*, July 27, 2018, www.haaretz.com/israel-news/netanyahu-israel-welcomes-softening-of-polish-holocaust-law-1.6219584.
76. Zeev Sternhell, "Why Benjamin Netanyahu Loves the European Far-Right," *Foreign Policy*, February 24, 2019, https://foreignpolicy.com/2019/02/24/why-benjamin-netanyahu-loves-the-european-far-right-orban-kaczynski-pis-fidesz-visegrad-likud-antisemitism-hungary-poland-illiberalism/; Raphael Ahren, "Yad

Vashem Slams 'Highly Problematic' Israeli-Polish Holocaust Statement," *Times of Israel*, July 5, 2018, www.timesofisrael.com/yad-vashem-slams-highly-problematic-israeli-polish-holocaust-statement/.

77 Sławomir Sierakowski, "Poland's Dictatorship of Myth," *Project Syndicate*, August 13, 2018, www.project-syndicate.org/commentary/poland-memory-law-amendment-by-slawomir-sierakowski-2018-08?barrier=accesspaylog.

78 To be sure, in August 2021, after Netanyahu was replaced as prime minister, the Israeli government changed its position regarding Poland. Israeli politicians publicly criticized new Polish legislation that would deny Holocaust survivors and their descendants the rights to property that had been stolen from them. In addition, Foreign Minister Lapid announced that he would review the Polish–Israeli joint statement that Netanyahu had signed in 2018. See TOI Staff and Agencies, "Israeli Leaders Pan 'Disgrace' as Poland Passes Law Curbing WWII Property Claims," *Times of Israel*, August 11, 2021, www.timesofisrael.com/israeli-leaders-pan-disgrace-as-poland-passes-law-curbing-wwii-property-claims/.

79 Chemi Shalev, "Netanyahu to American Jews: Drop Dead," *Haaretz*, June 26, 2017, www.haaretz.com/israel-news/.premium-netanyahu-to-american-jews-drop-dead-1.5488498.

80 Reuf Bajrovic and Tanya Domi, "Israel Just Dropped a Diplomatic Bomb into Bosnia's Politics," *Haaretz*, August 21, 2022, www.haaretz.com/israel-news/2022-08-21/ty-article-opinion/.highlight/israel-just-dropped-a-diplomatic-bomb-into-bosnias-politics/00000182-c04a-dc1b-a197-e3efc04f0000.

81 Sam Sokol, "Head of Bosnian Jewish Community 'Astonished' by Israeli Memo on Election Reform," *Haaretz*, August 11, 2022, www.haaretz.com/world-news/europe/2022-08-11/ty-article/.premium/head-of-bosnian-jewish-community-astonished-by-israeli-memo-on-election-reform/00000182-8d44-d68b-a3e2-ff454bfb0000.

82 Natasha Roth-Rowland, "How the Antisemitic Far Right Fell for

Israel," *+972 Magazine*, September 7, 2022, www.972mag.com/antisemitic-far-right-israel-orban/.
83 Ibid.
84 Ibid.
85 Jelena Subotic, "Antisemitism in the Global Populist International," *British Journal of Politics and International Relations*, 24/3 (2022): 458–74.
86 Ronald F. Inglehart and Pippa Norris, *Trump, Brexit, and the Rise of Populism: Economic Have-Nots and Cultural Backlash*, Harvard Kennedy School Working Paper RWP16-026 (2016).
87 Naomi Dann, "Richard Spencer Might Be The Worst Person In America. But He Might Also Be Right About Israel," August 17, 2017, https://forward.com/opinion/380384/richard-spencer-israel/; Peter Beinart, "The Real Reason So Many Republicans Love Israel? Their Own White Supremacy," July 29, 2019, https://forward.com/opinion/428488/the-real-reason-so-many-republicans-love-israel-their-own-white-supremacy/.
88 Mark S. Weiner, "Trumpism and the Philosophy of World Order," July 23, 2018, www.project-syndicate.org/commentary/trumpism-is-carl-schmitt-in-action-by-mark-s--weiner-2018-07.
89 Johann Pautz, "Death Panels on the Prison Planet: the New World Order Conspiracy and the Radicalization of American Politics," in Hisham Ramadan and Jeff Shantz, eds, *Manufacturing Phobias: The Political Production of Fear in Theory and Practice* (Toronto: University of Toronto Press, 2016), p. 214, quoting Arjun Appadurai, *Fear of Small Numbers: An Essay on the Geography of Anger*, ed. Dilip Parameshwar Gaonkar et al. (Durham, NC: Duke University Press, 2006), p. 52.
90 Lewin, *Patriotism: Insights from Israel*.
91 Ibid., p. 21.
92 Ibid., p. 22.

Conclusion

1 Jonathan Haidt, "The moral emotions," in R. J. Davidson, K. R. Scherer, and H. H. Goldsmith, eds, *Handbook of Affective Sciences* (Oxford: Oxford University Press), pp. 852–70.
2 Ezra Klein, *Why We're Polarized* (New York: Simon & Schuster, 2020).
3 Martha C. Nussbaum, *Political Emotions* (Cambridge, MA: Harvard University Press, 2013).
4 Hannah Arendt, *The Human Condition* (Chicago: University of Chicago Press, 1958).
5 Ibid., p. 242.
6 Jürgen Habermas, "The Public Sphere: An Encyclopedia Article (1964)," in *The Idea of the Public Sphere: A Reader*, ed. Jostein Gripsrud, Hallvard Moe, Anders Molander, and Graham Murdock (Lanham, MD: Rowman & Littlefield, 2010), pp. 114–20.
7 Ibid.
8 Ulrich K. Preuss, "National, Supranational, and International Solidarity," in Kurt Bayertz, ed., *Solidarity* (Dordrecht: Springer, 1999), pp. 281–9.
9 Kurt Bayertz, ed., *Solidarity* (Dordrecht: Springer, 1999).
10 Kurt Bayertz, "Four Uses of 'Solidarity,'" ibid., p. 14, https://doi.org/10.1007/978-94-015-9245-1_1.
11 Preuss, "National, Supranational, and International Solidarity."
12 Paul Spicker, *Liberty, Equality, Fraternity* (Bristol: Policy Press, 2006), p. 130.
13 "Solidarity," as defined in the *Cambridge Dictionary*, https://dictionary.cambridge.org/us/dictionary/english/solidarity.
14 H. Tristram Engelhardt, "Solidarity: Post-Modern Perspectives," in Kurt Bayertz, ed., *Solidarity* (Dordrecht: Springer, 1999), p. 296.
15 John Rawls, *A Theory of Justice* (Cambridge, MA: Harvard University Press, 1971); Véronique Munoz-Dardé, "Fraternity and Justice," in Kurt Bayertz, ed., *Solidarity* (Dordrecht: Springer, 1999), pp. 81–97, https://doi.org/10.1007/978-94-015-9245-1_5.

16 Danny Kaplan, "Commemorating a Suspended Death: Missing Soldiers and National Solidarity in Israel," *American Ethnologist*, 35/3 (2008): 413–27.
17 Tamar Hermann et al., "The Israeli Democracy Index, 2021," Israeli Democracy Institute, 2021, https://en.idi.org.il/media/17276/final-madd-d2021-eng_web.pdf.
18 Munoz-Dardé, "Fraternity and Justice."
19 Wolfgang Palaver, "Fraternity versus Parochialism: On Religion and Populism," *Religions*, 11/7 (2020): 319.
20 Ibid.
21 Ibid.
22 Ibid., p. 326.
23 Ibid.
24 "Document on 'Human Fraternity for World Peace and Living Together' Signed by His Holiness Pope Francis and the Grand Imam of Al-Azhar Ahamad al-Tayyib (Abu Dhabi, 4 February 2019)," https://press.vatican.va/content/salastampa/en/bollettino/pubblico/2019/02/04/190204f.html.
25 Jane Kramer, "The Carpentras Affair," *New Yorker*, October 29, 2000, www.newyorker.com/magazine/2000/11/06/the-carpentras-affair.
26 Edward Cody, "Jews' Graves Desecrated in France," *Washington Post*, May 11, 1990, www.washingtonpost.com/archive/politics/1990/05/11/jews-graves-desecrated-in-france/f208e408-5af9-413e-bc7e-ba80fd003c9b/.
27 Patrick McDowell, "200,000 March in Anti-Semitism Demonstration in Paris," May 15, 1990, https://apnews.com/article/e6c96df3bfbabcdc4f8f120642de92de.
28 Munoz-Dardé, "Fraternity and Justice."
29 Quoted ibid., p. 85.
30 Ibid., pp. 81–97.
31 Spicker, *Liberty, Equality, Fraternity*.
32 Quoted in Palaver, "Fraternity versus Parochialism: On Religion and Populism," p. 8.
33 Quoted in Munoz-Dardé, "Fraternity and Justice," p. 90.

34 James Ingram, *Radical Cosmopolitics: The Ethics and Politics of Democratic Universalism* (New York: Columbia University Press, 2013), p. 15.
35 Ibid.
36 Ibid.
37 Henry Felix Srebrnik, "Introduction: American Jews, Communism, the ICOR and Birobidzhan," in *Dreams of Nationhood* (Boston: Academic Studies Press, 2010), pp. 1–28; https://doi.org/10.2307/j.ctt1zxsj1m.6.
38 Marc Weitzmann, "The Vanishing," *Tablet*, January 6, 2021, www.tabletmag.com/sections/arts-letters/articles/vanishing-jewish-liberal-modernity.
39 To put this into perspective, Zemmour received only 7.07 percent of the general vote. David Sadler, "Presidential Election 2022: The French in Israel Voted More Than 50% for Eric Zemmour," *Globe Echo*, April 12, 2022, https://globeecho.com/news/europe/france/presidential-election-2022-the-french-in-israel-voted-more-than-50-for-eric-zemmour/.
40 Mitchell Plitnick, "How Donald Trump Exposed AIPAC," *New Republic*, March 24, 2016, https://newrepublic.com/article/131994/donald-trump-exposed-aipac.
41 "U.S. Jews' Political Views," Pew Research Center, May 11, 2021, www.pewresearch.org/religion/2021/05/11/u-s-jews-political-views/.

Index

Terms and People

affect 7–13, 17, 39, 41, 119,
    165–6, 173
AIPAC 176
antisemitism 10, 22–3, 39–40,
    153–60, 172
Ashkenazi/Ashkenazim 75,
    94–104, 107, 109, 119, 145,
    149–50, 166, 169

Bannon, Steve 153
Begin, Menachem 14–15, 27, 39,
    96–7
Ben-Gurion, David 15, 36
Bennett, Naftali 84
Bharatiya Janata Party (BJP) 69
Bollore, Vincent 6
Bolsonaro, Jair 14
Breaking the Silence 32, 76,
    84–6

capitalism 2, 127, 165
Catholics/Catholicism 116, 171

civil society 9, 28, 30, 109,
    167–9, 171, 177
cohanim 63

Dayan, Moshe 25–6
Deri, Aryeh 81, 98–100,
    109–10
Duda, Andrzej 155
Duterte, Rodrigo 14, 36

Erdoğan, Recep Tayyip 118
evangelicals 69, 90

fascism/fascist tendency 1–6,
    14–15, 20, 38, 57, 81, 116, 160,
    164
Fidesz 69
flawed ideology 3–7, 11, 106,
    160
Fox News 6
fraternity 151, 168, 170–4, 177
French Revolution 128, 170–1

Index

Gantz, Benny 40, 87, 139
Gaza 25, 40, 42, 52–5, 76, 82, 85, 133, 139, 141

Herut party 14–15, 96–7
Herzog, Isaac 38
Hungary 13, 69, 142–3, 153–4, 157–8, 166

Ideologiekritik 3, 7
Islam/Muslims 23, 40, 60, 67, 81, 90, 127, 131, 155
Israel Hayom 6
Italian Brothers 69

Kaczyński, Jarosłav 140, 143
Kahane, Meir 66–8, 85, 136
Knesset 37, 50, 66, 68–9, 85, 87, 99, 118, 138–9
Ku Klux Klan 70, 116, 153

Lapid, Yair 100, 104
Law and Justice party (PiS) 154–5
Le Pen, Marine 163–4, 166
Lehava 67, 70
Lieberman, Avigdor 98
Likud 14–16, 38–9, 69, 79, 84, 96–8, 103–5, 107–8, 110, 136, 139, 144, 149

Mapai 35, 96, 130
Marxism 2–3, 176
Meloni, Giorgia 69, 163–4
Mizrahi/Mizrahim 12, 75, 94–110, 119, 121, 124, 144–5, 149–50, 166, 169
Modi, Narendra 14, 69–70, 140, 163

Morawiecki, Mateusz 155–6
Murdoch, Rupert 6

Nazism 10, 14, 23, 27–8, 36–7, 67, 118, 153, 155, 157–8
Netanyahu, Binyamin 13–17, 22, 36–40, 49, 68, 79, 84, 97–8, 103–4, 106, 109–10, 115, 117–22, 129, 136–40, 144, 148–9, 152–60, 164, 166

Operation Protective Edge (Zuk Eitan) 43, 85, 133
Orbán, Victor 14, 69, 118, 140, 143, 153–4, 156–7, 159, 163–4, 166
Oslo Accords 36, 136, 147, 152
Otzma Yehudit (Jewish Strength) 68, 145

Palestinian Authority 74, 79
patriotism 125, 127–31, 135–40, 145, 149, 151, 160–1, 163, 168–9
Poland 13, 86, 118, 132, 154–5, 158, 166
populism 5–6, 10–19, 36, 79–82, 94, 97–8, 101, 118–19, 123, 126, 138, 149, 152, 157, 160, 162, 164–6, 176–7
Putin, Vladimir 14, 156, 158

Rabin, Yitzhak 26–7, 36, 39, 45, 136
Reform Judaism 71–2, 156, 177
Regev, Miri 84, 107, 139
Republican/Republicans 117, 121–2, 138

settlers 68, 71, 78, 83–5, 111, 114, 117–19, 131–2, 135, 144, 163
Shaked, Ayelet 139
Shas 75, 79–81, 98–9, 102, 104, 109–10, 137, 144–5, 149
Shoah/Holocaust 22, 27, 36–7, 40, 45, 153–6
Smotritch, Bezalel 68, 70, 91
solidarity 163, 169–74, 177
structures of feeling 8–11, 166

thymos 114
Trump, Donald 2, 10, 14, 80, 110–11, 116–21, 152–3, 156, 158–9, 163, 166, 176
UKIP 80, 127

ultra-orthodox Jews/Haredim 66, 71, 75, 79–81, 88, 98, 144, 169, 176–7
universalism 65, 102, 105–6, 124, 128, 158–9, 165, 169–71, 173–7

white Christian nationalism 137

xenophobia 64, 80–2, 98, 150, 155

Yishai, Eli 80

Zemmour, Éric 6, 176
Zionism 14, 23, 25, 28, 38–9, 42, 67–8, 128–9, 132, 136, 144, 152, 156–7, 177

Authors

Adorno, Theodore W. 1–3, 5, 7, 19, 108, 119
Arendt, Hannah 15, 57, 122, 167–8
Aristotle 18, 92, 168–9
Asmir, Samara 29

Beinart, Peter 36
Bergman, Ronen 28
Bourdieu, Pierre 19
Brooks, Rosa 51–2

Douglas, Mary 60

Engels, Jeremy 108, 120
Estep, Kevin 116–17

Filc, Dani 13, 17, 97
Flam, Helena 7
Freud, Sigmund 45
Fukuyama, Francis 5, 114

Greenfeld, Liah 151

Habermas, Jürgen 168
Hammerman, Ilana 31–2
Hobbes, Thomas 21–2
Hochschild, Arlie 10, 121
Holmes, Stephen 142

Jabotinsky, Zeev 23

Kant, Immanuel 175
Kelly, Casey Ryan 117–19

Kierkegaard, Søren 92
Kimmerling, Baruch 28
Krastev, Ivan 142

Levitsky, Steven 5, 143

Machiavelli, Niccolò 21–2
Marx, Karl 176
McVeigh, Rory 116–17, 123
Mudde, Cas 152
Müller, Jan-Werner 19, 138

Nietzsche, Friedrich 92–4, 108, 114, 168
Nussbaum, Martha C. 19, 167

Palaver, Wolfgang 82, 171
Pedahzur, Ami 109

Robin, Corey 49
Rozin, Paul 59

Said, Edward W. 101
Scheindlin, Dahlia 37
Scheler, Max 93, 108, 114, 121
Schmitt, Carl 24, 49, 158–9
Shklar, Judith N. 21
Stanley, Jason 3, 81
Sternhell, Zeev 129–30
Subotić, Jelena 157

Weber, Max 126
Williams, Raymond 8

Zertal, Idith 27
Ziblatt, Daniel 5, 143